Fort Robinson and the American Century, 1900–1948

The monument to Fort Robinson namesake Lt. Levi H. Robinson, dedicated September 5, 1934. HP9902/6-20A. Unless otherwise noted, all photographs are from the Nebraska State Historical Society.

Fort Robinson and the American Century, 1900–1948

Thomas R. Buecker

For Howard with best regards of

Thomas R. Buecker
2005 USCA Bivouac
Fort Robinson Nebraska

University of Oklahoma Press
Norman

Library of Congress Cataloging-in-Publication Data

Buecker, Thomas R.
    Fort Robinson and the American century, 1900–1948 / by Thomas R. Buecker.
       p. cm.
    Originally published: Lincoln : Nebraska State Historical Society, c2002.
    Continues: Fort Robinson and the American West, 1874–1899.
    Includes bibliographical references and index.
    ISBN 0-8061-3646-4 (pbk. : alk. paper)
    1. Fort Robinson (Neb.)—History—20th century.
    2. West (U.S.)—History—1890–1945. I. Title.
    F674.F7B8 2004
    978.2'93–dc22

                       2004047892

The paper in this book meets the guidelines for permanence and durability of the Committee on Production Guidelines for Book Longevity of the Council on Library Resources, Inc.∞

1 2 3 4 5 6 7 8 9 10

Contents

Illustrations

Figures

frontispiece

Lt. Levi H. Robinson monument

following page 64

Fort Robinson, 1902
Col. Jacob A. Augur
Col. Henry P. Kingsbury
Col. Horatio G. Sickel
Tenth Cavalry officers and ladies, 1904
Tenth Cavalry sergeant and family, 1904
Tenth Cavalry football team, 1905
Capt. Carter P. Johnson
Tenth Cavalry inspection, 1905
Firing the reveille gun, 1905
Sgt. John Reid
Troop I in charge formation
Tenth cavalrymen in the Ute campaign, 1906
Eighth Cavalry band, 1908
Eighth Cavalry departing for the Philippines, 1910
Twelfth Cavalry dress inspection, 1912
Twelfth Cavalry soldiers at Pine Ridge, 1913
Twelfth Cavalry soldiers in the stable area
Maj. Carter P. Johnson and family, 1916
Medical Corps trainees, 1918
The west end during the remount years
Unloading new arrivals
Veterinary officers at work
The dip vat
Capt. Oliver L. Overmyer
Horse herd near White River
Pasturing horses
"Riding out" horses
Stallion stable
Stallion Gordon Russell
Veterinary personnel performing surgery
Stallion Irish
Interior of the branding chute
Fourth Artillery gun crew

Close-order drill with dogs
Agitation training
Wintertime view of kennel area
Attendants gathering food pans
Examining a war dog before deployment, 1942
Coast Guard trainees and their dogs
Arlene Erlanger at Fort Robinson, 1945
German PWs arriving, 1944
PW Karl Schlager
PW Fritz Eisenwein
PW camp headquarters, 1945
PW camp spokesman Wolfgang Dorschel
Varista Hall
Interior of guard company barracks
German cooks on duty
German prisoner on a work detail
Flagpole and garrison area, 1944
Capt. Lee O. Hill
USDA beef research headquarters
Beef research feedlot, about 1960
Surplus bull sale

Maps

Preface and Acknowledgments

This volume continues the story of Fort Robinson, Nebraska, which began with *Fort Robinson and the American West, 1874-1899* (Lincoln: Nebraska State Historical Society, 1999). It examines the fort's role in the twentieth century. The year 1899 is a dividing line between two distinct periods in the fort's history. As the new century began, the old frontier post was gradually transformed into an important quartermaster depot with a very different mission from that for which it was established. Nevertheless, the post's twentieth-century soldiers marched and worked on the same ground where Fort Robinson's nineteenth-century history unfolded, and their achievements are as worthy of recognition as those of their predecessors. Now, it is their turn to be remembered.

This volume is the first complete history of Fort Robinson in the twentieth century. For decades interest has focused on the fort's early years; in that era the fort witnessed such dramatic and tragic events as the death of Crazy Horse and the Cheyenne Outbreak. In Western literature, Fort Robinson's final half century as a military post often has been summed up in a few sentences. Notwithstanding this neglect, the stories of the later cavalry garrisons, the Robinson Quartermaster Remount Depot, and World War II K-9 training and prisoners of war are all worth telling, a fitting end to more than seventy years of army presence on the White River in northwestern Nebraska.

Fortunately, in the years since Fort Robinson's military role ended, the final chapters of its history have been well documented. Along with the official records, a growing collection of oral interviews, reminiscences, and other documentation provided by returning veterans has proved invaluable. Much of the following narrative was derived from such materials, and much of the resulting work can be considered the story of Fort Robinson's veterans, a priceless, but dwindling resource.

Most fort histories end when the military lowered the flag for the last time and the soldiers marched out, but Fort Robinson, occupied and used continuously for more than fifty years since the army abandoned it, has taken on new roles that would be unimaginable to its former army residents. That story, too, is told in the chapters that follow.

A project of this scope depends on information, suggestions, and criticism from many colleagues and friends. First, my thanks to the staff of my own institution, the Nebraska State Historical Society. Director Larry Sommer, Associate Director for Museum Programs Lynne Ireland, and Historic Sites Coordinator Brent Carmack have been very supportive. Over the years James E. Potter, associate director for research and publications, has offered suggestions that have improved my work; the present book is no exception. My longtime friend Eli Paul, formerly of the Society's research and publications division staff, was always interested in the Fort Robinson project. His suggestions and help over the years greatly contributed to the result. I will always appreciate the Society's Library/Archives Division staff for their research assistance. Deb Brownson designed and laid out the book, Steve Ryan designed the dust jacket, Dell Darling drew the maps, Don Cunningham helped with editing, and Pat Gaster compiled the index. My coworkers at the Fort Robinson Museum—Steve Scoggan, Rebecca Serres, and Terry Steinacher—provided vital assistance, cooperation, and support. Thanks to all of you, my coworkers and friends.

The archivists at the National Archives in Washington, D. C. were most helpful. Staff of the Nebraska Game and Parks Commission and the University of Nebraska Archives and Special Collections, both in Lincoln, provided materials when requested. Mark Hertig of the Agate Fossil Beds National Monument made available the James and Harold Cook papers.

The U.S. Army's affiliated resource and historical institutions were of immense value to this project. Staff from the U.S. Army Military History Institute at Carlisle Barracks, Pennsylvania; The U.S. Military Academy Library at West Point, New York; and Bill McKale at the U.S. Army Cavalry Museum, Fort Riley, Kansas, offered courteous and timely replies to requests for information. The U.S. Army Quartermaster Museum, Fort Lee, Virginia, supplied material from publications not readily available elsewhere. Dr. Frank N. Schubert, Office of the Historian, Joint Chiefs of Staff, and the acknowledged authority on the Buffalo Soldiers, was of great help. I can always count on calling the Pentagon and getting a straight answer from Frank.

Several World War II veterans' organizations were extremely helpful. Members of the Fourth Cavalry Association recalled the 1942 dismounting of the regiment at Fort Robinson. Thirteenth Airborne and Eighty-eighth Glider Infantry veterans readily provided accounts of the 1943 airborne maneuvers. Veterans of the Casual Dog Detachment that trained at Fort Robinson before departing for the China-Burma-India Theater in 1944, regularly returned to the post and willingly shared their K-9 Corps experiences.

Colleagues and friends with the National Park Service were always available to answer my calls. Jerry Greene, Arvada, Colorado; Douglas McChristian, Sierra Vista, Arizona; and Doug Scott, Lincoln, Nebraska, freely offered technical advice on army operations and equipment. James Denney, longtime reporter for the *Omaha World-Herald*, now retired, and the late Joe R. Seacrest, former publisher of the *Lincoln Journal-Star*, kindly provided information and photographs from the archives of their newspapers.

Valuable contributions also came from Robert M. Koch and Elvin F. Frolik, both of Lincoln, and from S. C. Eittreim, Scottsbluff, Nebraska, who provided materials and helped me understand the beef research phase of Fort Robinson's history. Austin DeMuth of Crete, Illinois, and J. K. Hollenbach of Rehrersburg, Pennsylvania, provided information on their fathers' service at the fort with the Twelfth U.S. Cavalry. The late Miller Stewart furnished key sources on the Quartermaster Remount Service. Ursula H. Armstrong of Chapman, Kansas, graciously provided translations of prisoner of war materials. Marlene Mohler, Crawford, Nebraska, city clerk, made records available upon request, and Vince Rotherham, retired superintendent of Fort Robinson State Park, shared his insights on early park operations. Thanks to former Nebraska State Historical Society Trustee Dr. James Wengert, and to fort veterans Robert McCaffree, Ed Bieganski, Homer Blank, and Jim Stratton for their particular encouragement and interest.

I also want to add a note of thanks to Wolfgang Dorschel, Afrika Korps veteran and prisoner of war at Fort Robinson from 1943 to 1946. Wolfgang took a personal interest in my research, and gathered information and materials from other PW camp veterans in Germany. On one trip back to Fort Robinson, he brought Dietrich Kohl, a delightful PW comrade. Dorschel's efforts added much to our understanding of this significant, but little-known phase of fort history. Special thanks go to Ron and Judy Parks, whose financial generosity and interest in the work of the Nebraska State Historical Society made publication of this second volume possible.

Over the years I have had the pleasure of meeting many former Fort Robinson "veterans," both military and civilian, along with their wives and children, who also spent part of their lives at the post. I will never forget a memorable afternoon in the company of Maj. Gen.(Ret.) Tommy Sawyer, Mary Bell Cooksley (a remount officer's wife), and Gordon

Humbert (a dependent). As we walked the fort grounds, they shared memories of a bygone era, an experience I have been privileged to share with returning veterans on many occasions.

The following is a list of veterans whom I will remember as being particularly gracious in relating their Fort Robinson experiences, and who were my primary sources of information. I became close friends with many of them, some of whom are now deceased, and I will always owe each of them my gratitude for their interest in and valuable contributions to preserving the history of Fort Robinson:

Raymond T. Abernethy, Lincoln, Nebraska	CCC
Edmund Bieganski, Chadron, Nebraska	Remount
Homer C. Blank, Ainsworth, Nebraska	Remount
Paul E. Burdett, Missoula, Montana	Remount
Fred M. Carrier, Portland, Oregon	Fourth Field Artillery
Leo C. Cooksley, Berwyn, Nebraska	Remount
Mary Bell Cooksley, Berwyn, Nebraska	Dependent
Milo W. (Bud) Dimock, Ventura, California	K-9 Corps
Wolfgang Dorschel, Bad Griesbach, Germany	Former PW
Royal E. Draime, Vincennes, Indiana	PW camp
Fritz Esenwein, Maulbronn, Germany	Former PW
Gordon G. Golden, Alliance, Nebraska	CCC
Lyman C. Gueck, Scottsbluff, Nebraska	Veterinary Corps
Robert D. Hanson, Albert Lea, Minnesota	PW Camp
Florabelle A. Hanson, Albert Lea, Minnesota	Civilian Employee
Lee O. Hill, Rogers, Arkansas	Remount
Gordon L. Humbert, Marion, Iowa	Dependent
Gordon Hurley, Ledger, Montana	Remount
Robert Johnson, North Conway, New Hampshire	K-9 Corps
William S. Koester, Anaheim, California	Dependent
Dietrich Kohl, Lohr am Main, Germany	Former PW
Jacob Langos, Crawford, Nebraska	Remount
Claude J. Lewis, Crawford, Nebraska	Remount
Robert H. McCaffree, Sterling, Colorado	Remount
Barton S. Moen, Rockford, Illinois	Dependent
George P. Mueller, St. Louis, Missouri	Medical Corps
Lorenzo E. Norgard, Crawford, Nebraska	Remount/PW Camp
Charles H. Poskitt, Ft. Lauderdale, Florida	Fourth Field Artillery
Doris Rawalt, Chadron, Nebraska	Civilian Employee
George W. Richmond, Hayden Lake, Idaho	Veterinary Corps
Frank P. Robinson, Broadus, Montana	Remount

Lowell R. Rosnau, Brainerd, Minnesota	K-9 Corps
Clifford C. Runge, Sidney, Nebraska	Remount
Margerete Runge, Sidney, Nebraska	WAC
Glen H. Schoneberg, Orleans, Nebraska	Remount
Donald L. Spray, Torrington, Wyoming	K-9 Corps
James C. Stratton, Lance Creek, Wyoming	Remount
Donald L. Stuber, Shakopee, Minnesota	K-9 Corps
Donald K. Theophilus, Norfolk, Nebraska	Veterinary Corps
Alfred A. Thompson, Bismarck, North Dakota	PW Camp
Doug Topham, Crawford, Nebraska	Remount
Arthur N. Tyler, Chadron, Nebraska	K-9 Corps
Hans F. Waecker, Cliff Island, Maine	Former PW
Eugene F. Wasserburger, Crawford, Nebraska	Civilian Employee
Luther H. Wilmoth, Lander, Wyoming	Medical Corps
J. Weston Woodbury, Nephi, Utah	K-9 Corps
Herman C. Wulf, Gothenburg, Nebraska	Remount
Richard J. Zika, Detroit, Michigan	K-9 Corps

To all these, and to anyone I have inadvertently overlooked, my most sincere thanks. And to my family, Kay, Michael, and Anne, my warmest appreciation for their cooperation and understanding while I undertook this most interesting and enjoyable task. Finally, I wish to dedicate this volume to all the veterans who served at Fort Robinson—they have earned their place in our history.

Thomas R. Buecker
Fort Robinson, Nebraska

Introduction

On the evening of January 3, 1906, James R. Church, the post surgeon at Fort Robinson in northwestern Nebraska, boarded a train for Washington, D.C. One week later at the White House he received the Medal of Honor from President Theodore Roosevelt. The ceremony's origins could be traced to the outbreak of the Spanish-American War eight years earlier, when Church enlisted as an assistant surgeon of the First U.S. Volunteer Cavalry, commonly called the Rough Riders. Five weeks later, in combat at Las Guasimas, Cuba, Church performed his duties "gallantly," and, under heavy rifle fire, carried wounded men from the firing line. For those actions he was awarded his country's highest decoration. Captain Church was the first soldier to receive the medal under President Roosevelt's executive order that the award "will be made with formal and impressive" ceremony, the medal to be presented by the chief executive or his representative, setting the precedent for later recipients.[1] After the White House presentation, Church returned to Fort Robinson, and eight months later he was transferred for duty in Cuba.

In a way, these events symbolized the changes that the twentieth century brought to the United States Army. No longer stationed only at isolated posts in the zone of the interior, the army assumed global responsibilities. And this change was reflected at Fort Robinson; for many years after 1898 soldiers and troop units at the post on White River arrived from or embarked for overseas duty, rather than to defend United States interests on a vanishing frontier. The military subjugation of the Plains Indian was complete, but the soldiers faced new wars with strange, foreign enemies, and the new century brought new missions for the army and for Fort Robinson.

Following the war with Spain, the regular army was larger and more dispersed than at any time in its history. Because of the war, Congress nearly tripled the size of the regular army to more than sixty thousand men, not counting tens of thousands serving in state volunteer or National

Guard units. By 1900 more than sixty thousand regular and volunteer soldiers were fighting in the Philippines, twelve thousand men were sent into China to protect Western interests there during the Boxer Rebellion, and thousands of soldiers remained on occupation duty in Cuba and Puerto Rico.

The new century also marked a renaissance of sorts within the army, as it reorganized its general staff to improve coordination and administration. Education programs were set up for both officers and enlisted men. Training schools for cooks, bakers, and farriers, as well as staff and war colleges, were established. New clothing, ordnance, field equipment, and horse equipment were tested and adopted. The familiar blue uniform that defended the Union was replaced with shades of khaki and olive drab, less colorful, but much more comfortable in the tropical areas to which the army was being sent. The army's response to problems of policy, equipment, supply, and training, was reflected in events at Fort Robinson.

During the first decade of the new century, the consolidation of the army in the West was being completed. Thirty years earlier, thirty-seven army posts dotted the northern Plains; by 1910, only five active Indian war-period forts remained. The Spanish-American War revealed the need for consolidation to enable rapid mobilization in times of national emergency, and large, modern posts were built, while selected older posts were improved to house larger garrisons. The process to determine which forts were to be maintained and which were to be abandoned was keenly watched by nearby civilian communities. In the last quarter of the nineteenth century, concerned settlers and townspeople pressured politicians to have the army establish posts to protect them from Plains Indians. After 1900 politicians, urged on by concerned constituents, petitioned the War Department to retain, improve, and expand many of those same posts, not so much for the military protection they afforded, but for the economic benefit they brought to local communities. Crawford, Nebraska, merchants and citizens were no exception and were successful, as soldiers remained at the post on White River until 1948.

The army also was becoming more concerned about adequately housing and providing for the comfort of its troops. The War Department pressed Congress for appropriations to construct substantial, well-designed brick barracks, quarters, and support facilities. Local chambers of commerce joined the call for the construction of new brick buildings at their nearby forts.

But why was the army still maintaining a military presence in northwestern Nebraska as late as 1906, when Captain Church went to Washington to receive his medal? Although the Spanish-American War and Philippine Insurrection had temporarily removed large garrisons, by 1900 Fort Robinson still had a military mission of national significance. The post was located on two major rail lines, allowing rapid transit of men and supplies. It possessed a large reservation for training and a good water supply. Barracks, quarters, and other support buildings remained in reasonably good repair. Within the army Fort Robinson had a reputation as a fine cavalry station. And, with the end of the insurrection in 1902, posts in the United States were needed to house returning troops. Some forts, like Fort Niobrara, Robinson's sister post in north-central Nebraska, remained in use only until better facilities were arranged.

The soldiers who served at Fort Robinson after 1900 were better clothed, equipped, and fed than those who first marched into the White River valley that wintry March of 1874. Although the twentieth century brought new duties and service in far-off and exotic places, some aspects of soldier life never changed. The men still rose by reveille bugle call, mounted guard, drilled, performed fatigue, attended to the stables, and lowered the flag at sunset, the same routine, day after day, year after year. In other ways, however, army life was much different. Officers of the line and enlisted men with Civil War service were gone, although the officer corps and enlisted ranks still contained Indian war veterans. New recruits, who had enlisted for the adventure of war and the excitement of overseas duty, became the first U. S. soldiers to fight outside our borders in more than fifty years. Many of those soldiers were greatly disillusioned with army life when faced with the daily monotony of regular garrison duty.

With the arrival of the Tenth United States Cavalry in 1902, Fort Robinson continued its role as a regimental headquarters post for the Buffalo Soldiers. The return of the black regiments from overseas duty again brought a large African American population to northwestern Nebraska. In a period of nationally changing race relations, the Tenth cavalrymen enjoyed a relatively quiet term of garrison duty at the post, a situation not always found at other military stations. Regardless of race, citizens and soldiers generally coexisted in harmony on the northern Plains, a fact continually demonstrated since the black regiments arrived there in the 1880s. Throughout the periods when Buffalo Soldiers garrisoned Fort Robinson, Crawford generally proved the rule in this attitude, rather than the exception.

As it entered the new century, Fort Robinson looked like most other frontier posts. The buildings were arranged around a large, central parade ground, with officers' quarters on one side, and barracks and stables on the other. The post had matured, with green, watered lawns and lines of cottonwoods bordering a network of well-maintained roads. The twentieth century brought new and improved buildings, but Fort Robinson retained the layout of a classic Plains army post. Robinson, of course, benefited by being on two railroad lines; troops no longer marched in from distant forts, but unloaded at depots in Crawford and at the post. The railroads, its good physical facilities, and a large reservation were reasons Fort Robinson remained active, while the 1890s and 1900s brought abandonment to many frontier army posts. Like its neighbors, Fort Warren at Cheyenne, Wyoming, and Fort Meade near Sturgis, South Dakota, Fort Robinson was a "survivor" post of the Indian war period. Although the post ceased to be a regular troop station after World War I, its physical attributes led to further service as a quartermaster remount depot to process and issue army horses and mules.

The West itself was much changed by 1900. Towns, cities, and settlers occupied the region, which, twenty-five years earlier, had been largely the domain of the warrior. Communities were linked by a rail network that expedited the movement of travelers and freight. The Plains Indians were restricted to reservations, left to remember the days of old when they destroyed Custer and resisted the erection of a flagpole at Red Cloud Agency.

The twentieth century solidified the interdependence of Fort Robinson and the nearby town of Crawford, which by 1900 was a well-established commercial center for farmers, ranchers, and soldiers. As its population grew from 731 in 1900 to 1,323 by 1910, Crawford developed the "post town" mentality that characterized other towns near military installations. It could best be described as a love-hate relationship that worked to the mutual advantage of both civil and military populations.

Fort Robinson brought many benefits to Crawford. Soldiers were always on hand to provide martial entertainment, march in parades, participate in patriotic events, and present band concerts. The post gave civilians a sense of security, even in the days when military protection was no longer a necessity. The fort was also a source of local pride and a tourist attraction, as a newspaper editor boasted in 1907: "No visitor or tourist in that vicinity neglects the opportunity of viewing and enjoying an afternoon at the Fort. Filled with sights so interesting and history so thrilling that the same never grows old or tiresome to the most familiar." The Crawford citizenry followed news of its former garrisons in overseas conflicts, cheering when they left, and cheering new replacements when they arrived.

But the bottom line for a post town was economic. The military payroll pumped thousands of dollars monthly into the Crawford economy. The post provided work for the local labor force by hiring civilian employees and through temporary work on construction projects. Army contracts for fuel, grain, forage, produce, and dairy goods meant a steady flow of cash for local merchants and farmers.

Conversely, the proximity of hundreds of single young men created problems. Inevitably, the large numbers of off-duty troops that came to Crawford for a night on the town led to frequent incidents of disorderly conduct and violence. Drunkenness and soldier-related crime were accepted prices paid by post towns. Often the reporting in local newspapers accentuated the negative side of the civil-military relationship.

Fort Robinson garrisons developed a similar dependency on Crawford. Military personnel and their dependents found nonmilitary amenities in town, including goods and services not available at the post, and enjoyed social interaction with a civilian population. Officers and enlisted men participated in civic and fraternal organizations, in addition to joining churches. Some retired soldiers bought property, moved to town, and became productive members of the community. After the 1890s, post children attended Crawford public schools. For off-duty enlisted men, Crawford provided saloons, gambling, and prostitution, institutions and entertainment found in every post town. As Crawford benefited from the post, so Fort Robinson benefited from the town.

In the early years of the twentieth century, Fort Robinson remained a major cavalry post, a graphic reminder of the struggle for control of the American West that had taken place in the previous fifty years, and in which the post had played so prominent a role. But change was on the horizon, in the army, in the West, and in the nation as a whole. Fort Robinson, in some ways a microcosm of all three spheres, was also about to change. It would become, as the next in its long line of duties, the nation's largest and best known remount depot, where thousands of horses, mules, and dogs were conditioned, trained, and issued for service worldwide.

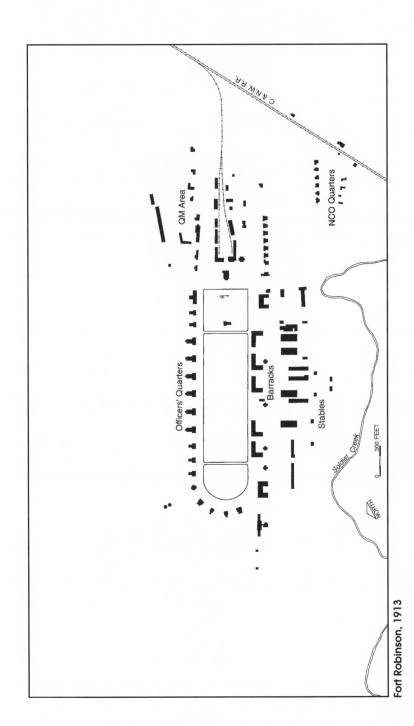

Fort Robinson, 1913

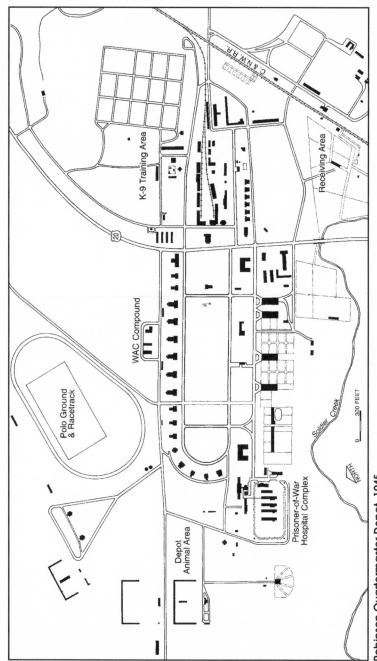

Robinson Quartermaster Depot, 1945

K-9 Training Area

Receiving Area

C & NW R.R.

WAC Compound

Polo Ground & Racetrack

Depot Animal Area

Prisoner-of-War Hospital Complex

Soldier Creek

NORTH

0   300 FEET

20

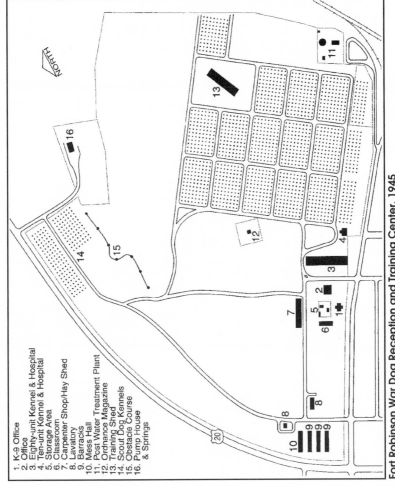

1. K-9 Office
2. Office
3. Eighty-unit Kennel & Hospital
4. Ten-unit Kennel & Hospital
5. Storage Area
6. Classroom
7. Carpenter Shop/Hay Shed
8. Lavatory
9. Barracks
10. Mess Hall
11. Post Water Treatment Plant
12. Ordnance Magazine
13. Training Shed
14. Scout Dog Kennels
15. Obstacle Course
16. Pump House
    & Springs

NORTH

Fort Robinson War Dog Reception and Training Center, 1945

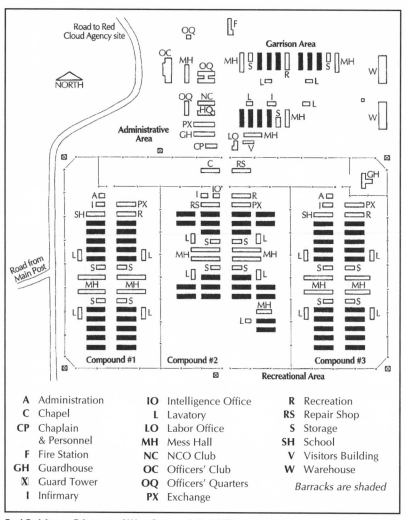

Fort Robinson Prisoner of War Camp, July 1945

A	Administration	**IO**	Intelligence Office	**R**	Recreation
C	Chapel	**L**	Lavatory	**RS**	Repair Shop
CP	Chaplain	**LO**	Labor Office	**S**	Storage
	& Personnel	**MH**	Mess Hall	**SH**	School
F	Fire Station	**NC**	NCO Club	**V**	Visitors Building
GH	Guardhouse	**OC**	Officers' Club	**W**	Warehouse
X	Guard Tower	**OQ**	Officers' Quarters		*Barracks are shaded*
I	Infirmary	**PX**	Exchange		

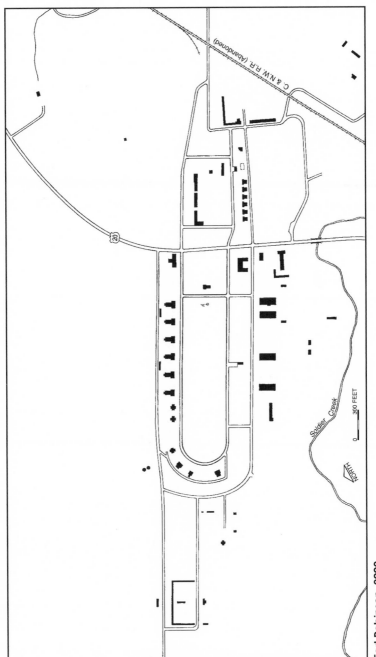

Fort Robinson, 2002

Chapter 1

The Last of the Cavalry

After the war with Spain the army's focus shifted overseas, with the Philippine Insurrection, Boxer Rebellion, and Cuban occupation tying up manpower. As a result, large garrisons did not quickly return to U.S. army posts. Forts were assigned smaller troop units that often rotated after short periods. By 1900 Fort Robinson housed only a single Tenth Infantry company. In 1901 the diminutive garrison increased with the arrival of two troops of the newly formed Thirteenth Cavalry regiment, along with the Twentieth Battery, Field Artillery. For several months the garrison at the post varied from two to three hundred men, an apparent return to prewar bustle.[1]

The two organizations assigned to the fort in 1901 resulted from a postwar expansion that saw the creation of the first new regular army units since the end of the Civil War. The Thirteenth Cavalry, organized at Fort Meade, South Dakota, in 1901, was one of four new cavalry regiments that joined the existing ten. The Twentieth Battery came from the reorganization of the field artillery that same year. Formed at Fort Riley, Kansas, where barracks and stables could not accommodate the unit, it was transferred to Fort Robinson, where winter quarters were available in 1901. The battery had a complement of two officers, 144 enlisted men, and 125 horses. Their armament consisted of six, 3.2-inch breechloading field-pieces. For a short time, area residents saw artillerymen hauling cannon and caissons, a novel sight in Nebraska's northern Panhandle.[2]

At the same time, the army was deciding which posts to keep and which to abandon. In 1893 Secretary of War Stephen B. Elkins concluded that the Indian wars were over, and during the 1890s several western posts were abandoned. In 1897 the Department of the Platte commander, Brig. Gen. John J. Coppinger, had to recommend one of three regional posts—Meade, Niobrara, or Robinson—for closure. Coppinger proposed abandoning Fort Niobrara and maintaining troops at the other two. Such talk was quickly cut short, however, as the army prepared for the Spanish-American War and overseas deployment.[3]

In 1901 the continuation question arose again. Secretary of War Elihu Root wanted to concentrate the scattered army for "economical administration and efficient training."[4] He ordered Lt. Gen. Nelson A. Miles, commanding general of the U.S. Army, to create a reorganization board to decide which posts were to be maintained, permanently or temporarily. While the board deliberated, rumors of abandonment ran rampant in communities near Indian war posts across the West. Post towns, including Crawford, anxiously awaited word of which forts would be retained. In June 1901 newspaper reports stated that forts Niobrara and Robinson in Nebraska were "no longer essential to the safety of their respective communities."[5] Many felt the only use for the old posts was "to give the soldiers a place of habitation and give certain officers a station to command."[6] Fort Robinson was then on the army's abandonment list. Naturally concerned over the post's future, Crawford businessmen lobbied officers formerly stationed at the post for support in keeping it open, and sent their letters on to sympathetic members of Congress.

Regardless of uncertainty about Fort Robinson's future, work began that year on a new hospital to replace the substandard 1885 building. Bids were opened at department headquarters on April 30 and construction started shortly afterwards. The new hospital was located at the west end of the barracks row. Built of brick, it was of standard plan and cost $22,000. Two years later a two-story annex was added; later an additional ward on the west side of the main building gave it a sixty-bed capacity.[7]

To the gratification of Crawford, army inspectors, including Brig. Gen. John C. Bates, commanding officer of the newly organized Department of Missouri, considered Fort Robinson an excellent location for cavalry. Bates promised to assign more troops there. Robinson's location on two railroad lines, the Fremont, Elkhorn & Missouri Valley and the Chicago, Burlington & Quincy, was a key factor in his decision. Early in 1902 the reorganization board decided to retain the fort as a permanent post, removing it from the abandonment list; Fort Niobrara would eventually be closed. Fort Robinson's future had been decided, at least for the time being.[8]

In support of this decision, word came that two squadrons of the Tenth Cavalry had been ordered to Fort Robinson. Earlier that spring the black regiments stationed in Cuba and the Philippines, including the Tenth, were due to be rotated to the United States. In the ensuing weeks, units then at the post transferred to other stations, while Fort Robinson awaited its new tenants. Meanwhile, on April 18, the Twentieth Battery boarded a

F.E.& M.V. train to return to Fort Riley. After the train had passed through Hay Springs, one of the artillerymen was seriously injured when he fell off one of the moving cars. The unconscious soldier was brought back to the Fort Robinson hospital, where he died several days later.[9]

On May 4, 1902, headquarters, staff, the band, and four troops of the first and third squadrons of the "Fighting Tenth" arrived by train. On May 6 the horses for the new garrison arrived, followed ten days later by the remaining four troops. Both squadrons came from Cuba; the second squadron, rotated from the Philippines, was assigned to posts in Wyoming. Fort Robinson again became a regimental headquarters post, with nearly seven hundred officers and enlisted men. The Crawford paper promised that the black soldiers "will rehabitate the town with its old-time business garb."[10]

On June 7 Jacob A. Augur, the son of former Department of the Platte commander Gen. Christopher C. Augur, took command. The younger Augur had graduated from West Point in 1868, and served as a line officer with the Fifth Cavalry before becoming the major and then lieutenant colonel of the Fourth Cavalry in 1897 and 1901, respectively. Augur, who was on detached service commanding Fort Leavenworth, Kansas, took an extended leave before arriving to take command of the regiment and post on October 14. He remained in command of the Tenth Cavalry while it garrisoned Fort Robinson.[11]

Like all new arrivals, the men of the Tenth quickly became an accepted and appreciated adjunct to the Crawford community. Baseball games were organized between town and post teams. Arrangements were made for the black cavalrymen to perform a program of military "evolutions," which included bareback riding, steeplechase, and a rescue race for the 1902 Fourth of July celebration. When in garrison, military mounted units were always a feature of any Crawford parade, and the Tenth Cavalry obliged on many occasions throughout their years at Fort Robinson. Local sports-lovers watched polo games between post officers and teams from nearby posts with keen interest. The Tenth Cavalrymen helped the local community in other ways. In July 1905 eighty troopers joined in a two-day search for a missing child, who eventually was found in the hills west of the post.[12]

As usual at military posts, the regimental band was greatly appreciated. The Tenth Cavalry Band was no exception, and its musicians performed for numerous public events in Crawford and at the post. By 1905 the band presented regular concerts in the Crawford public square. Its members also provided an excellent orchestra that frequently performed in local churches and at dances in the Crawford opera house. The Tenth Cavalry Band was called "one of the finest musical organizations in the United

States Army."[13] After one performance in Alliance for the annual Conductor's Ball, the local editor complimented "the famous 10th U.S. Cavalry orchestra, under the directorship of Professor George H. Kelley, [which] provided music and kept the dancers in high spirits from the time of the grand march till the end of the program."[14]

As elsewhere in the West, the color line had not been sharply drawn in Crawford for the buffalo soldier. Regardless of race, soldiers were soldiers, and the Crawford community and businessmen benefited from army payrolls and contracts. Soldiers patronized Crawford stores and establishments, apparently encountering little overt tension or racism. Rgt. Chap. William T. Anderson, himself an African American, presented guest sermons in white Crawford churches. Discharged and retired black soldiers frequently remained in Crawford, joining a sizable, yet segregated, black population in the community.[15]

After returning to the United States, army units faced less active field service so continuous training was required to maintain combat readiness. Pistol and carbine target practice occupied April and May of each year. The black troopers' work on the extensive Fort Robinson firing ranges paid off. In 1904 Troop I ranked third in the army for compiled range scoring. In 1906 the Tenth Cavalry ranked seventh out of all army combat regiments. Target practice did not come without risk. In May 1903 a soldier named Harriston of Troop C was accidentally shot and killed on the range.[16]

Field training for the Tenth Cavalry at Fort Robinson came in the usual form of practice marches and camps of instruction. It was not uncommon to see long columns of troops on the move, or camping along the waterways of northwestern Nebraska. Day marches were held throughout the summer, with one or two long-distance marches in the fall. Occasionally these marches coincided with public events. From September 26 to October 11, 1906, most of the regiment marched to Douglas, Wyoming, to participate in state fair activities. Just before this exercise, troops from Fort Robinson joined Sixth Cavalry units from Fort Meade and marched overland to Fort Russell, Wyoming, for several weeks of "camp of instruction" training.[17]

About this time the army realized the necessity of large-scale field and tactical training and in October 1903 the entire regiment participated in fall maneuvers at Fort Riley, Kansas. Several thousand regular army cavalry, infantry, and artillery troops trained alongside regional National Guard and state militia units at Fort Riley for more than a month. In a troop-wide baseball tournament, the Tenth Cavalry regimental team was defeated by the Twenty-fifth Infantry nine from Fort Niobrara for the championship of the Department of the Missouri. Unfortunately, while at the maneuvers, the Fort Robinson cavalrymen encountered the blatant racism of a white Texas militia regiment. The Texans refused to allow the black troopers to pass through their camp, "and the negro soldiers, who comprise one of the best cavalry regiments in the army" were displeased with the order.[18] Numerous fistfights took place, and on one occasion the cavalrymen briefly carried off one of the Texans, threatening him with bodily harm. Fortunately the vast maneuver camp broke up and the men returned to their stations before serious difficulties arose. But the ugly incident with the Texans illustrated the hardening racial attitudes of many whites after the turn of the century.[19]

During the Tenth Cavalry years at Fort Robinson, the army improved its equipment, clothing, and ordnance. The attractive 1902 dress uniform was adopted. Although the traditional blue was retained for dress wear, the plumed helmet was replaced by a more conventional cap. For summer wear, practical Khaki uniforms replaced blue field clothing. Firepower was improved as well, when the .30/40 Krag was replaced by the 1903 Springfield. The new arm, which featured a clip-fed, Mauser-type action, was issued about 1905. A new saddle, the 1904 McClellan model, was introduced along with other improved horse equipment. Individual field gear underwent testing and change. Russet or "fair leather" replaced the traditional black leather for accouterments and horse equipment, a change welcomed by the cavalry because the more natural finish was easier to maintain.[20]

Another change came to the Tenth Cavalry while it was at Fort Robinson. To increase firepower, machine gun platoons were organized for each cavalry regiment. In July 1906 one officer and twenty-one men from the first three troops were assigned to the new outfit. The soldiers were trained to provide overhead and indirect machine gun fire for cavalry support in combat.[21]

Several important visitors came to the vicinity during this period, including President Theodore Roosevelt, who made a whistle-stop in Crawford in May 1903. Colonel Augur had the troops and regimental band lined up along the tracks in town for the president's brief appearance. Roosevelt remembered the Tenth Cavalry from the Santiago campaign in Cuba and complimented the regiment on its fine appearance. Two years later the artist Frederick Remington returned to Fort Robinson (he first visited in 1897), and spent several days with his friend, Capt. Carter P. Johnson, who commanded Troop M. Remington had met Johnson years before when the regiment was stationed in the Southwest.[22]

In 1905 one of the most famous black officers of the United States Army served at Fort Robinson. Between the Civil War and World War II, Benjamin O. Davis, Sr., was one of only six black officers in the line of the regular army. Davis had served during the Spanish-American War as an officer with the Eighth U.S. Volunteer Infantry and decided to pursue a commission. After enlistment in the regular army, he was assigned to the Ninth Cavalry at Fort Duchesne, Utah, where Lt. Charles Young helped him prepare for the officer's examination. In 1901 while serving as squadron sergeant major, Davis became the first black enlisted man to pass examination for a regular army commission and became a second lieutenant in the Tenth Cavalry. Several years later he traveled from Fort Washakie, Wyoming, to Fort Robinson to appear before a regimental promotion board. After receiving his first lieutenancy, he returned to Robinson in April 1905 for duty with Carter Johnson's troop. After four months' troop duty, Davis went on detached duty as professor of military science at Wilberforce University, Xenia, Ohio. Ultimately, Benjamin Davis rose to become this country's first black general.[23]

Recalling the Tenth's years at Fort Robinson, the regimental historian recorded, "For the first time in its history, our men had the leisure and opportunity to take up athletics."[24] Boxing proved a popular participatory and spectator sport. During the fall, intraregimental football competition attracted keen interest. The 1904 Thanksgiving Day championship game between D and K Troops was "the most important feature of the day excepting the devotional services which were conducted by Chaplain William T. Anderson."[25] After the stubbornly fought contest ended in a 10-10 tie, the troops enjoyed a well-deserved Thanksgiving dinner. In the summer, Fort Robinson baseball teams played teams from other posts and civilian teams from Crawford and nearby towns including Alliance, Chadron, and Hot Springs. The construction of a substantial post gymnasium in 1904 greatly benefited soldier activities.

The YMCA (Young Men's Christian Association) was a major social and intellectual center for the Tenth Cavalry at Fort Robinson. When the regiment arrived it already had a branch of the YMCA, organized in 1900 in Cuba. At first the old amusement hall, on the east end of the original officers' row, was given to the club for a meeting place. After completion of the new gymnasium the group met there. Recitations, musical presentations, and debates were regular features for the membership, which met weekly. Most of the garrison belonged, with as many as 342 soldiers attending Wednesday evening meetings. Other forms of social activity came through several private troop clubs, and dances and other social events sponsored by the Dog Robbers and Syndicate clubs added off-duty diversions for the black troopers.[26]

Other diversions were found in Crawford, where saloons catering to soldiers drew a heavy business from the Fort Robinson garrison. As usual with post towns, prostitution flourished to the point of becoming quasi-legal, with several well-known (and well-patronized) houses in operation. Violence by off-duty soldiers in Crawford was generally the result of intraregimental bad blood and individual disorderly conduct rather than racial tensions. Soldiers committed several fatal shootings while visiting the "dives" in Crawford. As a result, the town marshal in 1904 made a conscientious effort to stop the carrying of concealed weapons by both citizens and soldiers.[27] Kipling was right when he wrote, "Single men in barracks don't grow into plaster saints."[28]

The most violent confrontation between the black cavalrymen and townspeople occurred in 1906. The previous year Crawford marshal Arthur Moss and Sgt. John Reid of Troop B had come close to blows as a result of participation in a July 4 horse race; animosity between the two evidently continued. The simmering hostility came to a head on the evening of May 13, 1906, when Moss was sent to break up a soldiers' beer party near the city park on the west edge of town. After he ordered the party to quiet down or disperse, an altercation broke out between Moss, Reid, and Pvt. Jordan Taylor, also of Troop B. During a brief scuffle Reid shot Moss with a .38-caliber revolver. He and Taylor then fled several blocks into town. There they took refuge in the house of Edna Ewing, an elderly black resident. While making their escape the soldiers were followed and fired on by several civilians, including J. H. Moss, the wounded marshal's brother; Art Moss died shortly after being shot.

As a crowd gathered at the Ewing house, Taylor suddenly bolted and ran toward the military reservation. But before he made much headway, he was fatally wounded by a "gun in the hands of parties unknown." Before he died, Taylor stated that Reid had shot Moss and was hiding in Edna Ewing's attic. The fugitive was captured and taken under guard to the city jail.[29]

Nervous townspeople heard a rumor that soldiers from the fort had threatened to storm the jail and free Reid. City officials feared that a civilian mob might seize and lynch the prisoner, so they decided to move Reid to the Chadron jail for safety. But before they could do so, word came from the fort that several men and rifles from Troop B were missing. Colonel Augur quickly sent Troops I and K into town to prevent further violence; soldier guards surrounded the jail. Tensions remained high into the next day. In a local bar a civilian named Murphy requested the loan of a gun, stating that he wanted to shoot someone. After being thrown out of the saloon, he went on a rampage and headed for the jail. When he failed to halt at the sentry's command, he was shot and killed.

Although the threat of soldiers storming the town never materialized, seven men who were reported absent from B Troop barracks were placed in the post guardhouse, and fourteen rifles were found concealed near the town limits. Reid was moved to the county jail at Chadron, where he was tried and convicted of manslaughter and sentenced to seven years at the Nebraska State Penitentiary. During the years the Tenth was at Fort Robinson there were several other homicides involving soldiers, but none created as much uproar as did the Moss shooting.[30]

The return of larger garrisons to Fort Robinson also brought increased business to the several houses of ill fame in Crawford. This development in turn brought an increased number of venereal disease cases at the post hospital. At one point Post Surg. Peter Field suggested that Crawford be declared off limits to the soldiers. Realizing the effect that such drastic action would have on local merchants, the town council appointed a village physician to examine all prostitutes periodically. Women found to be carriers of venereal infections were expelled from town; non-infected prostitutes were certified by the village physician. The city marshal made semimonthly tours of the establishments to check for certification. To finance operation of the inspection program, the council required all proprietors to pay a fine, or "whore-tax," for each prostitute passing inspection. Evidently the plan improved the health of the garrison; in January 1904 Surgeon Field reported Fort Robinson was free of incurable gonorrhea and had only one case of syphilis. Incidentally, the first inspecting physician was Doctor Anna Cross, who received the distinction of becoming the first woman to hold public office in Crawford.[31]

During this period narcotic use increased, perhaps in part because many soldiers had been exposed to opium in the Philippine Islands. The problem was caused by the over-the-counter availability of drug products containing morphine, cocaine, and laudanum in Crawford drug stores. One druggist's son explained that "narcotics could be purchased as readily as any other commodity," since the state had no laws controlling or preventing their sale or use.[32] Town officials made feeble promises to curb sales of drugs to soldiers, but took little concrete action.[33]

Chaplain Anderson and other officers, including Colonel Augur, realized the danger of drug use and its harmful effects on the garrison. On one occasion a soldier under the influence of morphine shot himself and later could not remember the incident. Others could not recall events after partaking of "drugged liquors" in Crawford saloons or houses of prostitution. Besides the enlisted men, others living on post were guilty of drug abuse. In 1904 several officers' servants were using a dangerous combination of cocaine and whiskey, sending one to the post hospital. Eventually, stricter national laws prevented over-the-counter narcotic sales.[34]

With the continuation of Fort Robinson assured for the moment, planning began for substantial building improvements. Thus far in its history, all the post buildings had been of log, frame, or adobe construction. During this period the army carried out an extensive rebuilding and expansion program at many of its military posts. Much of this improvement was due to the influence of congressmen who had army posts located in their states. Nebraska proved no exception, and yet another period of building activity began at Fort Robinson.

Between 1904 and 1906, numerous new structures appeared. Two squadron blacksmith shops, quartermaster shops, and a post bakery were built, and additions were made to the hospital, all of brick construction. In 1905 a substantially larger post headquarters building replaced the old 1882 administration building. The new, two-story frame structure on the east end of the parade ground contained five offices, a large lecture hall, and a room for the post library. Behind the east end of the barracks row a gymnasium gave the post a permanent recreation center. It contained a forty-three by seventy-two-foot floor area, and also featured a shooting gallery and bowling alley in the basement. In April 1907 the Crawford paper jubilantly announced, "Fort Robinson is destined to be one of the greatest army posts in the United States."[35] Clearly, Nebraska's congressional delegation was effectively looking after the military interests of the state.

By 1906 Secretary of War William Taft followed Elihu Root's recommendations for consolidation of the army in larger posts, to house regimental and brigade commands. Taft especially favored posts with recent construction, or ones with the potential for reservation expansion for added maneuver areas. Nebraska senators Elmer J. Burkett and Joseph H. Millard called on Taft, who told them that further improvements at Robinson were necessary if it were to be considered as a brigade or regimental post. That year Burkett introduced a bill for a $400,000 appropriation for building improvements at the post. Even so, when Taft's proposal for closing smaller posts hit the papers, nervous Crawford businessmen quickly contacted Senator Millard, who assured them that "Fort Robinson is a permanent post" and "large amounts of money will be expended on improvements."[36]

In July the War Department decided to expand Fort Russell at Cheyenne into a brigade post, and announced that Fort Robinson would be enlarged to a regimental-size post. One reason for Fort Russell's success was Wyoming's powerful senator, Francis E. Warren, who became chairman of the Senate Military Affairs Committee in 1905, a position he held for the next twenty-five years. It was no accident that from 1900 through 1910, $650,000 was spent on building improvements at Fort Robinson, while nearly $5 million was lavished on D. A. Russell.[37]

That September Secretary Taft and Gen. J. Franklin Beli, army chief of staff, visited Fort Robinson. They concluded that before the post could be considered for brigade-level expansion, additional reservation lands would have to be secured. Taft recommended the purchase of sixteen thousand acres between the main Fort Robinson military reservation and its ten-thousand-acre Wood Reserve, several miles west of the reservation boundary. Early in 1907 Senator Burkett attached an amendment to a sundry civil service bill for the sum of $140,000 to purchase the needed land. Unfortunately the provision did not survive the appropriation process.[38]

At this point, the War Department, responding to pressure from ranking officers and local politicians, attempted to make army posts more comfortable for soldiers. As part of this process buildings were constructed of stone, concrete, or brick, both for economy and durability. With hopes of expanding Fort Robinson to house a full regiment, quartermasters drew up an elaborate plan to completely rebuild the post with modern, standard brick buildings. The ambitious project called for the construction of twenty-four sets of officers' quarters, six double-company barracks, twelve troop stables, supply buildings, a riding hall, and other support buildings to accommodate a regiment of cavalry. According to the plan, almost all the existing Fort Robinson buildings were to be demolished and replaced. In the words of one quartermaster officer, "The War Department is not putting up any more temporary buildings these days."[39]

Coinciding with post renewal was a project involving the post cemetery established in 1875 when Robinson was considered temporary. Situated at the confluence of Soldier Creek and White River, the cemetery often flooded. A local editor urged the government to create a national cemetery north of the post at the foot of Red Cloud Buttes, and move the old burial ground there. "It would," the editor opined, "also be a very appropriate burial place for Red Cloud when he dies." An unnamed Fort Robinson officer followed up on the suggestion with a letter to the old chief, asking Red Cloud's consent to the plan. Red Cloud, who lived until 1909, politely declined on the grounds that he wished to be buried at Pine Ridge, next to other members of his family. Regardless of grandiose intentions, the post cemetery remained in its original location.[40]

As politicians vied for appropriations, Fort Robinson soldiers were involved in the last action between U.S. soldiers and Indians on the upper Plains. In 1906 many Ute Indians on the reservation in northeast Utah were unhappy over land allotment policies and the opening of reservation lands for white settlement. By late summer, about four hundred Utes under Red Cap and Appah left the reservation and headed northeast to Montana and South Dakota, seeking an alliance with tribes equally disillusioned. As they crossed Wyoming, the Utes ignored game laws and trespassed on private property; press reports claimed they caused damage and threatened citizens. In order to prevent violence, the governor of Wyoming requested federal troops to corral the wandering tribesmen.[41]

Secretary of War Taft wanted to send a large force to overawe the Indians and persuade them to return to their reservation. On October 21 Maj. Charles H. Grierson and Troops B and C from Fort Robinson, commanded by captains Robert Paxton and Carter Johnson, boarded a train for Gillette, in northeastern Wyoming, to block the Utes from entering Montana. Several days later Troops A and D left to join them, and a squadron of Sixth Cavalry was deployed northeast from Fort Meade. Ultimately more than eight hundred troops were in the field. Along with the soldiers went scouts from the Sioux reservation, including veterans Womans Dress and American Horse, old men called on to serve the army one more time.

On October 22 Johnson and two detachments of the Tenth Cavalry encountered the Utes fifty miles north of Gillette. Finding his quarry well armed, Johnson wisely decided to avoid conflict and called for reinforcements. As Johnson kept his men camped within sight of the Utes, the entire Third Squadron rushed up from Robinson, leaving only forty soldiers to man the post.

As additional troops arrived, tensions ran high, but several small incidents that could have resulted in violence were resolved peacefully. For several days Tenth Cavalry detachments patrolled the vicinity of the Ute camp to prevent any Crow or Cheyenne warriors from Montana from joining the Utes. On October 31 Johnson, an experienced negotiator, conferred with the Utes and eventually convinced them to move to a camp at Fort Meade, while their leaders went to Washington to argue their case. Johnson's able negotiations, and the level-headed actions of the Tenth cavalrymen prevailed. A potentially dangerous situation was resolved without a shot being fired.

As the Utes moved toward Fort Meade, the Tenth Cavalry remained in the field as a precaution, patrolling the Wyoming-Montana border. After the regiment returned to Fort Robinson, Johnson accompanied a Ute delegation to Washington, and assisted with the relocation of the Utes on the Sioux reservation near Thunder Butte. Several years later the Utes were ready to move back to Utah. On the return journey the Indians were escorted by the reliable Captain Johnson and ten enlisted men.[42]

The Tenth Cavalry's Ute incident was the last campaign for buffalo soldiers at Fort Robinson. The prejudices of civilians toward black soldiers were increasing in the early years of the twentieth century, and with incidents like the Moss shooting at Crawford in 1906, and more serious outbreaks of violence elsewhere, many whites were arguing for the removal of black regiments from stations within the United States. Conveniently, rotation to the Philippines of the black regiments, including the Tenth Cavalry, had already been planned. On February 28, 1907, five troops of the Tenth traveled by rail to San Francisco, then by steamer across the Pacific. In May the remaining three troops departed; the Tenth Cavalry had left Fort Robinson for good. With their departure, nearly twenty years of buffalo soldier garrisons at Fort Robinson had ended.[43]

For Crawford businessmen, the economic loss of two Tenth Cavalry squadrons was softened by the news that they were to be replaced by two squadrons of the Eighth Cavalry. On May 20 the field, staff, band, and first and third squadrons of the Eighth, under command of Col. Henry P. Kingsbury, arrived from Manila. Troops of the second squadron were stationed at forts Russell and Yellowstone in Wyoming.

The new soldiers settled into a routine characteristic of garrison duty in the first decade of the twentieth century. Lacking active field service, the annual practice march became an important training exercise, and the length and duration of the soldier "hikes" expanded on occasion. In late June 1910 seven troops of the Eighth Cavalry from Fort Robinson made a five-hundred-mile practice march to the sprawling Pole Mountain maneuver area west of Fort Russell. En route the troops participated in a Fourth of July celebration in Alliance. The soldiers were gone for eight weeks. Other types of training were also required for cavalry officers. All post officers, including Colonel Kingsbury, were required to make a ninety-mile annual ride.[44]

With a full garrison at the fort, the local citizens were well satisfied. On one occasion, after the troops returned from a lengthy absence, the local paper reported, "The return of the Eighth Cavalry to Fort Robinson has had the effect of enlivening the streets of Crawford in the evening." As expected, some nights were more lively than others. One night in the spring of 1908, a shooting fracas in the red-light district in northwest Crawford resulted in the wounding of "Mistress" Maud Adams. During the fusillade, two soldiers and two black civilians were also wounded.[45]

While the Eighth settled into its new surroundings, the campaign to modernize and rebuild the post was fully underway. Most of the $400,000 appropriated in 1906 was slated for new brick quarters and barracks as stipulated by the secretary of war. Reinforcing this policy, Q. M. Gen. Charles F. Humphrey added:

> There are, however, a number of garrisoned posts which were originally established and built thirty and more years ago with material and under methods of construction less substantial than now in use. The buildings at these posts have outlived their usefulness, and, aside from being cramped, inconvenient, uncomfortable, and in some cases insanitary, are in such dilapidated condition as to require large annual allotments to keep them in sufficient repair to be habitable.[46]

In the first phase of construction, four, ninety-horse troop stables and two stable guard quarters replaced older frame structures. Just south of the post gymnasium, a veterinary hospital, complete with offices, dispensary, operating room, and thirty-eight stalls for sick and convalescent horses, was built. The seven new buildings, completed in September 1908, cost just under $100,000.[47]

In 1908 work began on the quarters and barracks, the most imposing such structures ever to appear at Fort Robinson. Rounding out the west end of the parade ground were two duplex captains' quarters, one duplex lieutenants' quarters, and a single field-grade house for the post commanding officer. At the same time, a handsome, twelve-unit single officers' residence was constructed, anchoring the east end of officers' row. On the opposite side of the parade ground on barracks row were built two double-company barracks with spacious dormitory areas, mess halls, day rooms, and modern showers and toilets. They were the first and last units in a line of six projected barracks replacing older quarters. Both sets had high ceilings, a generous distribution of large windows, and were heated by steam, a far cry from the crowded, dark, log barracks of 1874.

By summer 1909 the buildings were completed and occupied by the men of the Eighth Cavalry. The new construction consumed almost all of Burkett's appropriation, and amounted to about twenty-five percent of the brick improvements planned in 1906. In 1910 a brick firehouse and hospital stewards' quarters were added. The new buildings were of standard quartermaster design and could be described as follows:

> Constructed from standardized plans and specifications developed by War Department architects, most army buildings raised between ca. 1890 and ca. 1915 exhibited uniform

design characteristics that represented the attainment of a
unique military utilitarian style widely replicated at posts
throughout the country. For lack of a better term, the type
might be designated Turn of the Century American Military.[48]

All masonry military construction in the early twentieth century
contained similar design elements, such as symmetry, repetitive window
openings, and pedimented entries. The impressive buildings added a
certain aura of dignity to the old fort. With new buildings planned and
built, and an efficient irrigation system that added trees and green lawns,
Fort Robinson was, in the words of a local newspaper, "one of the most
beautiful and attractive cavalry posts in the United States."[49]

Other forms of modernization came to the old fort. In 1908 a civilian
started a bus service between town and the post driving "a 55-horsepower
automobile, with a seating capacity for twenty-five people."[50] Boiler
systems were installed in the 1891 officers' quarters, providing more
comfortable and effective heating. And by 1910, the electrical age had
come to Fort Robinson. In 1909 wiring contracts were let, and the next
year the post received electricity from the Crawford power plant, lighting
building interiors and most of the streets.

About that time noticeable changes could be seen on the sprawling
military reservation surrounding Fort Robinson. As settlers moved to the
lands bordering the post, they cut across the reservation on their trips to
and from town, and a web of informal roads developed in addition to the
two main roads, which were originally the military trails that followed the
White River and Soldier Creek. Settlers were allowed the crossing privilege, but none of the informal routes were actually declared roads.
Settlers and townspeople were, however, forbidden to graze livestock or
harvest wood on the military reservation.[51]

Just after 1900 several small changes came to the Fort Robinson
reservation land allotment. Since 1889 the War Department had allowed
the city of Crawford to use a 134-acre tract in the extreme northeastern
corner of the reservation as a park and fairgrounds. In 1906 the military
declared this tract to have no value, and the secretary of war withdrew it
from the declared reservation and presented it to the city. Likewise, a
small parcel of rough, wooded land in the northwestern corner was of no
use to the government and was given up to settlement.

In 1891 legislation granted civilians right-of-way across military reservations to construct beneficial civil improvements. In the mid-1890s a
group of private investors received permission to construct an irrigation
ditch and holding reservoirs on the Fort Robinson reservation. The

project was intended to divert White River water west of the post and deliver it to irrigate farm lands east of Crawford. The ditch was completed across the fort before legal problems over water rights forced the project's abandonment. However, the smaller of the two holding reservoirs became the post ice pond, and the other provided the soldiers with a convenient place for fishing and duck hunting.

By 1900 Crawford citizens had become painfully aware of the consequences of being downriver from the fort. For years all the human sewage and stable drainage from the post went into the river and flowed past town. Crawford was growing and needed a source of unpolluted water. The town blamed the army for damaging its water supply, and in 1910 asked for fifty thousand dollars from the War Department for a new water system that would bring water to town from above the post lands. Secretary of War Jacob M. Dickson favored paying half that amount if an appropriation could pass Congress. The House Committee on Military affairs saw things differently and turned down the request, noting that the fort had been there before the town. Therefore the town's complaint was not the government's problem. If the issue were pushed, the fort simply could be abandoned. At the same time, other cities were complaining about damage to their water supply by army sewage, and the committee did not want Crawford's situation to set a precedent. Nebraska congressman Moses Kinkaid supported the town, but, according to newspapers, hesitated when the committee hinted about closing Fort Robinson. But when Crawford lawyer J. E. Porter went to Washington to lobby for the funds, he was assured that the army would take measures to check the dumping of solid wastes into the White River.[52]

A financial compromise was reached in 1911. The city built a dam and reservoir west of the post and was allowed to lay a twelve-inch wooden pipeline across the military reservation to bring fresh water into town. This system remained Crawford's primary water source for many years. Besides granting right-of-way for the pipeline, military authorities allowed local telephone companies and later electrical power companies to extend their poles and wires across the reservation. Civil projects such as these, and municipal land donations, represented the necessary cooperation between a town and its nearby military post.[53]

In early 1910 Crawford's approach to dealing with Fort Robinson by pandering to soldier needs for entertainment had severe economic and political consequences. At that time the state of Nebraska began a search for a western location for a new state normal school (teachers college). Along with Chadron, Alliance, and other communities, Crawford was in the running to host the institution. Local boosters stressed Crawford's advantages, including nearby Fort Robinson, where students "would derive extra benefits through observation of military life and tactics at the post."[54]

But others saw a negative influence in Crawford's history of luring troops to town by encouraging or tolerating an array of vices. The public perceived morality as lacking in many post towns, and Crawford was no exception. In 1906 saloon occupation tax and whore tax collections accounted for sixty percent of the town's local revenues. Although prostitution had been banned by city ordinance that year, Crawford residents were reminded three years later that "houses of ill repute are most [sic] too plentiful in our city." Likewise gambling, outlawed in 1903, continued in backroom clubs that also featured illegal liquor sales.[55]

In January 1910 the State Board of Education visited Crawford, and later called on Colonel Kingsbury at the fort. Although many residents were optimistic about Crawford's chances to gain the school, Chadron was selected. Crawford, seen by some (including many local residents) as "the stink pot of Northwest Nebraska," lost the opportunity to gain a respectable source of revenue, and the loss initiated a period of political tension and recrimination before the town finally clamped down on gambling and illegal houses, and gained more control over liquor sales. By then the school was lost and an opportunity for growth went along with it.[56]

Several years later the threat of the fort's abandonment arose again. The army general staff favored further consolidation of the army in large, division-sized posts. In 1912 a list of posts not "located with a view of securing economy of administration and supply, or a full measure of military effectiveness," was published.[57] Fort Robinson was on the list of posts that were not to be expanded, and its garrison ultimately would be sent elsewhere. That marked the end of the grandiose 1906 rebuilding project. Congressman Kinkaid reported to his constituents that although no money for continued construction would be allotted, the post probably would remain occupied.

In 1910, after three quiet years in garrison, the Eighth Cavalry was rotated to the Philippines. In November most of the officers held an auction to sell their household furniture, and several days later, Crawford citizens held a grand farewell banquet in honor of the departing officers. On November 27 six troops of the regiment departed, leaving the paper to comment, "They are a gentlemanly lot of soldiers, whose equal as to good behavior it will not be an easy matter to find."[58] Two troops remained at the post over the winter before joining the regiment.

In February 1911 Fort Robinson became regimental headquarters of the Twelfth U. S. Cavalry, commanded by Col. Horatio G. Sickel, Jr. On February 18 the first and second squadrons and band, numbering thirty-eight officers and 494 enlisted men, marched in. The third squadron went to Fort Meade. Before the new regiment arrived, Crawford citizens were advised, hopefully, that "the 12th Cavalry boys, who are to be stationed here, we understand, are equal to the 8th which we hope will prove to be a fact."[59]

Horatio Sickel, Jr., graduated from West Point in 1876 and transferred into the Seventh Cavalry after the Little Bighorn defeat. He served with the regiment through the 1890–91 Pine Ridge Campaign and the Spanish-American War period. He transferred into the Twelfth in 1902, became its lieutenant colonel and, later, its colonel. Like the other two cavalry regimental commanders who served at Fort Robinson in the years before World War I—Augur and Kingsbury—Sickel had graduated from the military academy soon after the Civil War, and served through the Plains Indian wars as a company-grade officer before receiving a field command after the turn of the century. The three were among the last of the old-line frontier officers to command Fort Robinson.[60]

The Twelfth Cavalry, a relatively new regiment, was organized in 1901, and did not have the longstanding traditions of service and esprit of other mounted units that had been stationed at the post. Many of the enlisted men probably had joined for the excitement of overseas service, not garrison duty at western U.S. posts. By 1913 the regiment had the second highest percentage of desertion of all U.S. Army regiments, and the highest percentage within the cavalry branch. This situation was attributed to the boredom accompanying interior guard duty, poor morale because of inaction, and inefficient personnel. In 1914 Fort Robinson had the fifth highest ratio of summary courts to average strength of eighty-nine installations in the continental United States. That year the Twelfth Cavalry also had the highest number of prisoners held in the disciplinary barracks at Fort Leavenworth of any cavalry or infantry regiment.[61]

Additionally the cavalrymen frequently resented the condescending attitude of some townspeople. As the soldiers saw it, Crawford was interested only in getting their money and continually expected them to be on their best behavior while in town on leave. Clashes with townspeople were frequent. One veteran later recalled, "I dealt Crawford a lot of misery and they dealt me a lot of misery. I always figured them a bunch of people that would take all and give nothing to the soldier. It's true."[62] On the other hand, the soldiers often displayed little regard for law and order. One night a sergeant found that two of his men had been arrested and held in jail:

> In them days they had a wooden jail, see. I said I'd be right
> down. Of course I had to get a hack, you know, from

17

Crawford, to take me down. I just got me a big round bar and I tore lock and all off. I said come on out. We ran across the street, had a glass of beer and had that hack driver bring us back home. The next morning a Crawford authority come up and wanted to find out who it was done it. . . And they told them that some of the soldiers went down there and broke the chain and made the prisoners escape. The commanding officer told them, "Damn lie, my boys wouldn't do anything like that."[63]

The Twelfth regiment seemed to have more than its share of off-duty disorderly conduct in town. In one incident in February 1916, three soldiers were jailed for indecent exposure, drunken and disorderly conduct, and breaking open the jail. Another time, after being told the car was full and refused a ride, an unruly soldier assaulted the driver of the passenger service between the post and town. Several days later drunken soldiers at the town depot attempted to force their way on to a passenger train without tickets. After a lively brawl with the conductor and train crew, they were forced to retire.[64]

Train-related accidents took a deadly toll when inebriated soldiers returned to post via the Chicago & North Western tracks. Following the rails was the shortest way back after a Saturday night on the town, and accidents occurred when drunken troopers attempted to hop passing trains for a lift to the fort. Other mishaps also took place. In the early morning hours of September 15, 1911, Pvt. William Raysner and a companion were returning to the post when Raysner got his foot stuck between the ties on the first trestle bridge west of Crawford. Although his friend tried to free the unfortunate soldier, Raysner was struck and killed by a special westbound passenger train returning fairgoers from the Dawes County fair.[65]

Drinking and carousing in Crawford saloons was a long-standing payday habit with Fort Robinson garrisons. After a 1912 payday, however, the Crawford newspaper reported there had not been a single arrest for disorderly conduct on the part of the soldiers, certainly an unusual occurrence.[66] To improve public relations, the troops gave military exhibitions and marched in local parades, and the band entertained at public celebrations. Nevertheless, the relationship between an army post and local community was ambivalent. While most soldiers were well behaved in their interactions with the civilian population, acts of misconduct often overshadowed the benefits the community received from hosting a military population.

During the Eighth Cavalry's tenure, moving picture shows were added to the entertainment available at Fort Robinson. Beginning in 1910 shows were put on by a private individual and were open to both soldiers and local civilians. As an additional attraction, in June of that year a weight lifter hoisted "the heaviest horse in the 8th Cavalry with the rider." By November movies were shown by the post engineer, featuring an hour and a quarter of films on six subjects, with a five-piece orchestra providing the music—all for ten cents admission. In August a movie featured the coronation of the king of England.[67]

In the fall of 1913 Fort Robinson soldiers appeared in a silent film. The day of the Wild West Show was over, and the premier western showman, William F. Cody, turned to this new form of entertainment. In September 1913 the Col. W. F. Cody Historical Pictures Company was formed in Denver to make movies from Western history featuring Buffalo Bill himself. The battles of Summit Springs, Warbonnet Creek, and Wounded Knee were to be reenacted.[68]

Cody's company arranged with the Department of the Interior to film on the Pine Ridge reservation, and even to make the Wounded Knee sequence on its original site. Gen. Nelson Miles, who had been in command during the 1890 campaign, came along to provide technical advice. Colonel Sickel, a Seventh Cavalry officer at Wounded Knee, went to assist "in placing troops in scenes of combat in reproducing the Battle of Wounded Knee."[69] Along with Sickel went Troops A, B, and D and a medical detachment from Fort Robinson. The troops left the post October 6 and marched to Pine Ridge. When they arrived, the producers issued them nineteenth-century army uniforms, equipment, and arms.

For several weeks the Twelfth cavalrymen played movie extras; the filming was not always enjoyable. General Miles, never an easy man to satisfy, caused substantial difficulties:

> Taking the job very seriously, he insisted upon literal truth. No incident which had not actually been part of his 1890 campaign could be pictured. There had been eleven thousand troops in the field; all must be shown. So the three hundred cavalrymen present marched past the cameras forty times; the General was not informed that after the first few repeats the lens was closed. Nor would he approve the picture unless the whole outfit were taken into the Bad Lands, miles away, in order to stage events which had originally occurred there, although the scenes might just as well have been filmed near the Camp.[70]

The filming was completed, and the troops returned to the post by October 31.

In 1915 Twelfth cavalrymen again worked in the movies, this time in a local production. A company was organized by Chadron residents to produce a "local talent" film. Their western adventure film, titled *In the Days of '75 and '76*, was a thrilling story of "Calamity Jane" and "Wild Bill" Hickok. The film featured a ride to the rescue by the U.S. Cavalry. Consequently in August several sequences were filmed on the military reservation with Twelfth Cavalry troopers again playing the cavalry of an earlier era. Although the movie's setting was 1876, the soldiers wore their 1915 uniforms and equipment. Despite such technical flaws, the movie is a valuable artifact, thought to be the earliest surviving film made in Nebraska entirely by Nebraskans.[71]

After two years of inactivity at Fort Robinson, the Twelfth Cavalry troop units began to respond to trouble looming in the Southwest. Civil strife and political unrest in Mexico brought a threat of violence along the border, and regular army units hurried south. Early in 1913 the Fourth Field Artillery and Eleventh Infantry at Fort Russell were transferred to Texas City, Texas. Troop E of the Twelfth Cavalry left Fort Robinson on April 22 to guard the Wyoming post in the absence of its regular garrison. In July Troop H departed for Cheyenne on the same temporary duty. Those units never returned to the post garrison.[72]

That fall, a dispute surfaced on the Navajo reservation in New Mexico, when eight Navajos resisted an order from the Indian agent. Newspaper accounts magnified the incident into a large-scale revolt, and in November the Indian department requested troops. The army did not want to divert troops already stationed along the Mexican border, so the first squadron at Fort Robinson was alerted for field service. On November 20 Troops A, B, C, and D, under the command of Capt. John W. Craig, started by train for the Navajo reservation. Shortly after their arrival, the dispute was resolved. Instead of returning to Fort Robinson, the first squadron was reassigned to El Paso, Texas, as part of the army buildup along the Mexican border.[73]

Other problems faced the army in 1914. Labor disturbances broke out in the coal mining regions of Colorado, Montana, and Arkansas requiring federal troops to quell the disorders. The Second Squadron of the Twelfth Cavalry was deployed to Fremont County, in south-central Colorado, to help maintain order during a strike by the United Mine Workers. In May Troops F and G and the Machine Gun Platoon left the post to join Troops E and H from Fort Russell in the strike districts. The Fort Robinson troops remained on this duty until January 1915. The army chief of staff complimented the troops on their performance of this undesirable duty, noting the soldiers preserved good order and "no overt acts of a serious character were committed in their areas of control."[74]

Barely a year later, on March 9, 1916, a large force of bandits under Pancho Villa raided Columbus, New Mexico, burning several buildings, killing eleven civilians and nine soldiers, and wounding many others. In retaliation the Punitive Expedition was organized under Gen. John J. Pershing, and additional troops hurried to the border. On March 14 the remaining Twelfth Cavalry troops at Fort Robinson, headquarters, the Machine Gun Troop, and Troops F and G, numbering 230 officers and enlisted men, quickly left the post for Columbus. Though no one knew it at the time, the last cavalrymen had left Fort Robinson.[75]

After the sudden departure, only eleven soldiers and five civilian employees remained at the post. A military station, regardless of its garrison, needs a commanding officer so on March 31, Maj. Carter P. Johnson came out of retirement to command the almost vacant post. This assignment was Johnson's fifth tour of duty at Fort Robinson. He had been there in 1877 as a Third Cavalry private at the time Crazy Horse was killed. In 1878–79 he again served at the post with the Third as a corporal during the ill-fated Cheyenne Outbreak. In 1882 he became one of the few noncommissioned officers to rise from the ranks to become an officer. As such, he was appointed as a second lieutenant in the Fourth Infantry, and again assigned to Fort Robinson. The next year Johnson transferred to the Tenth Cavalry, where he spent some years with the regiment on duty in the Southwest.

After serving in Cuba and the Philippines, Johnson arrived for duty at Fort Robinson with the Tenth Cavalry. Not desiring further overseas service, he transferred to the Eighth Cavalry, just before the Tenth left for the Philippines in 1907. In 1909 after thirty-three years of active duty, he retired at Fort Robinson as a major, and moved to a ranch west of the post on White River. Now, in 1916, he returned as commanding officer. Johnson was serving in that capacity when he died of heart problems at Alliance on December 12, while returning from a trip to Wheatland, Wyoming. As an efficiency report once said, Carter P. Johnson was "an excellent soldier and efficient officer."[76] To replace Johnson another retired officer, Capt. Frank Nickerson, a former quartermaster officer, was called up to command the post and served the next several years.

Just before the last Twelfth Cavalry units left Fort Robinson consideration had been given to using the post as a training center for regional National Guard units. When the removal of the regular garrison appeared imminent, support solicited by the Crawford Chamber of Commerce from commercial clubs in northwestern Nebraska stressed the post as an ideal location for guard training. The Nebraska congressional delegation in Washington approached the War Department's Division of Militia Affairs with this proposal. Although the officers appeared receptive, no such arrangements for training were made that summer. The next year, a board of officers visited Fort Robinson to look at matters "in relation to army preparations," and favored use of the post as a training camp. With America's sudden entry into World War I, however, the rush of war mobilization bypassed the old fort on White River, and any plan to use the fort for large-scale training was never implemented.[77]

After America entered the war, a small military presence remained at Fort Robinson. On April 1, 1917, Company I of the Fourth Nebraska National Guard, three officers and forty-one enlisted men, arrived to garrison the deserted fort. Under command of Capt. J. W. Leedom the guardsmen trained, performed regular garrison duties, recruited members, and guarded the Belmont tunnel on the C.B.& Q.R.R. from the threat of sabotage. With few exceptions, their tour of duty was relatively quiet. While on duty at the tunnel, one soldier died of cerebrospinal meningitis and was buried in the post cemetery. On another occasion, sentries shot and wounded a guardsman who was resisting arrest for drunkenness and desertion.[78]

In late July 1917 the troops were called out to help with a railroad accident on the North Western tracks crossing the military reservation. An eastbound train of full oil tank cars derailed near the post, causing one of the cars to explode into flames that created a huge cloud of black smoke. Men from Company I were the first on the scene. Under the direction of captains Leedom and Nickerson, they used a large span of mules to pull seventeen cars to safety. The engine crew managed to pull the first five cars away from the fire, but eleven cars of oil were lost. To reward their efforts the railroad company presented the guardsmen with twelve hundred dollars for their mess fund.[79]

Later that summer, a small detachment of soldiers who had been premedical students before enlisting arrived at Fort Robinson for basic medical training before their assignment to the army hospital service. After several weeks of training, the men were sent to staff a new army hospital at Jacksonville, Florida. Likewise, the use of the post by Nebraska guardsmen was short-lived. In the summer of 1917 the National Guard was federalized, and in mid-July, orders came for nationwide mobilization. Company I left Fort Robinson the last week in August for training at Camp Cody, near Deming, New Mexico. In a scene that had been repeated many times throughout Crawford's history, "a large crowd gathered at the depot to bid the boys farewell." The troops, again, were gone.[80]

Other possibilities were considered for Fort Robinson's role in the Great War. In October 1917 Gen. William H. Carter, commanding officer of the Central Division, inspected the fort for possible use as a Signal Corps training center. According to the plan, six hundred men would be sent there for signaling and telegraph training. While at the post, Carter reminisced about his first trip to Robinson as a young lieutenant in 1874, relating how at that time "there were over 1,000 Indian teepees between his camp and Crow Butte." Although the old soldier was optimistic about Fort Robinson's prospects, the training center never materialized.[81]

In May 1918 the War Department announced that the post would be garrisoned by the Fifth Battalion, U.S. Guards. This new organization was composed of men ineligible for the draft or overseas duty for physical reasons. The force was designed to protect major utilities, shipyards, arsenals, and key railroad tunnels. By 1918 U.S. Guards relieved all first-line troops protecting points in the United States considered essential to the war program. To the delight of the local community, word spread that as many as eight hundred men would be stationed at Fort Robinson, renewing local hopes for its continuance as a large military post.[82]

In early June the Fifth Battalion, less Company A, marched into the post. The new garrison, numbering some 450 officers and enlisted men, was somewhat smaller than anticipated. The men quickly undertook a regular schedule of drill, infantry training, and guard duty. Off-duty, they fished, skylarked in the buttes, and were guests of honor at Crawford's annual Fourth of July celebration. The townspeople were pleased with the new garrison, finding them "very gentlemanly" as they went about "becoming agreeably acquainted" with the local community and spending their money.[83]

The Fifth Battalion remained at Fort Robinson for only two months; on August 9 it was ordered to Rock Island Arsenal for guard duty. Captain Nickerson and his small, but vigilant, caretaker force continued to man the post. On one occasion, after statewide prohibition was declared, they successfully intercepted a car carrying eighty quarts of illegal whiskey as it passed through the post.[84]

Chapter 2

Robinson Quartermaster Depot, Remount

As the twentieth century unfolded, the U.S. Army found it increasingly difficult to secure suitable cavalry and artillery mounts. In the army's view, good animals had become scarce. In the West, the market for riding horses was in a slump and ranchers apparently stopped breeding their mares. As one officer recalled, "It was seldom, three or four years ago, that a real cavalry mount could be found in the ranch country under eight or ten years old, and these were the top horses of the cow hands and not on the market."[1]

The quartermaster branch had been responsible for providing for all of the army's needs, except horses. Traditionally, animals for the mounted services were purchased through agency branch requisition. For example, cavalry officers were detached periodically to purchase horses for their respective regiments. Securing acceptable mounts was the responsibility of that purchasing officer, in a long-standing, yet at times haphazard, procurement practice.

In 1907 Maj. Gen. James B. Aleshire, the quartermaster general, envisioned a more efficient process with the establishment of the Remount Service. Under this plan, all responsibility for purchasing and issuing horses for the army would fall under the jurisdiction of the Quartermaster Corps. Besides creating an efficient apparatus to control procurement and distribution, the army breeding plan was implemented. With increasing mechanization, both the army and the U.S. Department of Agriculture feared the American riding horse was in danger of disappearing. By implementing a breeding program the army hoped "ranchers would turn anew to the production of better horses."[2] If the mounted services, and particularly the cavalry, were to remain strategically viable, a dependable reserve of civilian-owned horseflesh needed to be maintained.

Aleshire's plan called for the establishment of several remount depots to handle horses the army purchased in areas of the country where they were commonly bred. At the depots, quartermaster personnel would be trained in handling animals, to prepare for needs arising from future military mobilization. Riding horses, draft horses, and mules would be processed and economically maintained until they were issued. Animals would also be purchased directly at the depots when necessary. Government stallions would be issued to qualified civilian agents for breeding to build up a pool of horses for future army purchase.

In 1908 the first remount depot was established at Fort Reno in central Oklahoma, to maintain horses for troops in the Southwest and along the Mexican border. The next year a similar depot was started at Fort Keogh, Montana, for the Northwest. A third depot was added in 1911 at Front Royal, Virginia, for eastern procurement and issue. At first, remount operations proceeded on a trial and error basis, but eventually official regulations and tables of organization were put into effect. A separate division of the Quartermaster General's Office was designated the Remount Division.[3]

By the end of World War I, it was a foregone conclusion that Fort Robinson had no future as a regular troop station. The large wartime mobilization saw the establishment of improved military posts in more strategic locations than the relative isolation of northwestern Nebraska. The facts were plain enough: Fort Robinson was obsolete and ripe for abandonment.

New life for the old fort came in 1919 when the War Department decided to establish a quartermaster remount depot there. Quartermaster officers were quick to realize Fort Robinson's natural advantages. It could "furnish more economical maintenance for some of the large accumulation of public animals at division camps."[4] This decision was the dawn of a new era of Fort Robinson's history, and ensured its use by the army for many more years.

Fort Robinson and its military reservation were ideal for remount operations. The post contained adequate housing with permanent barracks, officers' quarters, and other support facilities for the smaller remount garrisons. Its reservation was larger than those at other remount stations. The post lands were well watered by Soldier Creek and White River, and raised an abundant supply of prairie hay. If needed, bottomlands were suitable for farming. Most of the reservation terrain was quite hilly, which was good for building stamina in horses. In addition, the post had good rail connections to facilitate the shipment of animals in and out of the depot. As one officer later wrote, "The climate, terrain and pastures, all of those things desirable in a Remount Depot were available at Fort Robinson, in a more generous way than [at] either of the other two depots."[5]

On June 2, 1919, the adjutant general directed the commanding general of the Central Department to make Fort Robinson immediately available to the quartermaster general for remount uses. In early July 1919 Capt. Oliver L. Overmyer with forty-nine enlisted men arrived to form the first depot detachment. Several days later, between July 13 and 18, the first animals arrived, nine hundred mules from Fort Dodge, Iowa, and Camp Pike, Arkansas. On August 20 the first shipment of twenty horses was received from Fort Keogh. That fall remount officers purchased nearly two hundred riding horses locally. The remount era had begun.[6]

On November 25 Fort Robinson was officially placed under control of the Quartermaster Corps as a permanent remount depot. At first it was designated the Robinson Intermediate Depot, later becoming Robinson Quartermaster Depot, Remount. That month, depot commander Lt. Col. Edward Calvert arrived with instructions to prepare plans and estimates for construction and equipment necessary to begin remount operations. Calvert made a list that included loading pens, shelter sheds, feed bunks, a dipping vat, and farm machinery.

A major problem for remount operations at the post was the lack of fences. When Robinson was a troop station, post animals had been kept in corrals, or grazed under guard, and there was no need for division fencing. With a larger number of horses and mules at the post, however, it was necessary to guard the herds constantly to keep them from roaming. Unfortunately the depot component was too small to allow men to be detailed to ride pasture and maintain continuous control over the grazing herds. The lack of fencing along the railroad caused the loss of at least six animals that were struck by trains at night. Consequently, the horses and mules in the pastures had to be rounded up and brought into the stable corrals each night. Animals also strayed off the reservation and caused considerable damage to neighboring crops, requiring long rides by depot personnel to round them up. Fence-building became a high priority. Enlisted men cut posts on the Wood Reserve and used round wire on hand to make fences. The smooth wire served to restrain horses, but could not hold mules, and regular barbed wire was quickly substituted. By the end of the first year, thirty-eight miles of fence had been built.[7]

Another priority was the construction of shelter and feeding sheds in a pasture opposite the stables and south of Soldier Creek. All of Calvert's prepared estimates for new construction lumber were disallowed, but for the project to proceed, much lumber was needed. So, like the Fort Robinson soldiers of old, the remount troops cut the lumber from trees felled and hauled from the Wood Reserve. Six temporary, L-shaped sheds were built south of the post and provided more than fifteen hundred linear yards of feeding space. The locally-cut lumber was supplemented by surplus lumber shipped from Fort Meade, South Dakota, and Camp Dodge, Iowa.

By 1920, 927 horses and mules were on hand at the depot. The fort was garrisoned by Remount Squadron No. 9, three officers and 114 enlisted men strong, in addition to a small veterinary and medical corps detachment. With much of their time being spent on construction and animal care, the horse soldiers often neglected other aspects of military life. That year the depot experienced its first visit by the inspector general. The barracks squad rooms were found to be in a "disreputable" condition, with unmade beds, disorderly lockers, and poorly maintained surroundings. In the station hospital the inspector general found narcotics not under lock and key and records improperly kept; "the baker had not been examined for venereal disease within a month." Regardless of such shortcomings, the main purpose of the remount was the care and issue of army animals; Fort Robinson soldiers were busy converting the old cavalry post into what would eventually become the country's largest remount station.[8]

Between 1919 and 1931 the depot received ten thousand animals. Sixty-five percent were horses, most of them riding horses, the remainder draft animals. The remaining thirty-five percent were mules; one-third pack mules and two-thirds draft mules. The average number of horses and mules on hand on the first of January for each of the first twelve years was 848. The number of animals received annually varied from 1,810 in 1920 to a mere 70 the next year.[9]

Most of the animals received were bought by purchasing agents throughout the country "who were continually buying horses of suitable type when they could be found."[10] To better organize purchasing, the United States was divided into remount purchasing zones, where animals were bought and shipped to the various depots for processing. In a typical year (1925) the Remount Purchasing and Breeding Headquarters at Colorado Springs sent 216 riding horses and 98 draft horses to Fort Robinson. That year the Kansas City zone office sent 326 riding horses, while the Fort Douglas office sent 101 riding and 35 draft horses.

Horses purchased were thoroughbreds, fifteen hands and one inch high, and straight-gaited. Brown and black horses with a minimum of white markings were chosen; grays, pintos, and light animals were rejected because they were thought too readily visible to an enemy. Unmanageable horses were usually not purchased. The average price paid for a riding horse for cavalry issue was $165. For several years in the early 1920s, the government put a hold on horse purchases. When purchasing resumed in July 1924, agents apparently "used great care in buying and as a result very few poor animals were received."[11] In addition to horses purchased from remount zones, some animals were bought locally. At Fort Robinson, depot officers found that locally purchased animals were comparable to those shipped in. Local purchases had other benefits: the owner sold his animals on a home market at a fair price, and the seller learned just what type of horse the army would buy.

For riding, the army preferred thoroughbred and half-bred horses. The name thoroughbred was properly applied to a breed of running horse originally developed in England. The thoroughbred possessed a splendid walk and trot with bursts of speed, and had strength, courage, and stamina. The thoroughbred gave a more balanced ride, carrying the weight of the rider evenly between fore- and hindquarters. Half-bred horses were produced by crossing thoroughbred sires with half-bred or other well bred mares. By this time it was well-established that thoroughbreds could be produced in the West, and not just in eastern areas. Then, the horses and mules were sent to the depots, where "they have the life of pampered pets, properly fed, properly sheltered in the cleanest of clean stables."[12]

Meticulous records were kept on each army animal, and immediately after purchase a temporary identification number was painted on each horse in silver nitrate. The incoming animals were placed in isolation pens for forty-eight hours. The depot veterinarian closely inspected the new arrivals and made decisions regarding medical tests, beginning his overall supervision of animals while they remained at the depot. Medical records were initiated on each animal received, starting with where the animal came from, the date of receipt, and its condition at the time. During the processing of new animals, frequent inspections were made to detect any disease that might affect the health of other incoming animals and those already on hand. The post had six isolation corrals, each with the capacity of about fifty animals, located in the southeastern part of the fort next to the railroad tracks. After the initial isolation period, the animals were taken to the branding chute in the west stable area. Later, as the depot began to receive larger numbers of animals, a chute was built in the receiving area to expedite branding during the processing stage. Horses and mules were moved from one part of the post to another via twenty-foot-wide, double-fenced animal lanes that controlled and directed herd movements to the desired stable and pasture areas.

At the branding chute each horse and mule received the Preston brand that was an identifying mark for all remount animals. The brand was a combination of one letter and three numerals, A001, A002, and so on for as many numbers as were needed. Each animal carried its own unique number for permanent identification and recording. The hair was clipped on the left side of the neck below the head and the brand applied. After branding, the animals were given the intradermic mallein test to determine freedom from glanders, and were immunized against encephalomyelitis, or sleeping sickness. The animals were then taken back to the isolation area to begin a twenty-one-day quarantine, with subsequent medical checks.[13]

All newly purchased animals were run through a dip vat to stop the spread of ringworm and eliminate body lice. The dip vat used at the post was sixty feet long, three feet wide, and eight feet deep; remount men sometimes used electric probes to encourage the animals into the dip solution. The dipping process took place after seven days of quarantine. When the initial twenty-one-day receiving quarantine ended, the animals were moved to quarantine pastures or traps for sixty days of additional observation. At the end of this period the horses and mules went through the condition and issue stable, where remount personnel roached manes and trimmed fetlocks, hooves, and tails. In this area the animals were weighed and measured. A horse was classified partially by how much it weighed. During this process small injuries were observed and treated and the animals returned to pasture, ready for the conditioning stage of the remount procedure.

Conditioning for remount horses began when they were assigned to a specific pasture and put on a diet. Some remount officers believed that military horses could not be conditioned in fewer than 120 days. They reasoned that horses were very susceptible to diseases and sickness incidental to movement or changes in environment. Newly purchased horses frequently suffered bouts of strangles (a form of distemper), rhinitis, and other respiratory illnesses. Remount officials believed it was best to allow an animal to contract such ailments and recover on its own, after which most developed immunity. During this period the horses were fed a fattening ration of oats, corn, and bran to put them in good condition. Sick animals were held until they recovered.[14]

The training of cavalry riding horses began at the condition and issue (C & I) stable, where they were bridled, saddled, and ridden for the first time. Experienced officers recorded each new mount's characteristics, such as nervousness, its reaction to being ridden, and bad habits such as kicking. Horses were not thoroughly trained as cavalry mounts at the depots, but had to be tractable and easily handled when they left for troop service. The riding process started in an oblong breaking pen, about thirty by sixty feet, with flared sidewalls to prevent injury to the rider's knees. The floor was sand with salt added in winter months to prevent freezing.

Before a horse could be issued it had to be ridden under saddle and snaffle bit at three gaits, and be gentle enough to permit a handler to pick up each foot without the horse being restrained. Training riding horses was a year-round operation with men riding each day. Winter training was aided by the conversion of one of the old frame cavalry stables to a riding hall in the early 1920s. Before shipment, the training officer and depot commander observed the riding of each animal and certified that each met the necessary requirements. Following regulations, animals could not be issued without a properly approved requisition.

Gentle horses were marked as suitable for issue. Fractious horses were classified as "re-ride" and would have to be ridden until they passed inspection. Many newly purchased horses were already well broken, but had not been ridden for a time and were high spirited. Remount veteran Ed Bieganski recalled his service at the C & I stable:

> Actually we had a rodeo every day, or every day that there
> were horses to ride. Once a horse quit bucking, he'd walk,
> trot, gallop. We'd call them well broke and gentle. Some of
> the cavalry and artillery didn't quite agree with that classifi-
> cation, but that's the way they were issued out.[15]

Ideally, remount officers wanted all horses to receive at least some preliminary training prior to issue so that receiving organizations would not get totally green, unbroken animals. Enlisted men were expected to do much of the gentling and training rather than leaving the task to the civilian depot employees. In the army's view, "training of remounts in peace time coincides with the duties they [the enlisted men] would perform in war."[16]

The issue of an animal completed the remount cycle. Depot personnel were constantly reminded that their duty was to issue "animals to organizations in the line and get these animals to their destinations in a highly satisfactory condition."[17] During the final processing and just before issue, each animal was weighed and measured, and the descriptive records were corrected. The depot veterinarian made a final check within four hours of shipment and always within two hours of loading the animals into the railroad cars.

The first issue from the Robinson depot was in December 1919, when sixty draft mules were issued to the post quartermaster at Fort Leavenworth. For the next twenty-five years animals were issued to posts and organizations in the Fifth, Sixth, Seventh, and Ninth Corps areas, the mounted service schools, and foreign possessions where troops were posted. In 1923 the first lot of three-year-olds was selected for the cavalry school at Fort Riley. Suitable young horses were also sent to the Fort Sill artillery school in Oklahoma, and on occasion to West Point; issues were also made to ROTC units and National Guard cavalry and artillery organizations.[18]

By design, Fort Robinson remounts went largely to posts in the central and western zones of the interior. Animals were routinely shipped to forts Riley and Leavenworth in Kansas; Fort D. A. Russell, Wyoming; Vancouver Barracks and Fort Lewis in Washington; forts Bliss and Sam Houston in Texas; and the presidios of San Francisco and Monterey in California. The depot also made occasional issues to eastern posts, such as Fort Myer, Virginia, and Chanute Field in Illinois. Overseas shipments went to the Philippines, the Canal Zone, Hawaii, and Chilkoot Barracks in Alaska. Between 1920 and 1931 the depot issued 9,758 horses and mules. One third of the issues were draft and pack mules; the majority were cavalry riding horses.

Another key remount depot function was to establish a breeding program. The program was partially experimental, to test the virility of government stallions, and partially educational to acquire knowledge in breeding techniques. The army also gained valuable experience in the care and development of young horses, yearlings and two- and three-year-olds. Information gained by depot breeding programs could then be shared with civilian horse breeders, all in the interest of increasing production of suitable horses.[19]

The breeding program at the Robinson depot took several years to develop. Breeding stock, thoroughbred stallions and mares, was kept segregated from the newly purchased animals. Stallions were exercised and ridden during the breeding season to keep them in "hard" condition. Depot stallions were bred exclusively to the depot mare herd. The broodmare herd originated with the receipt of 125 mares from Fort Keogh depot in 1920.

During the first years, the depot animals produced thirty to forty foals annually. Depot colts were raised for special army purposes: half were to go to the cavalry school, a quarter to the artillery school, and a quarter made available for purchase by officers. Officers' purchases of colts were at the discretion of the depot commander. Depot colts were issued or sold annually at three, and later four years of age. The colts were classified and trained according to age: weanlings, yearlings, two- and three-year-olds.[20]

The depot stallions were the finest horse stock owned by the army, all of "high type," and exceedingly well bred. Famous remount stallions at Fort Robinson included Fitzgibbon, K of K, and Pillory, who arrived in 1931. The most outstanding and successful depot stallion may have been Gordon Russell, who produced splendid colts. Occasionally, retired race horses were loaned to the government for stud use. In 1933 Sir Barton, owned by Dr. Joseph Hylton of Douglas, Wyoming, was placed at Fort Robinson. Sir Barton is remembered as the first triple-crown winner in 1919. The inclusion of a highly regarded stallion into the breeding program did not guarantee results. This outcome was particularly true in the case of Dinter, a highly touted Prussian stallion that arrived at the depot in 1928. After three years he was removed from the stallion stable, as his offspring "could not compare with the colts sired by the excellent thoroughbred stallions that are available here."[21]

In line with the breeding program was the remount service, where tested stallions were issued to civilian breeders to improve western bloodlines. By this means, a reservoir of suitable horses would be created to meet future military needs. In one remount area, one hundred stallions were in the hands of civilian agents, "the cheapest subsidy the government ever put across," as one remount officer stated with satisfaction.[22]

The army wanted competent ranchers and stockmen, who had suitable broodmares, to receive its thoroughbred stallions. Interested civilians applied to their appropriate area purchasing and breeding office, which investigated applicants as to reliability, facilities to care for the stallion, and the opportunity to breed the horse to suitable mares. Once a civilian applicant was approved, he received agent status and was shipped a stallion at government expense. The agent was responsible for all other costs, including feeding and medical care. As compensation, he could charge a ten-dollar service fee for each mare bred. The agent was required to report to the depot the number of mares bred each season, and the number of foals produced. Owners of the new offspring were under no obligation to sell the colts to the army, although when the need arose, the remount would buy those meeting its strict standards.[23]

Stallion issues to civilians started at the Robinson depot in 1923, with twelve animals. The number gradually increased and by 1932, sixty-two stallions were issued to breeders in Nebraska, Colorado, the Dakotas, Montana, and other western states. In the early period of remount operations, civilians were permitted to bring their mares to Fort Robinson to be bred there by army stallions, but this practice soon ended and the stallions were sent out to the mares.

Most agents gave the government stallions excellent treatment because they appreciated the program and the opportunity to participate. However, others returned horses in poor condition, sometimes with incurable injuries. In 1930 three stallions were returned in such bad condition they had to be destroyed. Remount officers often visited agents to check on their care of issue stallions, and they frequently received tips on agent mistreatment from outside parties. Agents who continued to prove unsatisfactory were denied future participation.[24]

The remount service did much to reestablish horse raising in the western states. Better horses were produced and breeders paid more attention to care and feeding, all in the interest of providing a market for army horse purchasers. To remount officers, the re-emergence of horse production was "a most valuable asset to the army and Nation as well."[25]

By 1925 the Robinson depot was functioning efficiently and as expected. Depot operations were divided into six sections, the animal, veterinary, and breeding sections to deal with depot livestock, and the supply, administration, and personnel sections to manage and provide for the enlisted and officer complement.[26]

The animal section was responsible for receiving, pasturing, training, conditioning, and issuing all animals. The men of animal section were also responsible for the condition of the stable areas, and performed the regular maintenance required there. Manure and wastes from the large number of horses and mules had to be removed daily from the stables and corrals and be incinerated, or used for soil enrichment. Feeding occupied much of the men's time. In winter the animals were moved from the open pastures into sheltered areas along the White River. In addition to hay and alfalfa, they were fed a balanced ration of bran, oil meal, and cracked corn with a crushed oat base. They were fed at large circular feeders designed to prevent horses from kicking each other while feeding. A single feed area might require as many as 350 bales of prairie hay, thirty-five bales of alfalfa, and ten sacks of grain every day.[27]

At times during the receiving and processing stages, hundreds of horses and mules would be moved to different points around the post. Incoming shipments were often unloaded in Crawford, and the animals driven to the fort. The job of moving large numbers of horses called for planning. On one occasion, a routine movement turned into a wild stampede as man struggled to control horse:

> In January we were bringing in about 300 head of horses from the southeast pasture, as we approached the railroad track, the engine on the siding blew its whistle, and our

horses stampeded. Went through the fence, broke it like matchwood, another rider and I went through them and tried to head them off to keep them off the parade ground. We managed to turn them, and took them down in front of the veterinarians office, in through another fence, out into another pasture.[28]

In this melee seven horses were killed and numerous others seriously injured, but the soldiers managed to keep the animals from running through the NCO row and barracks area, thus avoiding human injury.

The veterinary section had charge of quarantine and testing of incoming animals, and was responsible for the general health and sanitation of all animals at the depot. Each day veterinarians closely inspected corrals and stables, always on the lookout for sick animals. Diseases generally encountered at the depot included enteritis, abscesses, influenza, and pneumonia, in addition to abrasions, sprains, and other injuries that were a daily occurrence in the corrals and pastures. In a typical year (1929) the veterinary section treated 633 animals with 791 conditions, which included 213 traumatic injuries, 310 communicable diseases, and 268 noncommunicable diseases. Seventy-five percent of the communicable diseases were respiratory. With animals coming into the depot from distant points, a variety of equine health problems appeared, often causing loss. For example, in 1921 eighteen mares and seven colts died from swamp fever, and in 1925 infectious anemia caused the loss of twenty-eight mares.[29]

The busy enlisted men of the Veterinary Corps divided their time between hospital work, cleaning pens, and pasture riding. Each day a veterinary officer and several soldiers rode to the pastures looking for sick horses. Pasture riders were able to spot sick horses at a glance; such animals often were lethargic. The soldiers would rope and lead them back to the hospital for care. After several days under cover receiving medical care, most improved and were sent back to the pastures. If a horse or mule was down, a horse-drawn (later motorized) trailer was used to bring in the patient.

Besides animal care, veterinary officers inspected all commercially purchased hay and grain. In 1929 Fort Robinson veterinarians accepted 2,500 tons of hay, rejecting 150 tons that were not up to specifications. They also were required to inspect and condemn animals for surplus sale, or, when necessary, for destruction. The veterinary section inspected all meat, food, and dairy products before issue to the troops. Depot veterinarians also provided a small animal practice for post residents, and, when no veterinary services were available there, in Crawford as well.

The breeding section had charge of depot stallions, broodmares, colts, and all breeding activity. While breeding represented only a small part of depot work, the men assigned there were capable and serious. Carefully selected enlisted men were on duty with depot animals at all times to attend to the proper feeding and handling of mares and colts. In the breeding section, "every effort is used to maximum extent for production of the best type and quality of army mounts."[30] All depot breeding was confined to thoroughbred stock.

Nonproductive and unsuitable broodmares were "ruthlessly" eliminated; the policy of the breeding section was to keep only regular producers in the nursery.[31] Non-producers were replaced with depot-raised fillies and the best three-quarter and thoroughbred mares purchased from civilian sources. One of the celebrated mares in later years at Fort Robinson was the famous jumper Jenny Camp, a silver medal winner at the 1936 Berlin Olympic games.

Colt production was important, and foaling time was a special event for depot personnel. Capt. Nels Christensen recalled the interest when colts were being foaled:

> If there was a party at the officer's club on a Saturday night, it was not unusual for the club to empty by nine o'clock because everybody had to go home and get to bed and be ready for tomorrow's work. When foaling time came in the broodmare barn, the telephone operator had a list of individuals that were to be notified when the mare was foaling. . . . [A] call would come to the officer's club. And when it came, everybody at the club, including ladies in formal gowns, rushed to the broodmare, to the mare barn where the foaling was taking place in order to see what the youngster or youngsters looked like.[32]

The young horses received extra care, with special stables for each age group. The colts' feet received particular attention and their hooves were trimmed when they were young to prevent crooked feet. Halter breaking often began as early as three months.

The administrative and personnel branch controlled the pay, mess, and welfare of all post personnel. It was also in charge of all remount depot and post records, and performed all headquarters staff duties, including enlistments. When there were vacancies in the enlisted component, new remount soldiers were often enlisted at the post. Many enlisted men with long careers in the U.S. Army enlisted at post headquarters, or were transferred to the Robinson depot just after enlistment elsewhere.

The supply section was responsible for all routine procurement and distribution and kept property accounts for the post. Like the administrative and personnel sections, this section was a basic adjunct of every military installation. Unlike at other posts, however, the supply section at Fort Robinson was in charge of farming activity. In the remount era, the post was self-sufficient for much of its food, both for human and animal consumption. By the early 1920s the remount farm consisted of a dairy herd of twenty cows and twenty-one head of other cattle. Hogs and chickens were also raised at the farm.

Livestock forage production began in 1920. Bottomlands were broken with the aid of four, fifteen to thirty horsepower Titan tractors that were received at the post still crated for wartime shipment overseas. It was soon determined that the tractors were heavier than necessary for bottomland farming, and by the 1923 season, mule teams were substituted. Several hundred acres of alfalfa were planted and harvested, and prairie hay was cut and baled. In 1929, when purchased hay cost twenty dollars per ton, the post farm crew could produce it for only eight dollars per ton, a substantial savings. Depot farming operations were "watched by the commanding officer as though the farm was his own investment upon which he desires as great a return as possible."[33] Working the depot farmland was also good training for draft horses and mules before issue.

In the 1920s the army made a cost-effectiveness study of its remount depots. Fort Robinson was the most economical of the three, located as it was in excellent farming country with a climate that afforded longer grazing periods. In 1927 it cost twenty-six cents per day to keep one animal at the Front Royal Depot; about twenty cents per head per day at Fort Reno. At Fort Robinson the cost was only seven (.069) cents per head per day. The study summed up, "As an institution it [Fort Robinson] fully justifies its operation and maintenance as serving a valuable function and as a unique instance of Government economy and efficiency." At Robinson, horses could be produced in the nearby regions at a low cost and at the depot they could be cared for and handled economically, all to the satisfaction of the army Quartermaster Corps.[34]

After the establishment of the Fort Robinson depot, the abandonment of remount activities at Fort Keogh became feasible. The Fort Keogh depot was expensive to operate because of its distant location and the activities there could be better handled at Robinson. In 1923 all the Fort Keogh broodmares and colts were transferred to Fort Robinson. In 1924 the quartermaster remount requested and received permission from the

War Department to close its operations at the old Montana post. After fifty years of army use, Fort Keogh was transferred to the U.S. Department of Agriculture for agricultural research work.

One of the benefits of closing the Fort Keogh remount station was the transfer of Eric "Bud" Parker to the Robinson depot in 1924. As a civil service horse trainer, Bud became a Fort Robinson institution. Born in 1893 in Texas, Bud grew up near Fort Keogh at Miles City, Montana. He served with the remount in World War I, and then came home to work for the remount as a civilian. Parker's expertise in handling horses and his horsemanship became legendary. He held a reserve lieutenancy in the Quartermaster Corps and performed with depot polo and exhibition teams. When recalling Bud Parker, one remount veteran remembered him as "one of the best horsemen he had ever known," and another called him "the most capable man in handling green horses that I have ever seen." The successful operation of the Robinson depot was largely due to the fine horsemen who worked there, and as the record shows, Bud Parker was the best.[35]

Remount officers were always seeking to attract new interest in horse breeding. Explanations of remount breeding operations were published in the local papers to inform the public. Stallion and mare exhibits were sent to area county fairs to "attract the attention of private owners to breeding privilege offered at remount depots." Interested civilian breeders were encouraged to visit the depot, where quartermaster personnel received them hospitably. In this era of increasing mechanization, the success of army breeding programs depended heavily on gaining and keeping the interest of civilian agents.[36] During the 1930s the depot held frequent open houses, where jumping competitions and horse exhibits were common fare. On occasion, members of the Fourth Cavalry from Fort Meade participated. Informal horse shows with hunter-jumper and working cowhorse competitions were held. Crawford businessmen attended dinners at the post, complete with tours and demonstrations.

Ultimately, the big public event became Quartermaster Day, celebrated on June 16, the anniversary of the founding of the supply corps. The first Fort Robinson Quartermaster Day was observed in 1924 to show the public the depot's accomplishments. The program included animal exhibits, foot races, a tug-of-war, an enlisted men's polo game, a chariot race, and a baseball game, with a free barbecue at noon and a public dance at the post gymnasium in the evening. Preparations were made for three thousand visitors, but four thousand showed up. The depot cooks prepared 150 gallons of stew and several hundred apple pies, enough food for all the visitors, and some left over. The day was a tremendous success, and the horse exhibits "awakened more interest than was believed possible" among local ranchers.[37]

Although later Quartermaster Days did not reach the same level as the 1924 celebration, it became an annual event. Subsequent celebrations featured barbecues held at the Wood Reserve or on the lower parade ground. On several occasions the Fourth Cavalry Band provided the entertainment, but the mainstay was always the horse events and exhibitions of depot animals.

There were other avenues to promote the remount and bring Fort Robinson activities before the public. In 1939 a veterinary clinic was held for area stockmen. More than two hundred attended the demonstrations on the use of a stomach tube, breeding, castration, and autopsy. A noon lunch was offered. Local school classes and groups from the nearby Chadron teachers' college made periodic visits. Each year the Rev. George A. Beecher, "The Bishop of the Great Plains," was permitted to hold his boys' summer camps on the Wood Reserve. Although not directly involved with remount operations, Beecher's camps provided camping, swimming, wood carving, games, and spiritual enrichment for young boys. As a part of each summer's session, the campers spent time at the post to see the army activities there.[38]

Although most personnel at the Fort Robinson Quartermaster Depot were military, civilian employees augmented the force. Some civilians were long-term, permanent workers, employed throughout the entire remount period. Baird Cobb, Roscoe "Shorty" Craig, A. Leon "Pat" Humbert, Ed Nyberg, and others spent many productive years at Fort Robinson, contributing to successful remount operations.

Civilian employment at the depot actually began from necessity. In the years after World War I, reductions in the strength of the army prohibited a full enlisted component at Fort Robinson, and civilian workers were hired to make up the difference. During 1920 and 1921 depot operations were almost totally dependent on civilian laborers, who did most of the farming and ran the condition and issue stables. By the mid-1920s, military replacements arrived and thereafter civilian labor was limited in large part to new construction and farming operations. By the 1930s only four civilians were working with the animal section because of their proven ability in training horses for the remount. Temporary civilian positions were maintained to perform clerical duties, carpentry, and farm work during the planting and harvesting seasons, and civilians were also hired as depot night watchmen.[39]

During most of the remount period, Fort Robinson's enlisted component numbered about one hundred men. In the early years, the personnel

section experienced difficulty receiving and retaining an adequate number of soldiers to garrison the station. Many of the first men who arrived
had enlisted for only one year, and others were transferred in without any
experience or interest in the remount service. Some felt Fort Robinson's
isolated location made it difficult to retain single enlisted men.[40]

Some of the new recruits had aptitude for animal work, while others
did not. In 1929 several recruits arrived with no experience or desire to
work with livestock; the recruiting service had promised that they would
be assigned to a motor transportation unit at Fort Robinson, and not an
animal depot.[41] Whenever possible, however, replacements with a background in animal husbandry were forwarded to the depot. Pvt. Elmo
Brangham received his remount assignment after basic training at Fort
Leonard Wood:

> He [interviewing officer] wanted to know if I wanted to be a
> truck driver, I told him the people, . . . there at Fort Leonard
> Wood, drove like crazy. . . . I thought I'd driven cars and
> trucks some but I didn't want to stick my neck out to be
> included in that group the way they drove there, so I told the
> officer that I didn't want to be a truck driver and he said,
> "How about being a clerk here?" I said I don't type. . . . He
> said, "Well, I see by your record that you used to break and
> train horses." Which I did at home, I was born and raised on
> a ranch in Idaho. So he said, "How'd you like to be trans-
> ferred to the Remount at Fort Robinson, Wyoming—or Fort
> Robinson, Nebraska, rather?" I told him that would suit me
> just fine.[42]

At Robinson, where animal work was the first priority, incoming
recruits seldom received formal military training. Kenny Hutson, upon
failing to salute a colonel, was asked, "Soldier, don't you salute an officer
when you meet one?" The rookie replied in earnest, "Yes, why, are you an
officer?"[43] At this point in Fort Robinson's history, military protocol was
secondary to riding and caring for horses and mules. Riding classes were
organized in the early 1930s to better prepare novice horsemen for their
new occupation. Not until much later was there any organized effort
toward soldier basic training at the post.

Along with receiving and issuing animals, the enlisted men performed
a daily routine of stable cleaning, replacement of clay on stall floors,
grooming, and feeding. In the summer, they often worked beside civilian
workers putting up hay. In addition to their regular tasks, remount soldiers

were occasionally called upon for special duty. In August 1936 soldiers guarded President Franklin D. Roosevelt's train while it stopped in the Crawford yard for several hours. The president was on a tour of drought-stricken states, and his train was delayed in Crawford while switching railroad lines. Because the halt was made in the early morning, Roosevelt was asleep and the soldiers never had an opportunity to see him. In November 1935, after being launched in the Black Hills, the Stratosphere Balloon set the world's altitude record before landing in central South Dakota. Several remount truck drivers were detailed to transport the balloon's gondola to Washington, D.C. Limited to driving only three hundred miles a day, the soldiers were absent for several weeks before returning to the post.[44]

As with earlier fort garrisons, the remount men cultivated an excellent post garden to supplement their regular mess. One year a ten-acre garden produced 10,985 pounds of potatoes, 550 pounds of kale, 3,666 pounds of carrots, and 307 pounds of kohlrabi, among other produce. Gardening was so successful that exhibits of post produce were sent to county fairs and once were part of an award-winning Dawes County exhibit at the Nebraska State Fair. In 1923 a canning outfit was purchased for the enlisted mess, and three thousand jars of vegetables were put up.[45]

Some enlisted men were hired by officers to serve as their "strikers" or "dog-robbers," the time-honored titles for part-time orderlies. Strikers often lived in the officer's house, shoveling snow and firing furnaces in winter and taking care of lawns in summer. As in the days of old, being a striker normally excused a soldier from part of his daily duties, and he received extra pay, usually about ten dollars a month, for his services to the officer.[46]

Other duties aside, most remount soldiers worked with the animals. Working around large animals, particularly newly received horses and mules, could prove dangerous and even fatal. In 1940 Pvt. Marvin Miller of the remount detachment was kicked in the face by a horse, putting him in the post hospital for several days. A few years earlier, Pvt. Clarence Chulk, a Chadron native, was fatally injured when a team of mules he was leading broke away. Chulk had the lead rope tied around his wrist, and he was dragged by the runaways. His funeral was held in the gymnasium and he was buried in the post cemetery.[47]

Various activities and diversions were initiated to improve troop morale. Outdoor sports, bowling, and triweekly movies provided amusement for all post personnel. Dances in neighboring towns and biweekly enlisted dances on post were a main form of entertainment. In the 1930s the Chief Red Cloud Post No. 2232 of the Regular Veterans Association provided social activity for the soldiers and local civilian veterans. Two playgrounds, one for enlisted men's children and the other for officers' children, were installed. Post children "find many forms of recreation and apparently in general enjoy good health and are happy."[48] The availability of off-duty diversions and adequate housing for married enlisted personnel raised morale and added to the contentment of Fort Robinson soldiers. Although its garrison was small, by 1938 the post held one of the highest reenlistment percentages of the entire army.[49]

During the remount period, six or seven commissioned officers were normally assigned to the post, with the post commander holding the rank of major or lieutenant colonel. Most officers were from the quartermaster branch, with an occasional cavalry or field artillery officer detached to remount duty. The officer complement included one or two Veterinary Corps officers. Some years three to six reserve quartermaster officers arrived for two weeks of active duty training. One of the notable reservists who served at Fort Robinson was Pierre Lorillard, Jr., millionaire tobacco heir and a lieutenant colonel in the quartermaster reserve, who frequently treated the enlisted men to beer and cigarettes.

Officers had to fill the nominal post commissioned positions, and perform all the other assorted tasks associated with remount operations. Officers had charge of the various stables for issue stallions, riding and training, and weanlings and directed farm and dairy operations. The officers' duties were combined as logically as possible in regard to the chain of command, all under the close supervision of the depot commander. Newly assigned officers found remount duty involved longer hours than was required at regular posts. Lt. Leo Cooksley described his day:

> My main duty was in the Animal Section, which included the Condition & Issue Stable, where issue horse and mules were processed daily. This included feet and manes trimmed and each animal ridden and rated as to state of training and readiness for issue to cavalry units in the field. In addition I was assigned duty at the Bloodstock stable [for depot-raised yearlings through threes], plus one trap [pasture] or more where my job was to look for sick or injured animals. Each trap held from 250 to 300 head of issue horses. A civilian cowboy plus one or two mounted enlisted men did most of the work, sorting off and catching the sick or injured horses, but an officer had the responsibility to see that all was accomplished properly, daily, leaving the stable area no

later than seven each morning. The Post Commanding Officer
usually monitored the stable area, starting at about 6:30 a.m.[50]

Incoming officers were advised that at Fort Robinson a private automobile was "a real convenience. Post is isolated." They were warned that
full-time servants were seldom available, but there was "good fishing near
the post: trout and bass are caught."[51] Officers assigned to remount duty
were dedicated, professional horsemen and soldiers, who served well in
the last years of the mounted services. Post commanders Capt. Lee O. Hill,
Maj. Edwin N. Hardy, and colonels Frank Carr and Edward M. Daniels all
went on to head the remount division in Washington. Capt. Edward W.
Sawyer, who served at the post in 1942 and returned in 1947–48, rose to
the rank of major general before his retirement in 1964. Lt. Col. Russell
McNellis, the depot veterinarian in the last years, later became a brigadier
general and chief of the Veterinary Corps.[52] While serving at the fort all
officers observed the long-standing tradition that whenever an officer was
thrown or fell off his horse, he had to buy drinks that night for the crowd
at the club. Some bragged about being treated to drinks by those with
reputations as exceptional horsemen—until they, too, fell and were
"fleeced" by the club.[53]

The remount years brought a number of changes to the physical layout
of the post, with many new structures being erected on the main post area
and in the various pastures, feedlots, and segregated corral areas. Many
old buildings, surplus to current needs, were removed between 1920 and
1930.[54] When the remount took over Fort Robinson there were about one
hundred major buildings at the post. But before 1919 the post had been
nearly abandoned; the older frame and adobe buildings were rapidly
deteriorating and some were in an advanced state of dilapidation. Small
outbuildings and wooden walks were "practically in ruins," and all
buildings needed exterior paint.[55]

The remount detachment quickly adapted the old cavalry station to fit
their needs, using five of the old wooden troop stables in a new role to
ready animals for issue. In the brick stables, box stalls replaced the narrow
standing stalls formerly used for the troopers' horses. Several of the old
frame stable guard quarters were converted to stallion stables. For its first
decade at Fort Robinson, the remount used what was available until new
facilities could be built.

In addition to a lack of fencing, one of the problems facing the new
occupants was the many public roads that crossed the reservation. Post
officers feared that civilian traffic would hamper remount grazing and
farming operations, and interfere with projected fencing projects. As a

solution, the War Department decided to allow only three routes to cross the reservation: the main east-west road along White River, a road running up the Soldier Creek valley, and a road running straight south from the post to Deadman Creek. Adjacent farmers and ranchers were not happy, and boundary fences were cut on several occasions. Eventually, the Deadman road was also closed because neighboring civilians became accustomed to the army's eminent domain over what was once open land. The state of Nebraska was granted a right-of-way along the old main road, which was rebuilt as a state and later federal highway.[56]

Another problem was that the entire Wood Reserve was under private lease to the Coffee Cattle Company, which denied the remount some ten thousand acres of additional grazing lands. For several years the army attempted to have the lease revoked, and the Coffee company made every effort to retain its grazing privileges for the full five-year term. Finally in 1924 the lease expired and was not renewed. Remount officers fenced the reserve into three grazing pastures and built a log cabin to house a herd caretaker.[57]

As division fences were built on the reservation, wells were drilled, and windmills and concrete water tanks installed to water stock in areas away from running water. Large hay sheds were built to protect hay harvested on the post or purchased for feeding. In sheltered areas along the White River, feed traps were constructed to hold animals for both winter feeding and gathering for shipment. The traps were fifty-to one-hundred-acre fenced areas that held several hundred head.

Beginning in the late 1920s work began on new stables for the depot animals. By this time it was apparent that the depot stock (stallions, broodmares, and colts) had to be totally segregated from newly purchased animals, which were "constantly infecting the Depot with various kinds of diseases which the animal kingdom is heir to."[58] By then, the frame buildings in the stable area, which had been condemned years before the remount arrived, were beyond repair. A large area west and northwest of the main post was designated as the new location for all depot animals.

In 1926 a seventy-four-stall, U-shaped broodmare stable and thirty-stall yearling stable were built just beyond the water towers. Two years later a mare stable was built just beyond the upper end of the parade ground. The new stables and adjoining corrals were built of lumber cut by the soldiers from the Wood Reserve. In 1930 a sixty-by-sixty foot stallion stable was added, as a home and showplace for the five depot stallions. Fenced paddocks for each animal radiated from the sides and back of the attractive, cupola-topped structure, which was landscaped with shrubs, a circular driveway, and stone walls. As this part of the post was now under the breeding section, a veterinary annex with office, examination room, and attendants' sleeping quarters was built just south of the mare stable. The west remount area was landscaped with trees, flower beds, and white frame fences. At the same time the receiving and conditioning areas were completely rebuilt, and an animal lane was completed to Crawford, removing the danger of trailing horses down the highway.

With new improvements came the demolition of older, unneeded buildings. In 1923 the last five remaining 1887 adobe troop barracks were demolished, clearing the south side of the parade ground. On the hill immediately above the warehouse area, a number of old quartermaster support buildings, including employee quarters, a gun shed, quartermaster stables, and the post chapel, were removed. The last of the wooden troop stables and adjoining stable guard quarters were gone by 1930. Below the old 1874 parade ground, five sets of NCO quarters, built between 1886 and 1902, were demolished or removed. Between 1928 and 1931, twenty-six post buildings, derelict relics of the old cavalry days, were torn down in the post's second great period of "urban renewal." And in 1929 the old salute gun left the post. Mounted on an iron tripod in the space opposite the east brick barracks, it was used for years by cavalry garrisons to fire the morning and evening guns. No longer necessary in the remount period, the gun was presented to the city of Crawford, and set up in the city park for martial ornamentation.

One relic of the old days that remained was the post cemetery, which had unfortunately fallen on hard times. In 1920 a flood inundated many of the markers, covering some with twelve inches of silt. In 1924 the soldiers rechanneled White River away from the cemetery to prevent further flood damage. But with the silt and neglect came weeds that practically obscured the white marble markers. To the rescue came Earl A. Brininstool, the famous chronicler of the Old West, who in 1926 visited the overgrown graveyard, and in an article was highly critical of its neglected appearance.[59] The article came to the attention of Q.M. Gen. B. Frank Cheatham, who informed Brininstool that the cemetery had been cleaned up and was then in good condition. A skeptical Brininstool commented in a note to his friend James Cook, "Wonder how long it will stay decent."[60] Several years later a concerned citizen wrote to the Crawford Chamber of Commerce, urging the cemetery be moved to higher ground to preserve "this graveyard of heroes."[61] Nevertheless, the cemetery remained where it was, though better tended than during the pre-Brininstool days, and it continued in use throughout the post's remaining years.

Other noticeable changes came to the old post on White River. After World War I motor vehicles were provided for the post quartermaster and officers and the number of private vehicles increased. Officers and enlisted men sometimes arrived with personal automobiles and soldiers began to purchase cars locally. The automobile age made nearby communities more accessible, and soldiers drove to Alliance and Chadron to watch football games or took pleasure trips to the Black Hills. Beginning in the late 1930s state patrol officers came to the fort to give license examinations as a convenience to soldiers. Twentieth-century progress also brought the air age to Fort Robinson. To aid pilots, "Fort Robinson" was painted in large white letters on the dark slate roof of the first brick stable. In the early 1930s post officers selected a suitable landing area two miles south of the post, and visiting officers flew in from distant army posts. In 1933 two cavalry officers flew from Fort Riley to visit remount friends, making the five-hundred-mile trip in four hours.[62]

By the 1930s Fort Robinson was considered the best maintained and policed post in the Seventh Corps Area. It looked like a large eastern horse farm, with green fences, trees bordering the parade ground neatly painted white four feet high on their trunks, and white frame buildings with green trim. About that time all interior post roads were regraded and graveled, and the major drives were oiled. Other changes came in April 1930, when the post flagpole was badly damaged by a team of runaway mules pulling a bull rake, and had to be taken down. Later that year it was re-erected on the main parade ground opposite the post headquarters. During the artillery period (Chapter 3), a French 75mm fieldpiece was shipped to the post, placed at the new flagpole, and used to fire salutes on special occasions.[63]

It was during the remount years that Fort Robinson became known as "The Country Club of the Army." This appellation derived from the post's informal atmosphere and the variety of outdoor recreational opportunities it provided for residents and visitors. As one newspaper reporter put it, "The longing to leave the recreational cabins, creeks bright with fat trout, and outdoor games isn't simply overpowering."[64]

With the advent of automobiles, the horse gradually became less essential to mainstream Americans, particularly the growing urban majority. To many citizens, riding, jumping, and other equestrian activities were recreational, almost elitist, pursuits, but with its horse-related mission, activities involving horses naturally became the main off-duty recreation at Fort Robinson. During the 1930s the equestrian sports of racing, competitive jumping, and other mounted contests were standard fare for both officers and enlisted men. All officers were issued riding horses and were expected to ride, whether they were with the remount or another service branch. Everyone on post, including dependents, was encouraged to ride, and a call to the riding stable would always produce a ready mount.

Interest in polo was revived at Fort Robinson in the 1920s. Polo provided competition, good training for men and horses, and maintained soldier interest in horsemanship. It also provided recreation, and gave the post and local community an exciting, fast-moving spectator sport. The post team played army teams from forts Meade, Russell (to become Fort F. E. Warren in 1930), and Logan, and civilian teams from Denver, Colorado Springs, and Hot Springs, South Dakota. Several officers from affluent families brought their own polo ponies with them when assigned to Fort Robinson.

Along with polo, the army saw the benefits of participation in hunt club activities. Riding to the hounds was seen as "bold riding" that gave soldiers experience in fast, cross-country travel. In 1932 the Soldier Creek Hunt Club was founded. That year the cavalry school and Arapahoe Hunt Club of Denver donated a pack of foxhounds to the post. Post commander Hardy, himself an avid rider and outdoorsman, became master of the hunt. Hunts were conducted on Wednesday afternoons and Sunday mornings, and were open to all enlisted men and officers. Interested local civilians also joined in. The dog pack was recognized by the Masters of Foxhounds Association, and by 1934 consisted of thirty-four English foxhounds and French staghounds. Because there were no foxes in the post vicinity, Fort Robinson hunts were "drag" hunts, whereby the trail of a pursued animal was simulated beforehand by dragging a coyote hide through the reservation countryside.[65]

Soldier Creek, White River, and the several post reservoirs provided fishing. In 1927 Herbert Hoover, then secretary of commerce, requested permission from the War Department to begin operations on the post reservation "for the propagation of trout and bass for stocking streams."[66] Permission was granted and the Bureau of Fisheries started raising fish below the post springs and in the Cherry and Soldier Creek basins. In 1936 the army constructed several new ponds and made them available as nursery ponds, doubling hatchery production. On one Thanksgiving Day outing three officers reportedly caught 120 trout in three hours.[67]

With fishing and hunting readily available, Fort Robinson became a favorite stop for traveling general officers. During his term as army chief of staff, Maj. Gen. Charles P. Summerall made several visits to the post to fish and ride in the hills. Likewise in 1932 Maj. Gen. Johnson Hagood, Seventh Corps commander, spent four days fishing at the post. During the remount era, a steady stream of quartermaster, cavalry, and artillery branch chiefs came to inspect, then relax. Besides high-ranking army officers, senators, congressmen, and notable civilians also visited. Taking time off from his work on Mount Rushmore, sculptor Gutzon Borglum and his family made several visits, staying with Maj. Sumner Williams and fishing the post streams.[68]

To supplement equestrian activities, other amenities associated with a country club lifestyle appeared. In the 1920s a nine-hole golf course was laid out north of the main post. When skeet shooting became a popular pastime, a range was built at the base of the buttes for use by soldiers and interested local civilians. By the 1930s new concrete tennis courts were built for the officers and their families, and a court was added near the barracks for the enlisted men. In 1935 a fine, reinforced concrete swimming pool costing five thousand dollars was opened. Although the pool had no showers or dressing rooms, it proved a welcome recreational addition for post residents. A favorite off-duty hangout, which contributed to the post's country club atmosphere, was the officers' club. Housed in the former 1891 commanding officer's quarters, it was the scene of parties, dinners, receptions, and other social affairs for officers and their guests. Life at Fort Robinson in the 1930s stood in sharp contrast to that of the frontier post of fifty years earlier.[69]

Because of its small garrison and noncombat mission, a casual lifestyle developed at Fort Robinson during the remount years. To outsiders, the fort might look like a military post, but for the soldiers stationed there, it did not seem like a regular army post. The relationship between officers and enlisted men was generally more informal than that found at larger posts where combat troops were stationed. Even the enlisted men's mess hall looked more like a fancy restaurant than an army dining hall. Along with important remount functions, the post truly was a country club for the army in the years before World War II.

An interesting bit of Fort Robinson folklore came from the remount period. On the east side of the old parade ground, a length of pipe can still be seen suspended a dozen feet in the air between two massive cottonwoods. A story developed that the pipe was used as a hitching post in the old days, and subsequently grew up with the trees. Although a botanical impossibility, this explanation persists to the present day. The pipe actually was attached to the trees to support a swing put up for the children in the 1890s, when black families were housed in the old log barracks. Besides the six original sets of officers' quarters on the old parade ground, the pipe is one of the oldest artifacts of Fort Robinson's nineteenth-century history.[70]

Chapter 3

The 1930s

For a time in the late 1920s and early 1930s, Fort Robinson became an artillery post as well as a remount depot. As early as April 1923 Maj. Gen. George B. Duncan and several other general staff officers visited the post to explore the possibility of a dual role for the old fort. Anticipating the return of economic prosperity due to a larger garrison, Crawford business-men supported the proposal and were encouraged to "see that everything . . . will be accomplished to bring about what will be considered best for the community."[1] However, the Quartermaster Corps, then in full control of Fort Robinson, was hesitant to support the proposal. In a 1927 report, Brig. Gen. Harry F. Rethers, the acting quartermaster general, mildly opposed the idea of incorporating two military activities at the post, but added if the "exigencies of the service demand it," there would be no objection. In addition to the remount detachment, he believed that forty officers and three hundred enlisted men and their dependents could be housed at Fort Robinson.[2] By 1928 the War Department decided to station a pack field artillery unit there.

Fort Robinson's physical setting offered several benefits for this type of artillery. The broken terrain and buttes on the reservation provided an excellent locale for pack training. Because pack artillery was dependent on horse and mule transportation, the local availability of forage and water was a natural asset. In addition, if the need arose, there was a possibility of expanding the military reservation. And, as General Rethers had noted, housing and support facilities for hundreds of extra soldiers were available at the nearly vacant post.

The unit slated for the post was the Fourth Field Artillery, then stationed at Fort McIntosh, Texas. One of the batteries created in 1901, the unit was designated the Fourth Field Artillery Regiment and reorganized into battalion rather than regimental format. The Fourth Field Artillery saw service in Texas, Mexico, and the Canal Zone before its transfer to Fort McIntosh. During this period, pack artillery units were designed for use in difficult terrain, with guns and men being transported entirely by pack animals. In combat, pack artillery was deployed much like light artillery, and was especially suitable for operations in mountainous or jungle regions, or to provide support for landing parties. The battalion was subdivided into batteries, each with four mountain howitzers with gun crews and support personnel.[3]

On May 1, 1928, the battalion received orders to leave Fort McIntosh for northwestern Nebraska. Three weeks later Headquarters, Headquarters Battery and Combat Train, and Batteries A, B, and C of the Fourth Field Artillery marched into Fort Robinson. The battalion numbered just over three hundred officers and enlisted men. With the arrival of the new troops and their families, the population of the post returned to the higher prewar levels.

Before their arrival, post commander Maj. Sumner M. Williams had been instructed to divide the post and reservation into separate areas to accommodate both the artillery and remount operations. The artillery battalion was given the bulk of the quarters and animal facilities, receiving both brick barracks, six stables, blacksmith shops, adjoining stable guards, and most of the officers' housing. The artillerymen were assigned the rough, northern part of the reservation for training and firing activities; the rest of the post and Wood Reserve were for remount use. Remount enlisted personnel were moved from the east barracks into the bachelor officers' quarters.[4]

More than thirty thousand dollars were allotted to prepare the post for the new tenants. The station hospital, which had been closed for fifteen years, was opened and readied for service. The barracks and officers' quarters were renovated by civilian carpenters hired from Crawford and Chadron. Noncommissioned officers and the civilian employees who had been permitted to stay in vacant units on officers' row were bumped to other housing on post or in town. To provide additional housing for noncommissioned officers, several of the old troop latrine buildings, which had remained after the adjoining adobe barracks were demolished, were moved to other locations and remodeled into living quarters.

Following military protocol, Lt. Col. William F. Morrison, the higher ranking artillery officer, assumed command of the post; Major Williams continued to command the remount operations. Morrison worked with Williams to iron out housing arrangements and "other details for the occupancy of the post."[5]

Several months later Morrison was replaced by Lt. Col. Laurin L.

Lawson, a longtime artillery officer who had won promotion from the enlisted ranks after the Spanish-American War. Unfortunately, the transfer of command and the specialized needs and responsibilities of the remount and artillery complements at times caused "a very delicate and difficult command problem." Although army inspector generals noted the two separate and distinct activities were "cordially and harmoniously carried forward," a degree of friction remained.[6] After Lawson was transferred, Williams wrote in his annual report that "the unnecessary friction and interference that had persisted during the more than two years that he had been in command of the post disappeared. . . .[B]oth the official and social life of the garrison were greatly improved."[7]

The field artillery required additional support structures and facilities at Fort Robinson. A new ordnance storage area was laid out north of the main post in the part of the reservation assigned to the artillery. A substantial concrete and brick magazine was built there in 1928, followed in 1930 by six smaller tile brick magazines. In the stable area a large rigging shed was constructed to store pack equipment, and several other structures were later built specifically for artillery use.

Although artillery training was a distinct departure from the normal remount routine at Fort Robinson, in one aspect it was similar. Artillery troops spent much of their time caring for horses and mules. As in the cavalry, there was a daily cycle of stable and husbandry duties, with soldiers performing blacksmithing, feeding, grooming, and herding. Just as in the days of the cavalry garrisons, after the animal chores were done, the Fourth artillerymen spent their time on military drill and artillery training.

Field artillery training was intended to develop tactical efficiency, with map problems in winter, field exercises when possible, and battery firing during the later spring and summer. The Fourth Field Artillery was armed with two types of pack howitzers. Their primary weapon was a 2.95-inch Vickers-Maxim mountain gun of British and American manufacture. It was a light, compact weapon, easily separated into four loads for pack mule transportation; it fired a twelve-and-one-half pound projectile a maximum of 4,800 yards. One battery was armed with a newly designed 75mm pack howitzer, which could be separated into six loads, or could be pulled by two mules in tandem. Aparejos or Phillips pack saddles were used to transport both types of guns.[8]

Range firing usually took place in spring and summer. Notices in the Crawford newspapers warned civilians not to leave the roads passing through the military reservation during the firing. In addition the Wood Reserve road was frequently closed during practice and civilians were warned not to pick up fired shells or fragments. Practice took place with both the mountain gun and the 75mm howitzer with a subcaliber 37mm tube insert; subcaliber shooting was done at ranges from 2,000 to 2,500 yards.[9]

Firing took place northeast of the post, toward the western butte area, and from the south across the Soldier Creek valley to the north buttes. At times each battery fired twice weekly with shrapnel and high explosive. For example, in March 1931 Batteries D and E fired two hundred rounds of shrapnel and then fired additional rounds for record. Several times the Crawford businessmen were invited to watch the firing and have a field-prepared meal with the troops. During firing season the artillerymen eagerly sought to qualify as first-class and expert gunners for the extra pay the ratings brought.[10]

In 1928 the chief of artillery directed that a pack artillery board be established at Fort Robinson to supervise field testing of new ordnance and equipment. Under the direction of Maj. Herman Erlenkotter, the board made recommendations on the Phillips pack saddle, 75mm pack howitzer, Thompson submachine gun, and a variety of 75mm ammunition. In 1931 new high explosive shells were tested for accuracy, transportability, penetration, and fragmentation. In March 1930 in a test of shrapnel shells with an improved time fuse, gunners fired them at a rate of ten rounds per minute. Officers and engineers from Rock Island and other arsenals frequently came to Fort Robinson to observe test firings.[11]

Besides ordnance, field equipment such as communications gear and training saddles were field tested by the Fourth Artillery. In February 1931 a detachment was detailed to Fort Riley to test the maneuverability of pack artillery while supporting cavalry units. Battery E made a fourteen-day march to the Black Hills to test new pack equipment under the supervision of the artillery board. On that trip the new 75mm gun was taken along.

Practice marches were a frequent and year-round aspect of artillery training at Fort Robinson. Overnight "hikes" to the post Wood Reserve featured physical competitions and games while the soldiers were in camp, and each battery made an annual march that lasted up to two weeks. Usually the marches were to towns where county fairs and rodeos were being held, and the artillerymen put on exhibitions and firing demonstrations, and set up camp displays. While stationed at the fort, units marched to fairs at Hemingford, Chadron, Harrison, and Lusk, Wyoming. In September 1931 Battery D participated in the "Battle of St. Mihiel" at the Box Butte County Fair. The show, based on the first American offensive in France during World War I, was a great success, after which the public was "still talking about the realistic appearances of the battle, given by the battery, whose officers worked out a very excellent form of combat including infantry, artillery, and grenade throwing."[12] Through participation in such local events, the public better understood the role of pack artillery in modern warfare—and the soldiers had a good time.

In its new role as an artillery post, Fort Robinson was often visited by general officers; chiefs of artillery, corps commanding generals, and the quartermaster general made visits between 1928 and 1930. Inspectors also examined the post, often reporting infractions by the artillery battalion. A report in 1929 found Battery A with "kitchen generally not well policed. Ranges not polished, and too many roaches in evidence." A check of the Battery C squad room found that the men's shoes were not neatly arranged beneath the bunks.[13]

During the summer of 1930 reserve officers from the 341st and 342nd Field Artillery came to Fort Robinson for training. The officers, most from the Lincoln-Omaha area, usually trained in Wisconsin, and now had a shorter distance to travel and a battalion of men to work with. In July forty-three officers came for two weeks training in signaling, formations, field set-up, measurements, and sights and bearings. Several weeks later a small group of officers from western Nebraska towns arrived for similar training. The reservists received the complete cooperation of the Fourth Field Artillery; upon departure they showed their appreciation for help received from the enlisted personnel by leaving boxes of cigarettes and cigars for them. The next summer two groups of officers from the 340th Field Artillery Regiment from Kansas came for training, forty-eight in one group and thirty in another. The reservists were housed in tents behind the west officers' quarters. Extra facilities for summer trainees were built for the 1931 session. A combination bathhouse/latrine and brick mess hall were added to "make the reserve officers more comfortable during their stay here."[14]

In April 1930 the Fourth Field Artillery at Fort Robinson was redesignated the Second Battalion, Fourth Artillery Regiment, and assigned to the Second Cavalry Division. The reorganization brought no personnel changes, but the firing battery designations were changed to D, E, and F.

The larger artillery garrison brought to Fort Robinson aspects of military life commonplace at posts housing line troops. New recruits regularly arrived as replacements and immediately began the school of the soldier. In addition to battery firing and pack training, the artillerymen had infantry drill two mornings a week and trained with gas masks for chemical warfare. And on former cavalry firing ranges, the men worked on small arms marksmanship and the batteries competed in pistol championships. With more troops at the post, a formal military routine returned. The morning gun was fired each day, and soldiers were assigned guard duty, held daily guard mount, and marched in weekly reviews. As in the past the neatest appearing soldier at guard mount was selected as orderly for the commanding officer. In winter, details were sent out to harvest ice. Along with the expected training, one duty was a direct result of the new garrison. On many occasions troops were sent to fight prairie fires caused by practice firing of their artillery pieces.

One reminder of an oft-repeated scene, when sons of officers left western army posts to attend West Point, occurred at Fort Robinson in 1930. That year two Fourth artillerymen were sent to Fort Snelling, Minnesota, to take the preliminary examinations for entrance to the United States Military Academy. The next year, one of the candidates, Pvt. Raymond C. Adkisson, was accepted and left for the Point. He graduated in the class of 1935 and became the only known Fort Robinson enlisted man to enter West Point directly from the post.[15]

One alarming problem that faced the Fourth Field Artillery at Fort Robinson was desertion. In its first year there, the battalion had eighty-two desertions, a high number for a garrison of only four hundred men. The lack of off-duty recreation was one reason for desertion and low morale at isolated posts. Colonel Lawson admitted that the most important need was additional recreational facilities, and he submitted proposals for a new recreation building to supplement the existing post gymnasium. He also encouraged an active athletic program and other off-duty diversions. Gradually, troop morale and discipline improved, and the number of court-martials decreased. By 1930 desertions at Fort Robinson dropped to sixty-one; there were forty-two in 1931.[16]

Athletic events were popular, and both the artillerymen and the remount detachment followed boxing with considerable enthusiasm. Large exhibitions were held, with proceeds often going to the Army Relief Fund. On several occasions, crowds of up to one thousand watched outdoor matches held on the officers' tennis court. Besides soldier and local civilian participants, boxers came from across the state to fight at the fort. One 1929 bout featured "Kenny Auston, the Nebraska Whizbang," who thrilled the crowd with a win over an opponent from Lincoln.[17]

During the winter the troops played basketball with teams from nearby towns, and each year saw a post championship among all organizations. For outdoor recreation soldiers ice skated on the reservation ponds and at nearby Whitney Lake. About this time the fort's winter sports program provided a novel form of recreation—skiing. Skis and poles were ordered, as anxious soldiers anticipated that with adequate snowfall they could hit the slopes surrounding the post. Unfortunately, the local terrain proved too broken and with little snow, skiing was generally restricted to being pulled by horses across the valley flats.[18]

For summer sport, an improved baseball field, complete with a grandstand and dugouts for opposing teams, was constructed on the northwest corner of the original 1874 parade ground. Other year-round diversions included Saturday night dances at the enlisted men's service club, and excursions to dances at nearby towns, including Whitney and Van Tassell, Wyoming. To improve the quality of post entertainment, "talkies" made their debut at the post movie theater in May 1930, with a crowd of 442 attending the first showing. With more officers on hand, polo flourished during the artillery period. In 1931 Fort Robinson won the tri-state championship in an exciting tournament watched by several thousand spectators.[19]

In November 1929 the twenty-six-member Seventy-sixth Field Artillery Band was permanently transferred from Fort Russell to Robinson. Having a band at the post once again benefited both the post and the local community, and Crawford people were "more than pleased to have such a splendid band at the fort." Directed by WO Gregorio Trapolino, the band added martial music to reviews and formations, and performed weekly concerts in the summer. The bandsmen also organized a swing band named the Syncopators that played for local and post dances.[20]

The threat of abandonment that appeared intermittently in Fort Robinson's history resurfaced in 1929 when several old frontier posts, including forts Russell and Robinson, were mentioned in a congressional proposal to cut military spending. Two years later a list of posts to be abandoned was released, but Fort Robinson was not on it. Although it would never again house a large peacetime garrison, the old post's importance as a quartermaster remount depot had insured continued army occupation. Although the local citizens were relieved the fort was spared, rumors surfaced that the Fourth Field Artillery would be moved out.[21]

Finally, in August 1931, the artillery was ordered to Fort Bragg, North Carolina. Before the transfer was effected half of the men in the battalion were transferred to other artillery units in the Seventh Corps Area. On September 10 the Seventy-sixth Field Artillery Band was reassigned to Madison Barracks, New York. In early October all the artillery horses and pack mules were loaded and shipped out. On the tenth, the last remaining members of the Fourth Field Artillery boarded the train, where they found boxes of cigars, cigarettes, and candy left for them by appreciative Crawford businessmen. A local paper mourned their departure: "The citizens of Crawford regret very much to have the artillery and band moved from the fort as they have enjoyed both social and business association with them."[22]

With the departure of the artillery, the entire post and reservation returned to Major Williams's control. Crawford leaders quickly lobbied to have other troops assigned at the post, and a delegation met with Congressman Robert G. Simmons to urge him to use his influence to regarrison Fort Robinson. Their efforts were to no avail, and the post reverted to its preartillery population. However, Williams and other quartermaster officers were content with their sole occupancy of the fort, remarking that its use by two organizations with different duties and objectives had been "unsatisfactory."[23]

The loss of the large garrison at the post was not the only economic problem facing the local community as the Great Depression began. In October 1931 both banks in Crawford closed. It was a calamity for the community, and, with unit and detachment funds in both institutions, the bank failures also seriously affected Fort Robinson. Following established procedures, a board of "disinterested" officers came from Fort Meade to investigate. Though the post suffered a substantial loss, the board determined that no officers could be held at fault.[24]

In addition to depression and hard times, 1931 was reported to be the driest and hottest year on record in northwestern Nebraska. The post's hay crop was only one-third that of previous years. Although horse purchases began to be limited by a cost-conscious Quartermaster Corps, in 1932 depot capacity for breeding stallions and mares was increased. To prepare for this expansion the post managed to retain, and even increase its complement of civilian employees. By the summer of 1932 sixty civilians were on the payroll, building new stables and preparing additional alfalfa fields. For the rest of the decade, federally-funded post improvement projects provided most of the employment for civilian workers in the area.[25]

In late spring 1932 Williams was promoted to lieutenant colonel and ordered to other duties. In June his replacement, Maj. Edwin N. Hardy, arrived from Fort Riley. Hardy, a native of Tennessee, had graduated from West Point in 1911. A career cavalry officer, he also attended the army's Command and General Staff School, and spent several years with the general staff. An excellent rider and knowledgeable horseman, "Pink" Hardy's equine expertise was a contributing factor to Fort Robinson's reputation as a great horse center.[26]

During the Depression the charitable activities of the Army Relief Society drew heavy support from the post. Although created to support soldiers who "through unfortunate circumstances have become destitute," the society also helped nonmilitary families. In 1933 post women quickly gathered two large boxes of clothing for a needy civilian family. Special entertainment, including boxing tournaments, variety shows, movies, and casino parties, were held in the post gymnasium to raise funds for relief society work. At other times, army regulations were sidestepped as the post assisted the local community. In the early 1930s, portions of the eastern military reservation were leased to cattlemen to provide additional winter grazing. As part of a federal relief project, Crawford was permitted to use gravel from pits on the reservation to resurface roads in the city park. In another departure from military rules, volunteer workers, organized by the Crawford American Legion, were allowed to gather firewood on army land and distribute it to needy families during the harsh winter of 1932-33. Whenever possible, Major Hardy sought to cooperate with the local community as civilians and the army coped with hard times.[27]

Throughout the 1930s Civil Works Administration (CWA) and Works Progress Administration (WPA) projects at the post aided hundreds of unemployed men in northwestern Nebraska. Late in 1933 CWA construction and conservation projects provided ninety days of work for more than one hundred men. A new sixty-four-stall broodmare stable and new colt stable were built, replacing earlier native pine structures built by the soldiers in the 1920s. A major project in the Wood Reserve was construction of the officers' cabin complex in 1934. Built of sawed logs on a low, pine-covered ridge above the north fork of Soldier Creek, the complex consisted of the cabin, stables, dog kennels, and a private swimming pool. Described as a "real monument to the West," the roomy, story-and-a-half cabin was the scene of countless parties, picnics, and receptions, and it frequently served as the commanding officer's summer quarters. A recreation cabin for the enlisted men was available on the middle fork.[28]

On the main post, Fort Robinson's physical plant also benefited from the three-lettered relief programs of Roosevelt's New Deal recovery plan. Civilian work projects repaired the interiors of quarters and renovated the post sewer, electric, and water lines. Behind officers' row, multiunit garages were built, and single garages went up behind the brick quarters and NCO row. Warehouses and other utility buildings were refloored and repaired, roads were paved, and concrete sidewalks were poured. By the mid-1930s Fort Robinson was much improved from the days when the remount began operations.[29]

At the height of the Great Depression, Fort Robinson was involved in one of the most successful relief programs in American history, the famed Civilian Conservation Corps (CCC). Organized in April 1933, the program took young, unmarried men off relief rolls and put them to work at hundreds of camps across the country. For several years in the 1930s the fort played a key role in northwestern Nebraska CCC operations.

The army, with its resources for mobilization and supply, was put in charge of the new relief measure; within seven weeks the army mobilized 310,000 men into 1,315 camps across the country. The prevailing army attitude was that the program was "necessary but disruptive." In the army's view, the CCC program drained personnel, as regular army officers were assigned to run each camp, but eventually reserve officers were called up for the task. Many civilians were critical of the military administration of a civilian program, and rumors surfaced that the CCC was the first step toward forcing individuals into the army. Although the program had military overtones, the army never intended to insert military training in the CCC agenda.[30]

The CCC targeted unemployed youths between eighteen and twenty-five. Once enrolled in the program, each corpsman allotted a substantial portion of the thirty-dollar-per-month wage, usually twenty-five dollars, to assist his family. In addition, a veterans' CCC was established for older men who were World War I veterans. Most enrollees at the Fort Robinson camp came from the Nebraska Panhandle, and with few jobs available elsewhere, young men volunteered eagerly. One former corpsman recalled joining "because of the depression and employment was hard to find. Thirty dollars a month looked good and clothing thrown in."[31]

Although it organized and managed the program, the army had nothing to do with the selection of Fort Robinson as a work site. Work sites were selected by federal and state forestry officials, with the stipulation that all work was to be done on government land. Consequently, plans were hurriedly made to begin CCC operations at the post. In April 1933 Fort Robinson was designated as headquarters for the Nebraska District, as well as for the subdistrict of northwestern Nebraska. Besides providing shelter, clothing, food, and medical care, the army was also responsible for program administration. As post commander, Major Hardy was initially given charge of all Nebraska CCC operations. Along with Fort Robinson, camps at Chadron State Park and later at Valentine were included in the subdistrict. As with his regular military duties, Hardy accepted the new responsibilities with enthusiasm and energy.

When area enrollment began in late April, Fort Robinson was expected to serve as a conditioning center for new enrollees before they were sent to other camps. By the middle of May several hundred men had arrived for medical examinations, conditioning, and preliminary training. Most of the men, however, were to remain at the post. From the new arrivals, the 798th CCC Company was formed on May 16, 1933. The new "garrison" found the post's remount detachment willing to help them adjust to their new lifestyle, which "made CCC duty at the post pleasant."[32]

Generally, company strength was 100 to 150 men, with several detached for cooking and kitchen work. Two or three army officers, one civilian superintendent, and two civilian foremen were attached to each company. More experienced men were assigned as leaders and assistant leaders, with the bulk of the manpower organized into work squads. Military uniforms were issued: blue denim fatigues for work and olive drab shirts and trousers for dress. Emulating the army, a camp patch was designed, and stripes were worn on uniforms to denote rank among the corpsmen.

Some corpsmen were assigned post duty, and quartered in the east brick barracks along with the remount detachment. Others soon moved to a side camp that was established on the Wood Reserve in June, where they lived in tents while the buildings of the permanent camp were constructed. The camp, near a sawmill on the south fork of Soldier Creek, was aptly christened Sawmill Camp. Workmen immediately began cutting lumber to build accommodations for sixty men. The camp, completed in October, consisted of two barracks, a combined mess hall and recreation building, a bathhouse and latrine, and separate quarters for camp supervisors.[33]

With company organization completed and housing arranged, work projects began. In the early days many local residents complained about the CCC at Fort Robinson, fearing it would replace civilian employees at the post; others thought the CCC would become a supplemental work force for the army. Major Hardy gave assurances that there would be no conflict with the jobs that could be done with local labor.[34] Work projects were carefully planned and progress was thoroughly reported. Civilian inspectors from the state made regular inspections of work projects and camp conditions. CCC officials took care to avoid habitually incorporating CCC workers into the regular military activities of the post, but on occasion, corpsmen were called on to help the remount soldiers move large horse herds or bales of hay.[35]

Because forestry was one of the main objectives of the CCC and a large portion of the fort lands was tree-covered, timber management became a prime occupation for the 798th Company. In the fall of 1928, a week-long blaze destroyed much of the south half of the Wood Reserve. During its tenure at Fort Robinson, the "Tree Army" planted thousands of seedlings in that area and on other fort lands. Crews also removed diseased trees and cleared dead wood to lessen the fire danger. Conservation work also occupied CCC crews, who built many rock check dams to control erosion along waterways. Corpsmen also removed underbrush along Soldier Creek and White River, cut weeds, and dug yucca plants out of pastures. Several crews kept busy working at prairie dog eradication in the cultivated fields and pastures on the military reservation. Northwest of the main post, CCC workers cleaned up and filled shell holes on the old Fourth Artillery firing ranges. A major project was repairing the dam on Lake Crawford to prevent seepage, and building smaller dams on the branches of Soldier Creek to create fish ponds. CCC crews also improved roads and bridges and constructed trails into the buttes.[36]

Along with forestation and conservation, some work was allotted to the post proper, where corpsmen manned the gas pumps and telephone switchboard. Several old fort buildings were demolished and the materials salvaged by CCC crews; trees were planted and a rock curb installed around the huge parade ground. CCC workers also helped cremate dead horses, not one of the popular assignments. All in all, the Fort Robinson company kept busy with constructive and useful projects.

Various diversions were available for off-duty CCC boys, including sports, which occupied much of their leisure time. In the summer, softball teams, nicknamed the Woodpeckers, played teams from Crawford, Whitney, and Marsland. In the winter of 1934 the Crawford Sanitary Laundry sponsored a CCC basketball team, which played teams from Lusk, Wyoming, Harrison, and Chadron Normal School. Boxing and wrestling matches were held with the Chadron company. The men played tennis on the new enlisted men's court just west of the brick barracks. Sawmill Camp CCC men participated in archery and nature study, and made overnight hikes. Because the CCC was considered part of the post, members joined in annual Quartermaster Day celebrations and Memorial Day observances. They were allowed to attend the post theater and use the bowling alley in its basement.[37]

Other pastimes were available for corpsmen. Early in 1934 Company 798 formed Deadwood Camp No. 1 of the United Conservators of the United States. The purpose of this organization was to preserve ties of comradeship and work for the preservation of the nation's resources. Capt. F. P. Strickland, who commanded the 798th, encouraged wood carving and photography among his charges. On weekends, CCC boys often walked to town and saw the sights, and several members organized a dance band called the Rhythm Rockers. Transportation was arranged, enabling corpsmen to attend dances in Chadron. In February 1934 six boys from the camp were injured when the truck returning them from a Chadron dance was struck by a car. Although none of the boys was killed, the driver of the car died in the accident.[38]

On April 1, 1934, the district CCC headquarters was moved to Fort Crook at Omaha and the 798th Company was transferred to a new camp at the Nebraska National Forest near Halsey. On July 5 a new unit, the 2744th Company, was organized at the post. Initially, enrollees for the new company came from all over the state, with more than forty from Omaha. Several days later, eighteen men from the 762nd Company arrived to form an experienced cadre to help the rookies. Subsequently, new members came only from the counties adjacent to Fort Robinson.[39]

The new company was organized much like the 798th, and work projects continued. However, the 2744th Company's major project was building a massive dam on Soldier Creek, about three miles above the post. The new dam, 470 feet long, 55 feet high, and with a base 210 feet wide, was the largest single CCC work project undertaken on post lands. Intended to store creek water for irrigation, the dam was to impound more than six-hundred acre-feet of water. For months CCC workmen with Caterpillar tractors and fresno scrapers moved dirt for the required fill. During cold weather, a night crew kept fires burning to keep the ground from freezing. Eventually nearly eighty thousand cubic yards of earth were hauled. By the summer of 1935 the dam was completed and began to fill with water. The corpsmen named it Lake Bertha, in honor of the wife of Maj. Gen. Louis H. Bash, the army quartermaster general. However, the name did not stick, and by the late 1930s the lake became more familiarly known as Carter P. Johnson Lake, in honor of the long-serving Fort Robinson cavalry officer.[40]

The 2744th Company continued at the post through most of the fall of 1935, but the days of the Civilian Conservation Corps at Fort Robinson were numbered. On October 25 the company was demobilized and its members transferred to camps at Mitchell, Nebraska, and in the Wildcat Hills south of Scottsbluff. In the two years the CCC operated at Fort Robinson, the workers made valuable contributions to the physical appearance and conservation of post grounds and the military reservation. Although the regular corpsmen were gone, the post hospital continued to serve for several years as a regional CCC hospital. Up to fourteen CCC men were assigned to hospital work and as ambulance drivers under a district surgeon. Injured or sick corpsmen from camps as far away as three hundred miles were brought there for medical care. In addition the hospital was used by members of the veterans' CCC.[41]

In the mid-1930s, the glamour of the Olympic Games came to Fort Robinson, when the post was a summer training site for the United States Army equestrian teams. For both post personnel and local civilians, it was a rare opportunity to see the finest of horses and horsemanship, as a new dimension was added to Fort Robinson's already varied history.

The first Olympic equestrian competition occurred at the 1900 Paris games, but the regular program of three main events was initiated at the 1912 Stockholm games, where one of the members of the United States' bronze-medal-winning, three-day event team was Capt. Guy V. Henry, Jr., born at Camp Robinson in January 1875.[42] The Olympic equestrian program of three main events was divided into individual and team competitions. The first was the grueling three-day event, or overall equestrian championship, with dressage, endurance, and jumping competition. The second was the Prix des Nations with spectacular jumps over banks, ditches, and the triple bar. Dressage was the third event, which put the horse through a series of movements "which displayed a degree of communication and cooperation between horse and rider."[43] Beginning in 1920 U.S. equestrian teams for the Olympics were selected, organized, and trained at Fort Riley, the home of the cavalry school. The team was composed of the best riders from the cavalry school and the field artillery school at Fort Sill, Oklahoma. The army team had made an excellent showing at the 1932 Los Angeles games, winning one gold, two silver, and two bronze medals in the five events entered. The next year preparations began for the 1936 games, scheduled for Berlin, Germany.[44]

During the summer of 1934, Maj. William B. Bradford, team captain for the 1936 games, visited Fort Robinson. He was greatly impressed with the summer climate of northwestern Nebraska, compared to the conditions at Fort Riley. He discussed the possibility of moving the summer training session to Fort Robinson with post commander Hardy, who was enthusiastic about hosting the Olympic team, and quickly received permission from the quartermaster general and chief of cavalry. The higher altitude, cooler climate, and rugged topography, made Fort Robinson an ideal training site for both men and horses.[45]

On June 4, 1935, the finest riders in the U.S. Army arrived at Fort Robinson. Seven cavalry officers, five field artillery officers, and twenty-five Ninth Cavalry enlisted men with thirty-five horses composed the team. One member was Capt. Earl F. Thomson, who later held the American record for having won the most Olympic equestrian medals. Family members accompanying the officers were housed in vacant quarters on the officers' row, and the enlisted men quartered with the remount personnel in the brick barracks. The extensive course required for three-day event training was laid out, running from the east side of the military reservation west along Soldier Creek to the Wood Reserve. Training at the post would center specifically on the jumping events.[46]

Summer training quickly settled down to a daily regimen of riding and horse care. The team's enlisted men served as grooms, feeding, exercising, and preparing the horses for shows, and during their off-duty hours played softball. The Olympics, as their team was named, joined the local softball league, playing games against town teams, CCC, and post remount teams. Meanwhile, the officers played tennis and socialized with post and town residents.

Jumping horses were a novelty in western Nebraska, and in response to local interest, the Olympic team gave several exhibitions. On June 30 they presented a show at the Alliance Panhandle Stampede. CCC corpsmen eagerly volunteered to help with the shows, loading hurdles and obstacles on trucks and assisting with set-up work. This duty gave the boys an opportunity to see world-class jumping horses and be a part of their popular exhibitions. Later the Crawford Fourth of July celebration was capped by a jumping exhibition. The local community felt honored by the selection of Fort Robinson as training quarters and appreciated the shows put on by the team.[47]

On August 18 nearly four thousand spectators crowded Fort Robinson to watch an equestrian exhibition and view a depot exhibit of remount stallions, mares, and colts. The Fourth Cavalry Band from Fort Meade entertained the crowd and invited dignitaries, including Maj. Gen. Frank C. Bolles, commander of the Seventh Corps area from Omaha. The next day the Crawford Chamber of Commerce hosted a banquet for the Olympic team.[48]

Summer training concluded with the team's departure on September 7, and the next summer Fort Robinson personnel anxiously watched for the results from the Berlin Olympics. As if they had followed Hitler's orders, the German entrants dominated the equestrian events. In the three-day individual event, Captain Thomson, riding Jenny Camp, won a silver medal, while the gold went to a German rider. The course was so difficult that three horses died, and only twenty-seven of fifty entrants finished. The great Jenny Camp set an Olympic record for the endurance phase of the three-day. In the individual Prix des Nations, Lt. Carl Raguse on Dakota gained fifth place after jumping to break a tie, while in the team competition, Raguse, Bradford, and Capt. C. C. Jadwin placed fourth. The 1936 showing was mediocre compared to the victories won at Los Angeles in 1932, and team members were determined to do better at the 1940 games to be held in Tokyo.[49]

Summer training at Fort Robinson continued in 1937, with four officers and twenty horses. In the 1938 season, six officers, accompanied by their families, arrived for training with twenty-eight horses, including Dakota, veteran of the 1936 games. As usual, training followed a rigorous daily schedule, and, despite requests from neighboring towns, only one local exhibition was presented. The Fort Robinson Labor Day show brought more than six hundred cars and a crowd estimated at two thousand to the grounds. A local reporter described the event: "Getting to see the 'cream of the crop' of horses and riders in action, proved quite a thrill to the large crowd and everyone expressed themselves as being highly pleased with the show, as the applause following the jumps testified."[50] The summer training season had ended, but the rumblings of World War II had begun. Japan already was fighting a war in China, and the site for the 1940 games was changed to Helsingfors, Finland.

A larger group of Olympic candidates arrived on June 19 for the 1939 season. The cavalry team consisted of eight riders, twenty enlisted men, and thirty-four horses from Fort Riley. The same day the field artillery team of eight officers, nine enlisted men, and twenty horses came from Fort Sill. From this group ten members and sixteen horses would be named to the 1940 Olympic team by the selection committee. Five of the horses on the cavalry team were products of the Fort Robinson remount depot.[51]

Training and activities for the team continued as in previous summers, and again only one exhibition was held. In conjunction with the dedication of the new Crawford Post Office, between five and six thousand spectators attended the September 4 exhibition in the city park. One observer reported, "The show lasted close to two hours and consisted of an exhibition of the three-day horses, a fine schooling exhibit by Major McMahon, and an intensive showing of the jumping horses. The major share of the horses used were bred and raised at Fort Robinson."[52]

Three days later, both the cavalry and artillery teams returned to their stations. Tragedy struck the cavalry team in October when Lt. Scott M. Sanford was injured in a fall and died a short time later. Sanford had trained at Fort Robinson for three summers and had many friends there and in Crawford. Several days later, all hopes for Olympic glory in 1940 ended for the army teams. On October 22, 1939, word came that because of the war in Europe, the army's training program had been canceled and team members reassigned for regular military duties. Fort Robinson's brief but exciting stint as an Olympic training center had ended.[53]

The 1930s, a period of frontier nostalgia in the nation, also saw the placement of historical markers at Fort Robinson. The initial recognition of fort history came in 1930, when stone gatemarkers were erected where the highway entered the post grounds. Bronze plaques commemorated the establishment of the fort and its namesake, Lt. Levi Robinson. In 1931 Major Williams located what was thought to be the site of the guardhouse where Crazy Horse was killed, and later a stone marker was erected there.

Post personnel had long realized that significant Indian war events had occurred at the fort, and in an area filled with "Indian and pioneer traditions," it seemed natural to commemorate "some of the most important incidents and characters" with suitable monumentation.[54]

In 1932 the Captain Christopher Robinson Chapter of the Daughters of the American Revolution in Crawford erected a marker at the old Red Cloud Agency site. Foundation stones from agency buildings were gathered and formed into a core for the marker, which was then covered with large chunks of petrified wood, gathered north of town. That May the marker was formally dedicated, unveiled by Jim Red Cloud, the grandson of the famous chief.[55]

In 1934 Major Hardy became interested in historical markers. For several years he had wanted to put up a monument for Crazy Horse on the post; he envisioned a pyramid, eight feet square at the base and nearly twelve feet high, made of Black Hills native stone. He believed the monument "will prove of great interest in the years to come in perpetuating the rich historical traditions of this part of the country."[56] However, some thought there were other reasons for his interest in history. Shortly after assuming command of the post, Hardy had ordered the removal of an old cabin below the fort on White River that remained from the early days. Some area residents were critical of his actions in removing "a fine old monument to the ingress of civilization." After hearing the complaints about destruction of the cabin, Hardy evidently gained a new interest in post history.[57]

Major Hardy enthusiastically pursued the marker project, including the pyramid marker for Crazy Horse and a similar one for Lieutenant Robinson in the open area between post headquarters and the highway. The army provided funds and manpower, and a local subscription paid for the bronze plaque for the Crazy Horse monument; the plaque for the Robinson marker came from the 1930 gatepost. In early August the monument cornerstones were laid with ceremony.[58]

With the cooperation of the Crawford Chamber of Commerce and interested individuals, the army planned a celebration for September 3–5, 1934, centering on the monuments' dedication. The elaborate event would involve elements of both Indian and white ceremony, with relatives of Crazy Horse and many Indians invited from the South Dakota reservations. Other guests included Quartermaster General Bash from Washington and the Reverend George Beecher. The Fourth Cavalry Band from Fort Meade would furnish music. Among the invited guests who could not be present was Dr. Valentine McGillycuddy, who had attended the mortally wounded Crazy Horse in 1877. The three-day event was touted as "The Last Great

Fort Robinson from the south, 1902. RG1517:13-3

Col. Jacob A. Augur, Tenth Cavalry. RG1517:93-6

Left: **Col. Henry P. Kingsbury, Eighth Cavalry, shown here as a captain in the Sixth Cavalry, 1899.** (U.S. Military History Institute, Carlisle Barracks); right: **Col. Horatio G. Sickel, Twelfth Cavalry.** RG1517:60-2

Tenth Cavalry officers and their ladies relax on an officers' quarters porch, 1904. RG4893:1-3

An unidentified Tenth Cavalry sergeant and his family, about 1904. Courtesy Bob Sandstrom, RG1517:93-36

Troop K football team, Thanksgiving Day, 1905. The 1884 post commander's quarters is in the background. RG1517:93-23

Capt. Carter P. Johnson, Tenth Cavalry, was stationed at Fort Robinson five different times from 1877 to 1916. RG2411-2712

Troop I, Tenth Cavalry, at a Saturday morning inspection in front of the 1887 barracks row, about 1905. RG1517:93-5

Tenth Cavalry troopers firing the reveille gun, 1905. RG1517:93-9

Nebraska State Penitentiary mug shot of Sgt. John Reid, Troop B, Tenth Cavalry. Reid was sentenced to seven years for manslaughter for shooting Crawford city marshal Arthur Moss, 1906. RG2418-4747

Troop I, Tenth Cavalry, in charge formation. RG1517:93-12

Tenth cavalrymen pose with a young Ute boy during the closing days of the 1906 Ute campaign. Northwest Museum of Arts & Culture/Eastern Washington State Historical Society, Spokane

The Eighth Cavalry band on parade, about 1908. RG4911:1-30

Eighth Cavalry troops depart for the Philippines, November 27, 1910.
RG1517:78-12

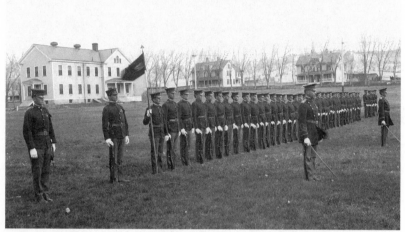

Troop A, Twelfth Cavalry, on dress inspection, 1912. In the background (left to right) are the 1905 post headquarters, 1892 officers' quarters, and 1909 bachelor officers' quarters. RG4891:1-1

Twelfth Cavalry soldier extras pose in and out of costume on the set of Buffalo Bill's movie at Pine Ridge, South Dakota, October 1913. RG3132-24

Left: **Twelfth cavalrymen clowning in the stable area.** RG3132-36

Below: **Maj. Carter P. Johnson with his wife and niece at the bachelor officers' quarters, May 1916. The combination post chapel/school-house is in the background.** *VMI Alumni Review,* Winter 1990.

Medical Corps trainees on close-order drill, 1918. Courtesy Mrs. Ned Tecker, RG1517:114-3

The west end of Fort Robinson during the remount years. The condition and issue area is at lower left, with the depot mare and colt stables in the background. RG1517:15-15

Unloading new arrivals at the Robinson Quartermaster Depot. RG1517:45-47

Veterinary officers carefully examined and measured all new animals.
RG1517:45-31

All animals were periodically run through the dip vat to eliminate external parasites and prevent skin disease. RG1517-0432

Capt. Oliver L. Overmyer, commanding officer of the Robinson Quartermaster Depot from 1919 to 1924, in a 1942 photograph. Courtesy Donna Nix, RG1517:114-2

Horse herd in the White River feed traps. RG1517:45-57

Pasturing horses during the conditioning phase. RG2731:7-42

"Riding out" horses for inspecting officers before issue. RG1517:45-33

Fort Robinson stallion stable, built in 1930. Attendants' quarters and grain shed at right. RG1517:114-1

Two of the noted depot stallions: above, **Gordon Russell** (RG4967:42-6); opposite, **Irish** (RG4967:49-17)

Veterinary personnel frequently performed surgery in the open, as in this 1943 view. RG1517: 20-6

Interior of the branding chute. Irons were heated in the furnace at left and applied to the animal in the chute at right. RG1517:22-1

A full gun crew of Fourth artillerymen poses with a Vickers-Maxim mountain howitzer. RG1517:64-3

Battery A section preparing to fire. RG1517:76-6

Fourth artillerymen in the barracks mess hall. RG1517:84-11

The team from Battery A, Fourth Artillery, won the post basketball championship in 1930. RG1517:86-3

A Soldier Creek Hunt Club outing at the Wood Reserve. RG1517:25-1

Maj. Edwin Hardy, master of the hunt, at right center. RG1517:25-2

Polo at Fort Robinson. Maj. Ralph G. Kercheval and Private McLean override
the ball close to the goal. RG1517:45-25

Above: **Re-erecting the flagpole on the main parade ground, 1930.** RG1517:45-23

Right: **Civilian Conservation Corps men lounging at the Saw Mill Camp on the Wood Reserve.** RG1517:114--6

Left: **Entrance to the Saw Mill Camp.** RG1517:114-5

Below: **Mess hall at the Saw Mill Camp.** RG1517:114-4

Company 789, Civilian Conservation Corps, in front of the east barracks, 1933. RG1517:61-26

The U. S. Olympic equestrian team at Fort Robinson, summer 1935. Team captain Maj. William B. Bradford is fourth from left. RG2918:Album 1

Dedication of the Crazy Horse and Levi Robinson monuments, September 5, 1934. RG1517:90-2

Marianne Wenzlaff, daughter of remount Lt. Ted Wenzlaff, unveils the Levi Robinson monument. Gathered around (left to right) are Lt. Wenzlaff, Maj. Edwin Hardy, two unidentified enlisted men, and QM Gen. L. H. Bash (at microphone). RG1517:90-4

Pipe ceremony following the unveiling of the Crazy Horse monument. RG1517:90-10

Gathering of the Sioux Nation." By the end of August, nearly twelve hundred Sioux from the Pine Ridge and Rosebud reservations had arrived and camped at the old agency site. Local subscription provided twenty-four beef cattle, thirteen hundred loaves of bread, eight hundred pounds of sugar, 240 pounds of coffee, and loads of candy for the guests. One enterprising individual from Harrison was intercepted with twenty-two pints of whiskey before he could reach the camp.[59]

In town the celebration featured daily parades followed by Indian dancing, horse racing, and contests of all kinds. The reservation visitors won a softball game with the locals, 6–5, and also the archery contest, while the city park held concessions, including "the famous mummy, owned by Homer Sherill, which has puzzled scientists of world-wide repute." Thousands of visitors from Nebraska, South Dakota, and Wyoming took part in the festivities.[60]

Dedication of the monuments on September 5 was truly a memorable occasion for Fort Robinson. Before the elaborate ceremony, the post held an open house of all depot operations, a horse show, a jumping exhibition, and a concert by the Fourth Cavalry Band. Visitors also toured the enlisted and CCC barracks, bakery, and post headquarters. The ceremony proper began at 4:30 P.M., when several hundred Sioux gathered north of the Crazy Horse pyramid, while military and civilian observers met south of the Robinson monument. Leaders of both groups then met at a tipi erected in the center of the square to hold a council and smoke a pipe of peace. Captain James H. Cook, the noted frontiersman and former army scout, represented the whites; the Indian contingent was led by Short Bull, White Bull No. 2, and Jim Red Cloud. After the council (in Lakota) was completed, all participants moved to the seating area and the formal program began.

The back porch of the post headquarters served as the speakers' stand. Among the special guests seated on the porch were several retired soldiers from Crawford, including Caleb Benson and William C. Beckett, two old sergeants who had served with the Tenth Cavalry at the post. After the invocation, Major Hardy welcomed the crowd, and newspaper editor Karl Spence read John G. Neihardt's "The Death of Crazy Horse." The program included an address by General Bash and orations by Bad Wound and the Reverend Mr. Beecher, interspersed with musical selections by the band.

At the end of Beecher's remarks the crowd gathered around the Robinson monument. After the Crawford Male Quartet sang "Tenting on the Old Camp Ground," the monument was unveiled by Marian Wenzlaff, daughter of Lt. Ted Wenzlaff, a cavalry officer then on duty with the remount. Attention then shifted to the Crazy Horse marker, where tribal leaders performed the Chief Song and Medicine Man Breast gave a ceremonial invocation. The marker, covered with a red blanket, was unveiled by Black Medicine, a nephew of the famed warrior. The Indians then held an Omaha dance, followed by a salute of eleven guns, the same salute rendered for a brigadier general. As the last gun was fired, the crowd stood, and on the main parade ground the flag was lowered while the Fourth Cavalry Band played the National Anthem. The ceremony had ended; a poignant moment in Fort Robinson history was over. The dedication program noted, "It is the first time in history that an Indian Warrior west of the Mississippi River has been honored by the erection of a monument to his memory through government agencies."[61]

Although the monument dedication and celebration was a great success, some of the Indian participants were dissatisfied with the choice of those selected to represent the Crazy Horse family. Indian people believed to have had a closer relationship to the famed warrior were not invited to speak, prompting some to walk off during Bad Wound's oration. Henry Standing Bear later remarked, "It [the ceremony] was considered by many Indians to be a failure I am sorry to note."[62] Nevertheless, the fact remained that "the Indian killed by his one-time enemy the white man was honored, just as the white man who was killed by his red enemy was honored."[63]

With the monuments completed, grander projects were planned. Local residents approached Hardy with a plan, resurrected from 1906, to have Red Cloud's remains buried atop the buttes above the post. The major thought this would be impractical and thoughtfully suggested that the chief instead be buried at the old agency site, halfway between the town and post.

In March 1935 he wrote General Bash about the scheme, and suggested building another pyramid marker, honoring Red Cloud, at the agency site. Red Cloud's remains would be placed in a nearby concrete sarcophagus, and a fence built to enclose twenty-five acres around the grave. Hardy stated that local people wanted the site set aside as a national park, eventually with a museum exhibiting Captain Cook's personal collection of Red Cloud paraphernalia and other Indian arti-facts. Hardy claimed that the whole project, including a new road from Highway 20, could be completed for ten thousand dollars. He added, "Such a plan would represent a proper commemoration of pioneer and Indian history in this part of the country."[64]

Bash was less enthusiastic, but more realistic, and instructed Hardy not to use quartermaster funds for any additional markers. It had been difficult enough to cover the costs of the two pyramid markers and the general hoped "nothing further will be heard of it." He also informed Hardy that national parks and monuments were no longer under army control, and the ten thousand dollar estimate was too low for such an ambitious project. In conclusion, he added, "I am telling you all this frankly as I see it here. There is very little, if anything I can do except to help it along if my advice is asked." The army built no more monuments at Fort Robinson.[65]

Chapter 4

War Comes to Fort Robinson

By the end of 1939, Fort Robinson had been a remount depot for two decades. In the 1920s and 1930s the nation's defense budget dictated the number of animals, primarily riding horses, the army would need each year. The twenties brought austere budgets, and in the thirties, the country had priorities other than maintaining a large cavalry force. During those years, modest numbers of horses were received, cared for, and issued. Ironically, in the last years of the horse cavalry, remount activity peaked at Fort Robinson when World War II brought new, unforeseen roles.

Although mechanization of the armed forces had begun in 1930, half of the army's cavalry regiments were still mounted or retained a horse section, and the field artillery was largely horse-drawn ten years later. Many National Guard units also still used horses, and the post furnished mounts for the Wyoming National Guard cavalry, which, according to one officer, did not mind receiving unmanageable horses. At the time, no National Guard mounted unit had all the horses it needed, and if the guard were ever to be called into federal service, the remount's work at Fort Robinson would increase considerably.[1]

As war clouds loomed over Europe, the army general staff planned for the probable mobilization of the army and National Guard. Plans in 1939 projected a massive increase in quartermaster remount operations, to provide more than 200,000 horses and mules. An increase of this magnitude would require four new depots and a significant expansion of the three existing installations.[2]

Maj. James M. "Jumping Jimmy" Adamson, who replaced Hardy as depot commander in 1937, did not favor expansion of the Fort Robinson depot. The new plan called for the depot to accommodate 7,200 horses, an increase Adamson doubted could be achieved. He felt that winter weather posed many problems for the conditioning and issue of animals, effectively restricting depot operations to eight months a year. Nor could the reservation handle such an increase in grazing pressure, and forage would have to be shipped in. He was apprehensive of the costs of materials and labor that would be required for such a dramatic expansion of depot facilities. Maj. Gen. P. P. Bishop, the area corps commander, agreed with Adamson, and recommended that expanding the depot be reconsidered and the present capacity be maintained.[3]

Adamson's and Bishop's concerns became moot because horse and mule procurement never approached the levels called for in the army's initial mobilization plan. With the outbreak of war in Europe, the general staff re-evaluated and modified war plans to increase mechanization. As a result, in fiscal year 1941, the army authorized the purchase of some twenty thousand additional animals: 16,800 horses and 3,500 mules. Because this influx of newly purchased animals would be passed on to the remount depots, they had been warned about the new procurement program in September 1940. Depot commanders at Front Royal, Fort Reno, and Robinson, were alerted to plan for a larger number of receipts and an increased workload. In calendar year 1941 the army actually purchased about 24,000 horses, a fraction of the 1939 projection, but, nevertheless, much higher than prewar levels.[4]

The impact of the 1941 purchases was sharply felt at Fort Robinson, where in the first half of the fiscal year, more than six thousand newly purchased horses and nine hundred mules were received. Of that number 1,446 horses and 662 mules were shipped out. In 1939 Fort Robinson had an average animal strength of 1,323; by 1940 it was reported as 5,790. Due to adverse weather, purchasing was reduced in early 1941 and shipments exceeded gains, with more than five thousand animals being issued. During the second half of 1941 purchasing was on the upswing, with the post receiving 12,832 horses and 1,234 mules; at the same time issues totaled nearly the same. On the eve of America's involvement in World War II, Fort Robinson was approaching its heyday as a quartermaster remount depot.[5]

The increased numbers of horses brought a corresponding need for more personnel. In the late 1930s the post's veterinary detachment consisted of only two officers and fifteen enlisted men; by December 1941, six officers and forty-one soldiers were on duty, with more arriving weekly. A key addition to the veterinary staff came in August 1940, when Lt. Col. Floyd C. Sager arrived and began his duties as chief veterinarian. Sager, a graduate of Cornell University with a degree in veterinary science, was also a decorated veteran of World War I. He spent several tours of duty in the Philippines and served briefly at Fort Robinson in the 1920s. Sager was a skillful veterinarian, very popular with both officers and enlisted men. He was quick to praise his men, and was recalled as being more of a father figure than a commanding officer. Sager was proud of the low animal mortality rate achieved by his men in spite of the constant changes in horse and mule population. With ever larger numbers of animals arriving at and leaving from the depot, Colonel Sager's veterinary force eventually grew to more than one hundred officers and enlisted men.[6]

The increase in all phases of remount operations taxed depot facilities. The veterinary hospital, built during the 1908–9 brick expansion period, proved too small. In 1941 a twenty-stall, L-shaped frame annex was constructed behind the main building. Shortly afterwards, two frame hospital ward stables were built just north of the annex. Each ward had a thirty-horse capacity and was heated. South of the hospital, permanent feeding shelters were added for animals in the observation pastures. To facilitate the processing of animals in the condition and issue area, a frame and concrete handling chute was built in 1942. Eighteen horses or mules could be run through the chute at one time.[7]

Most of the construction projects were accomplished through WPA programs and funding. In 1940 alone, $24,000 had been allocated to projects that increased feeding facilities and improved forage storage. Relief program laborers also built new porches on quarters, and painted and repaired the interiors of most post living quarters. The eighty-one civilian workers employed on those projects also found time to build flower boxes and lawn furniture. The WPA projects put the post "in the finest condition at the present time that it has ever been." In addition, WPA labor was used for feeding, after animal numbers increased without a corresponding increase of animal section enlisted personnel.[8]

During the summer of 1940, the cavalry equestrian team returned to the post for training. The team, though much reduced in size, continued its training even though the war in Europe eliminated any possibility of international competition. The next year, the army's famous Olympic horses were brought to Fort Robinson, including Dakota, still considered the finest jumping horse in the world. Some of the veteran animals showed the scars from years of training and competition in world-class meets. The prized horses were turned into the pasture between the post and buttes and kept at Fort Robinson for the duration.[9]

As the threat of war became imminent in 1939, many in the local community thought larger numbers of soldiers would return to Fort Robinson. Rumors circulated that the fort might be used a training area. In January Crawford residents heard there was a possibility that the Fourth

Cavalry regiment from Fort Meade might come to the fort for maneuvers that summer. Reflecting views similar to those from the pre-World-War-I era, the newspaper urged that "the local grounds would afford an ideal setting for the staging of army maneuvers."[9] Despite such optimism, no prewar maneuvers were held at the post. Later that fall, it was rumored that nine hundred infantrymen would come to the post for training. The community soon learned, however, that the troops were to go to Camp Robinson, Arkansas, not Fort Robinson, Nebraska. By 1940 it had become clear that without the assignment of combat troops, the post would not play an active part in national defense, but would continue in its long-standing role of quartermaster support.[10]

Excitement over the prospect of more soldiers coming to Fort Robinson surfaced briefly in 1941. That spring the army announced that three hundred new units were to be organized, including several quartermaster remount squadrons. The new remount units were to support troops in the field on a divisional level. On April 1, Troop B, 252nd QM Squadron, under command of Capt. James P. Burns, was activated at Fort Robinson. The strength of the new unit was two officers and 185 enlisted men. Part of the training cadre came from Fort Reno, while the balance was made up of three-year enlisted men from Fort Robinson. The troop itself was composed of 165 green recruits, many from Missouri, with backgrounds varying from Harvard graduates to Ozark farmers. Colonel Hardy, visiting the post as chief of remount, thought the new recruits had potential, "most of them having a farm background with some knowledge of horses. . . . I believe they will be developed into an excellent organization."[11]

With the remount detachment already housed in the east brick barracks, the troop moved into the west barracks. Extra support facilities were built behind the quarters, including a blacksmith shop, granary, saddle room, and wagon shed, all for the exclusive use of Troop B training. After arrival, the men immediately began training and took over the feeding and care of a large portion of the depot livestock. In addition to learning remount duties, the troops received basic military training, where they organized guard details and mastered the fundamentals of marching and drill. Much of their time was spent riding and polishing their horsemanship. By July the entire troop completed a thirty-mile ride and several days later joined the Crawford Fourth of July parade. It was a throwback to the old cavalry days, and local residents were delighted to see horsemen march again in town.[12]

By August their training had been completed, and the troop received orders for field deployment. On August 5 Troop B departed for the extensive Louisiana army field maneuvers then underway, before being transferred to Fort Bliss, Texas, for duty with the First Cavalry Division.

With depot activity on the increase and the country facing a national emergency, post security became a concern. By November 1941 the fort's security force consisted only of three civilian night watchmen. With remount personnel too busy to perform guard duty, the new post commander, Lt. Col. Edward M. Daniels, asked for the assignment of four trained military policemen to augment post security. "Critical areas," including the motor pool, electrical substation, water towers, and main water springs, were secured with high, chain-link fences. Some areas were illuminated at night for extra security. Wartime conditions had come to Fort Robinson.[13]

Throughout 1941 small groups of reserve quartermaster officers were called to active duty and began to arrive at the post for training. Most of the new officers had recent ROTC commissions, and Fort Robinson was their first active duty station. The new men were trained through observation, then by participating in daily post and depot operations. Colonel Hardy wisely directed that their work schedules be arranged to keep them busy and the "shavetails" were regularly rotated through most post duties. Coinciding with "hands on" remount training, the trainees were required to attend officers' school, where classes covered equitation, military customs and courtesy, company administration, procurement, and the articles of war. The post commissioned staff served as instructors.[14]

The usual period for reserve officer training was three months of fairly intense work. Most of the men, who were recent college graduates, arrived at the post without basic household items. At times newly married couples "arrived with all their possessions in a small car and were assigned to rambling quarters of seven or eight large rooms."[15] Post officers helped the rookie officers adjust to their new environs. Some alumni of Fort Robinson training later advanced to field grade rank by the end of World War II.

Regardless of these preparations and anxiety that the U.S. might be drawn into the war, life at the post retained its relaxed lifestyle in the fall of 1941. During the 1941 World Series radio broadcasts, all work, except the care of sick animals, was suspended. A popular pastime that fall for the soldiers was hunting pheasants on the military reservation, with shotguns and ammunition provided by the remount detachment. Limits on the number of birds that could be taken by a hunter were governed by the number of dead cats he turned in beforehand. Common housecats were the worst predators on the post because of their destruction of young wildlife and their potential as carriers of rabies. Three cats destroyed qualified a hunter for one pheasant—pet cats were required to wear a small bell, or risked being killed. In addition to wild domestic cats, skunks, hawks, and crows could be exchanged for pheasants. For other outdoorsmen, fishing on the Wood Reserve was prohibited that fall, because fish had been released to spawn in upper Soldier Creek.[16]

The sporting event most anticipated by officers was the Kentucky Derby. The officers' club, nicknamed the Ratcatcher's Inn, was transformed into a racetrack clubhouse, complete with a toteboard posting odds. On race day, officers and wives gathered to hear the prerace coverage and listen to the broadcast. Several remount officers had former racing associations, and it was expected they could provide "insider" information. As the race progressed, "we all cheered or groaned during the radio report of the race."[17] West Point alumni followed the Army-Navy football game with keen interest, but the Derby was the most popular event.

Like Americans elsewhere, Fort Robinson soldiers were shocked by the news of Japan's attack on Pearl Harbor. Lt. Robert McCaffree recalled how he heard:

> Suddenly, Lieut. Kercheval, who lived in the second quarters northwest, bounded in in great excitement. "Come over and listen to the news on the radio. The Japs are bombing Pearl Harbor!" We went to Kercheval's quarters and listened, stunned, to reports of the attack. We could hardly believe it. We didn't talk much, just stared at each other. Later, as we learned of the attacks the same day on Nichols Field in the Philippines, we probably discussed a shipment of horses and accompanying detachment of soldiers from Fort Robinson, who arrived in the Philippines in November.[18]

The sudden sense of emergency sparked orders for the military police to call men back to the post from Crawford. They found one group of soldiers in a local bar. When told to return to the fort immediately, one soldier asked, "What are we going to do now? We don't even know how to shoot a rifle or carry a gun or handle anything but a pitchfork and scoop shovel!"[19]

Back at the post, details were quickly organized to guard the recently fenced critical areas from possible sabotage. Some remount men took a more realistic attitude in the face of the sudden wave of war hysteria. They didn't believe that if Axis agents came to America, the first thing they would do was poison the Fort Robinson water system.[20]

Nerves were on edge at Fort Robinson for days after Pearl Harbor. Once, in the middle of the night, a second lieutenant shot at a coyote while making the rounds of the guardposts in the staff car. The shot precipitated a general alarm. When a senior officer pointed out that the alarm had roused the whole post, the offending lieutenant, who had a reputation of acting rashly, was repentant.[21] Although some areas were off limits, U.S. Highway 20 ran directly through Fort Robinson, and incoming soldiers, used to more restricted posts, were amazed at the civilian traffic passing daily.

Although Fort Robinson's normal remount operations continued, the end was near for the horse cavalry. The rapid and concentrated firepower of World War I fighting had brought changes in the role of cavalry. It could no longer be used as an attack force, but was limited to reconnaissance, scouting, and harassment. Another setback for the cavalry came in 1930, when army Chief of Staff Douglas MacArthur directed each service branch to mechanize. Throughout the army, in both line regiments and support organizations, motorized vehicles gradually replaced horses.[22]

Included in this modernization was the Fourth Cavalry, since 1924 stationed at Fort Meade. In 1940 mechanization had come to that historic regiment, which, in the 1876–77 Sioux War, had been assigned to Camp Robinson. That year the Fourth became a two-squadron, horse-mechanized corps reconnaissance regiment. Although the first squadron retained its horses, two troops of the second squadron converted to transport in scout cars and jeeps, and one troop was mounted on motorcycles. To give the horse section more mobility, "portee" trailers were utilized, each carrying one squad of eight men with their horses and equipment. More change came in the early spring of 1942, when the army planned to fully mechanize three regular and seven National Guard cavalry regiments, including the Fourth, which would enable them "to better fulfill their function of army corps reconnaissance units."[23]

Still unaware of the coming change, the Fourth Cavalry prepared to march in Omaha's Army Day parade on April 6, 1942. The long trip from Fort Meade to eastern Nebraska was planned as a training maneuver. Some 1,250 men and 487 horses were transported in nearly four hundred vehicles on the three-day trip. The regiment camped at the Ak-Sar-Ben race track in Omaha on Friday, April 3. The next day regimental commander Col. Joseph M. Tully was summoned to Seventh Corps headquarters, and informed that the regiment was to be dismounted and fully mechanized. Later that day the rest of the regiment was told the news, and for many a cavalryman, it was quite a shock.[24] On their return trip, the troops were to leave the first squadron's horses at Fort Robinson.

On Monday the regiment marched proudly in the parade, to the excitement of more than sixty thousand spectators. The Fourth Cavalry horse section stole the show, as it clattered along the streets in a last public appearance. For both the riders and the appreciative crowd, "there was a poignant realization that it might be the last time Omaha streets would ever echo to the hooves of horse cavalry."[25] On Tuesday morning the regiment began the long journey to Fort Robinson, making overnight stops at Kearney and Alliance. While on the road, the long column averaged fewer than twenty-five miles per hour.

At 2 P.M. on the afternoon of April 9, the regiment's vehicles began to arrive in Crawford, and camp was set up just west of town on the military reservation. Preparations were made for a last mounted review before the regiment turned in its horses. As word spread quickly, most of the Fort Robinson garrison and many local citizens gathered on a hill southwest of town to view the end of the Fourth horse cavalry. "It was quite a treat for the Crawford people to see a large number of soldiers again, as it had been a number of years since Fort Robinson was full of soldiers," a local paper remarked.[26]

At about five o'clock the horse section mounted, crossed the highway, and formed for its last review. The horse section passed in review three times in front of the mechanized section and the crowd of spectators: the first pass was at a walk; the second was at a trot, while the regimental band played "Oh, Susanna;" and the third was at a canter as the band blared "Garry Owen," the rollicking, traditional march of the cavalry. Spectators admired the precision exhibited by the cavalrymen and horses as they moved from column to flank formations. After the mounted troops were reviewed, they formed up and the mechanized troops passed them in review, led by Colonel Tully who saluted the horsemen from the lead vehicle. As the jeeps, scout cars, and motorcycles slowly went by, the band played "Auld Lang Syne," the finale to what one cavalryman recalled as "really a sad day and most of the horse troops were understandably distraught."[27] After many years of preparing horses for cavalry use, the Fort Robinson personnel realized they had witnessed a historic moment.

After receiving the salute, the horsemen moved off, dismounted, and removed bridles and saddles so the horses could be turned into a nearby feed trap. For many troopers, the review was an impressive and emotional occasion, and that night in Crawford bars many cavalrymen mourned the loss of their horses. Others looked forward to new training in a "mechanized cavalry where we could win the war."[28] That night many Fourth Cavalry officers visited the post officers' club, "trying to forget what they considered a tragedy at the time."[29] The next morning, the troop farriers removed the horseshoes and turned the horses over to the remount; the men then boarded vehicles for the trip back to Fort Meade. Many of the regiment's animals had now come full circle, having originally been issued from the Robinson Quartermaster Depot. From that day on, more horses would be turned in to the remount depot than would ever again be issued.

The end of the mounted cavalry brought a significant change to the long-standing role of the remount—the days of preparing and issuing cavalry horses were over. The remount depots, including Fort Robinson, became holding facilities, where army horses were maintained until they could be sold as surplus. Although the horse herds no longer held their traditional value to the army, they remained public property and had to be cared for.

The dismounting of the Fourth Cavalry was the first in a steady stream of horse returns to Fort Robinson, and many animals prepared and issued by the remount in 1941 came back to the depot as other regiments were dismounted. During the remainder of 1942, five thousand horses were returned, and in 1943 an additional twenty-two hundred head came in. With the 1942–43 returns, and with a large number of horses and mules already on hand, Fort Robinson neared its peak capacity. At the end of 1942, average animal strength was 9,085; by mid-spring of 1943 the average was 11,402. For one brief moment the number reached twelve thousand head, the largest total of horses and mules ever recorded at Fort Robinson.[30]

Depot feeding and care facilities were taxed. Along with the existing feeding areas along White River, two new areas were set aside and soon filled. The East Big Butte area, with a twenty-five-hundred-head capacity, was located along the highway just west of Crawford. The largest was the Glen feed area, just west of the post between the railroad and the river bottom. This area stretched for more than a mile and could hold six thousand head. Living quarters, called "shacks" in the remount vernacular, were built in the new areas to house the enlisted men assigned to care for the animals.

Hay harvested on the reservation could not begin to feed the vast herds, and huge contracts were let by the post quartermaster for stacked and baled hay during the summer months. After delivery, the hay was inspected by veterinary officers and stored in hay sheds or stacked in the open. Enormous amounts of feed were purchased, 55,415 tons of hay and 208 tons of cereal grains in 1943 alone. Eight large, open-side hay sheds were added for long-term storage.[31]

Before 1942 the main job of the remount branch had been the procurement of cavalry horses; after the cavalry was dismounted, liquidation of surplus horse herds became a priority. Between July 1943 and

December 1945 more than twenty-eight thousand riding horses were turned in at the remount depots for sale. In the winter of 1943–44, preparations began for horse sales at Fort Robinson. Animals to be sold had their feet trimmed and fetlocks clipped, then were branded with an "S" for surplus. In a two-day February 1944 sale, 1,067 surplus horses and 500 mules went through the ring at the rate of three animals per minute. Bidding was "spirited," with an average price of $132 being paid for the mules; half-bred riding horses brought an average of $61.11 per head. In 1944 alone, four thousand cavalry horses were sold at Fort Robinson, with the average price dropping to $34 per head by October. Hundreds of horses were purchased by the Eli Lilly Company, which used horse blood in the processing of various serums.[32]

Although Fort Robinson no longer issued horses to army combat units, other military agencies needed riding and draft horses. In 1942 the United States Coast Guard began to order hundreds of horses. The German submarine menace was at its peak, and mounted patrols were used to guard against saboteur landings. Fort Robinson horses were sent to the New Jersey coastline, and to Coast Guard stations in Oregon and Washington. In total the remount service issued some three thousand horses for coastal mounted patrol. By 1944 the submarine threat had abated, and the Coast Guard horses were returned to the depots.[33]

During the war, and particularly in the spring of 1945, especially gentle remount horses were sent to army hospitals, where riding became part of convalescent therapy. Hoff General Hospital at Santa Barbara, California, and the army air forces convalescent hospital at Fort Wright, Washington, were among those receiving horses from the Robinson Depot. Hundreds of horses were eventually issued for use by military hospital patients, an instance where the traditional role of the horse in warfare was somewhat reversed.[34]

Draft and riding horses were also put to use at the growing number of prisoner of war camps in the United States. Animals processed at Fort Robinson were sent to various camps in the Seventh Service Command area for mounted perimeter patrol, and prisoner work with draft teams. Fort-issued animals went to camps built near Midwestern towns, including Altoona and Clarinda, Iowa, Indianola and Atlanta, Nebraska, and Douglas, Wyoming.

Horse and mule teams also were in daily use at Fort Robinson. In line with wartime conservation of rubber and gasoline, the animal transportation stable was one of the busiest places on the post. As many as thirty-five teams were used each day for feeding, hauling refuse, and other tasks whereby tires and gasoline could be saved.[35]

The massive horse and mule herds produced thousands of tons of manure that accumulated in stable and feeding areas. In wartime, even this undesirable byproduct found a military use. Work details moved truckloads of manure to sites along the railroad, where it was then loaded by dragline into gondola cars. Wartime building brought the construction of dozens of ammunition depots, air bases, and other installations in areas of dry, loose soil. The army shipped the manure to be used as ground cover to stabilize and prevent the recently disturbed soil from blowing. A crisis came to post manure hauling operations when Herman Wulf, the NCO in charge, was transferred to Camp Lee:

> [In] October of 43 I was on my way overseas when I had a call to come back to Fort Robinson, they needed my services. So, I was transferred from Camp Lee, Virginia, back to Fort Robinson. . . . The C.O. had told me they didn't have any success with anybody else being able to take care of the equipment and take care of manure at the same time.[36]

Although mechanization reduced the need for army animals, it did not, as some thought, make them obsolete. The mule, with his surefootedness and stamina, was in demand for pack use, and remount mule purchases increased dramatically. In 1941 horse purchases had outnumbered mule purchases five to one; by fiscal year 1942 the ratio was two to one. In mid-1942 the army remount began a large scale mule-buying program. In 1943 the army purchased only four riding horses and more than ten thousand mules.[37]

By the fall of 1942 the Robinson depot began to feel the impact of this program when two thousand mules were received for pack training. In 1943 the number of mules on post grew to nearly four thousand. The objectives of mule training at the fort were twofold: to train them to carry packs and follow a bell mare on a trail. In preparing them for issue, mules first had to be gentled enough to stand quietly while their feet were picked up and handled, then their feet and manes were trimmed and clipped. Remount soldiers then acquainted the animals with packs and began training over the rugged terrain north of the post. Pack trains of fifty mules were taken into the buttes, where their training included exposure to 75mm artillery fire to prepare them for combat. After ten days to two weeks of this daily ritual, officers examined the mules to see if they showed nervousness or signs of rebellion. Animals passing those checks were ready for issue. By the end of the war, mules were being readied for service at the rate of five hundred per month.[38]

The largest single shipment of mules from the fort came in March 1943, when 1,082 animals were loaded into forty-nine railroad cars in three hours. Remount soldiers used "all techniques of persuasion" in the loading, which was finished in what they considered record time.[39]

In 1943 mountain troops training at camps Hale and Carson in Colorado received thousands of pack mules from the depot, and the first overseas shipments began to the China-Burma-India Theater. In addition to mules, soldiers from the post often were sent overseas. In the fall of 1943 a detachment from Fort Robinson accompanied a mule shipment to perform remount duties for American forces in Asia, including the noted Merrill's Marauders. Veterinary Corps personnel were frequently assigned to accompany railroad shipments to care for the animals until they reached the ports of embarkation. Sometimes this duty extended beyond the shipping ports. In March 1944 a detachment consisting of Lt. Harold Cleveland, T5 John Hinkle, and privates Clarence Corliss, Lyman Gueck, and Archie Seacrest accompanied 250 mules to the port of Jersey City. From there, they sailed for India, caring for the mules in transit. After arrival, the men and mules were moved to mainland China, where the men were permanently assigned as a field veterinary detachment for the Chinese army.[40]

By 1944 there were more mules than horses at the Fort Robinson depot; 4,932 mules and 4,441 horses were on hand. One important customer for American mules was the British army; thirty-five hundred mules were transferred to United Kingdom forces under lend-lease. Because they desired small mules, British officers came to Fort Robinson to select animals from the vast herds.[41]

Following established procedures, many remount soldiers enlisted at the fort, and consequently had received little or no basic training. To correct this deficit, in the spring of 1943 a six-week basic training program was initiated for all general service men on post. The first of two recruit training sessions began on April 2, and included some men who had been in the army for several years. Remount soldiers without previous basic training spent the mornings at their regular work, and assembled in the afternoons for combat exercises and drill. Other post personnel who had completed basic training were required to devote four hours each week to military training and drill.[42]

Basic training at Fort Robinson followed the rudiments fondly remembered by veterans. Helmets, packs, and rifles, strange equipment to the remount troops, were distributed. Besides drill and the manual of arms, hand-to-hand fighting techniques were presented by an experienced professor of martial arts from Denver. The unused post firing range was revamped, and after several weeks of target practice, forty percent of the trainees qualified for marksmanship badges. Antiaircraft training was later provided using .22-caliber rifles that were fired at ascending and descending targets operated by a rope and windlass. The soldiers also attended films and lectures at the post theater. Part of the training involved crawling through an infiltration course, complete with exploding charges and machine gun bullets flying overhead, certainly the most exciting part of the process. After several officers tried the course, one commented on how they "suddenly developed an intimate fondness for mother earth—like the closer down we nestled into the soil, the safer we felt."[43]

The end of basic training was marked by a hike to the Wood Reserve for a field day. After an inspection and drills, the men competed in athletic events and the winning platoon was feted at a dinner dance. The officers who served as judges were impressed by the spirit of cooperation shown by the men of the first training group.[44]

The Second Provisional Training Company completed its six-week basic training and made the Wood Reserve march on July 5. This group consisted of 104 men from all sections of the post. Field day winners received three kegs of beer provided by the losing platoons. That evening the troops gathered around a fire, singing, drinking beer, and relaxing—at least until a "commando" attack suddenly came at nine o'clock. Although little is recorded about the defense of the camp by the trainees, it was later noted the "men had an opportunity to put into practice the knowledge which they had been learning for the past six weeks." With its soldiers now better prepared, the only basic training provided at Fort Robinson during World War II had ended.[45]

After arms and field gear were put away, the regular post routine resumed. Once again, the remount soldiers adopted the casual clothing they liked for working with livestock. Many wore Levis, western boots, and rode western stock saddles; everyone generally enjoyed relaxed requirements for wearing the regulation uniform while on duty. All wore the familiar campaign hat, but often creased it in a nonregulation fashion to suit individual fancy. Incoming regular army personnel, including M/Sgt. Samuel Mitchell, were at first amazed by the look of Fort Robinson soldiers:

> Enroute to the camp I noted that the Fort Robinson enlisted men wore cowboy boots, blue jeans, army olive drab shirts, and either cowboy or campaign hats. This was an odd sight to me because in the infantry, strict military dress was a daily ritual. However, the initial shock soon wore off and I came

to respect the men of Fort Robinson and their western traditions.[46]

At times, higher ranking officers were not impressed with the men's cowboy duds. A visiting general once asked a saluting group of veterinary men if they were soldiers or civilians. The next day at roll call Colonel Sager admonished his men to wear regulation fatigues for the next several days while the general was on post. He added, "After he leaves, carry on."[47]

Perhaps the most unusual activity at the post during the war was the 1943 airborne maneuvers, recalling prewar visions of Fort Robinson's possible use for large-scale training. In March 1943 a delegation of Fort Robinson officers went to Alliance Army Air Field to confer with officials there about a proposed airborne operation on the Fort Robinson reservation. They agreed to hold battle maneuvers that summer in the rugged hills west of the post, which presented an excellent venue with trees and rough terrain, features not found on the sand hills of the Alliance military reservation. A glider regiment would land west of the post on Soldier Creek, to be followed by a regiment of paratroops.

As summer came, an airborne engineer unit arrived from Alliance and constructed a five-thousand-foot landing strip along the Glen feed area to support the maneuvers. The dirt strip, large enough to handle C-47 aircraft, was completed in one week. On July 23 sixteen transport planes landed to pick up the tractors and other equipment used to build the airstrip, and return them to Alliance.

The maneuvers, slated for early August, involved two glider regiments and a battalion of parachute infantry. One of the glider regiments was the Eighty-eighth Glider Infantry, which had been stationed at Fort Meade since the mechanized Fourth Cavalry left. Because there was no airfield near that fort, training for the Eighty-eighth had emphasized infantry tactics. The men of the dismounted glider regiment arrived at Fort Robinson by truck on August 5 to serve as the defending enemy in what became known as the "Battle of Fort Robinson."[48]

The real airborne troops, the 326th Glider Infantry and a battalion of the 507th Parachute Regiment, were flown in from the Alliance base. The glider regiment employed the CG-4A, the most widely used army transport and assault glider. Constructed of wood with steel tubing and a fabric skin, each could carry fifteen soldiers or one jeep. In addition to the airborne infantry, the 253rd Field Artillery Battalion supported the red defending force. All the airborne elements were transported from Alliance by four squadrons of the 434th Troop Carrier Group.

On Tuesday afternoon and Wednesday morning, August 10 and 11, the sky south and west of the post was full of planes as the airborne landings began. Most Fort Robinson soldiers were told nothing about the operation, and although not officially involved, many men hurried west up the Soldier Creek valley to watch the gliders come in. Wave after wave of C-47s towing gliders turned east down Soldier Creek from the Wood Reserve, releasing the gliders into the hay meadows just west of Carter P. Johnson lake. Unfortunately, the landing zone was on private property over which the army had no control. On the day of the landing, the area was covered with numerous small haystacks. The gliders crashed-landed into haystacks, fence lines, ravines, and each other. The remount observers were amazed there were relatively few casualties. The infantrymen quickly tumbled out of smashed gliders and prepared to engage their adversaries from the Eighty-eighth Glider Infantry.[49]

The next morning paratroopers jumped west of the post, and with both airborne units on the ground, the "battle" began in earnest. The maneuvers lasted several days and involved thirty-five hundred men, not including one hundred officers to observe the show. One night the Eighty-eighth troops moved into a gap between the 326th and 507th regiments, gaining their rear. The next morning the two units from Alliance fired on each other, believing they had found the enemy. The elusive Eighty-eighth seemed to have had the best of the war games.[50]

Although remount soldiers did not participate in the maneuvers, K-9 handlers and dogs from the war dog training center at Fort Robinson did. The dogs and handlers served as sentries and scouts to locate airborne soldiers. An airborne colonel, who landed in a tree, was captured by a K-9 soldier and his dog. As K-9 soldier Robert Fischer remembered, "The airborne troopers were surprised by the ferocity of the dogs and wouldn't have anything to do with them."[51]

By August 15 the maneuvers ended and the airborne troops returned to their posts. Much equipment including parachutes, drop test dummies, and life preservers, was lost. Some remount soldiers, who had never seen nylon, were quick to pick up the tow lines used to pull the gliders, and later used them for throw ropes to catch horses and mules. Almost all the sixty-two gliders that landed at Fort Robinson were badly damaged; some beyond repair. The battered gliders were hauled to the landing strip, where men from the 537th Service Squadron at Alliance spent two months repairing or reclaiming them. The only large-scale wartime maneuver at Fort Robinson was over. Less than a year later, many of the airborne troops who dropped on the post participated in the Normandy invasion.[52]

By 1943 activity at the fort was increasing. Besides an escalation in remount operations, a war dog training center had been established in 1942 and a prisoner of war camp was nearing completion. The post fell under the jurisdiction of the Seventh Service Command, with headquarters in Omaha, for administrative and logistical support. To assist with office work, the number of civil service employees increased, particularly in the post headquarters staff, motor pool, engineer, and supply sections. A regularly-scheduled bus service was initiated between Crawford and the post using a twenty-nine-passenger army bus.

In 1944 more than one hundred officers were on duty with the various post departments, including remount, K-9, medical, and PW camp. By this time all available post housing was full, forcing many married officers and enlisted men to live in apartments and motels in Crawford. Others had to commute from Chadron, where soldiers, regardless of rank, carpooled for the twenty-eight-mile trip.[53]

One section of the post that was greatly expanded during the war years was the medical staff. Eventually, the post hospital was commanded by a lieutenant colonel, with a staff of four surgeons, three dentists, and three administrative and laboratory officers. To care for larger numbers of post personnel and hundreds of German prisoners, female army nurses began to arrive. The nurses were housed in the old 1891 commanding officers quarters, for many years the home of the Ratcatcher's Inn. The officers' club moved to the basement of the 1909 bachelor officers' quarters, which had been named Comanche Hall in honor of the famous horse that survived the Battle of the Little Bighorn. The enlisted ranks were advised, "To clear up any doubt on the matter, army nurses are commissioned officers and are greeted with a salute."[54]

New facilities were needed and quickly built in the central post area to serve the larger number of soldiers. A new post office was operational by April 1943. Located just west of the east permanent barracks, the structure was a temporary, theater-of-operations-type building. Across the street to the west, a combination post exchange and recreation building was completed late in 1942. It contained a sales and lunch area with booths, and replaced the smaller PX in the east barracks. Across Highway 20 from the east barracks, a post chapel was completed in May 1943. The impressive building had a capacity of 180 people and replaced the post gymnasium as a place of worship. In the warehouse area, an engineers' warehouse/office and other support buildings sprang up. All the new construction was completed by civilian contractors, many driving from Chadron because of the shortage of temporary housing in Crawford.[55]

In 1943 a Women's Army Corps (WAC) detachment was assigned to

Fort Robinson. For the rest of the war, the women performed a variety of post jobs, relieving men for other duties. Although some enlisted men lost "plush" jobs or were transferred to other stations, for most "the anticipation of single women at Fort Robinson was a cheering note."[56]

The WACs lived in a separate compound constructed behind the officers' row. The new WAC area was mobilization-type construction, a more permanent type of wartime quarters than the theater-of-operations buildings. Besides a two-story barracks, the women had a mess hall and combination recreation and beauty shop. The WACs soon became a vital part of post operations, some holding secretarial positions while others ran the filling station, worked in the motor pool, and served as dispatchers. Many were truck drivers, and one motor pool sergeant admitted that "some of them were real good at it."[57] They drove loads of salvaged items to the Fort Warren depot near Cheyenne, while other women hauled manure or made daily deliveries of German prisoners to work sites on post.[58]

Some WACs enjoyed Fort Robinson's western atmosphere and like their male counterparts, were anxious to learn to ride horses. On one off-duty outing, a WAC from the Pacific Coast learned what "mountain oysters" were, after expecting her order to consist of the more conventional marine variety. Although fraternization between the ranks was discouraged, several post enlisted men married WACs they met while serving at Fort Robinson.[59]

During the war a small number of Japanese American soldiers arrived for duty in the officers' club and Comanche Hall as cooks, kitchen police, and dining room orderlies. Wartime prejudice against citizens of Japanese descent followed these soldiers to Fort Robinson. The men were under close surveillance for any remarks or comments they might make that seemed pro-Japanese. The post director of security and intelligence sent confidential reports to the quartermaster general's office on any evidence of subversive acts. One report told of a soldier who did not want to fight in the Asiatic theater—he had two brothers in the Japanese army. Another private stated he was willing to fight and made no preference as to theater. Regardless of their different nationalities or backgrounds, Fort Robinson soldiers generally performed their tasks in harmony and with efficiency.[60]

Throughout the war Fort Robinson remained a small post by comparison with other U.S. military installations. By 1943 only thirty-seven officers and 429 enlisted men were assigned as its regular post complement, including the remount, veterinary detachment, and other support branches. Although adjunct activities, in addition to horse and mule work, would bring more men to Fort Robinson, post strength did not increase significantly. With a limited number of quarters, the post was at capacity. But because of its small population, it was a close-knit post, and brothers were often able to serve there together. At one time, four Runge brothers (Clifford, Lester, Vernon, and Walter) from Sidney, Nebraska, were stationed with the remount at the post, working in administration and in the feed areas.[61]

As one form of entertainment for the men, United Service Organization camp shows made frequent visits. Traveling programs such as "Breezing Along," "Hullabaloo," and "Cavalcade of Music" brought the soldiers fast-moving shows of songs, dances, and jokes. The 1943 menu included "Keep Shufflin," a musical variety review described as a "Red Hot blues chaser."[62] The special services office also arranged post variety shows, dancing, card lessons, and other wholesome entertainment for the enlisted men. Dances and parties were organized on the post with girls brought in from nearby towns. Mrs. George "Sadie" Barker from Chadron was a well-known chaperone, who escorted hundreds of girls to activities at Fort Robinson. At one dance, eighty-five young ladies came from Chadron. The girls were required to have parental permission and be between sixteen and twenty-one years old to join the post trips.[63]

The war years brought a period of particularly close cooperation to the often rocky relationship between the post and town. As with civilian populations across the country, the Crawford citizenry paid special attention to servicemen at the fort. With so many of their sons and daughters in uniform, the townspeople's attitude toward the soldiers became one of concern and appreciation, rather than viewing their contributions in strictly economic terms.

Crawford businessmen and townspeople organized and then entertained the soldiers at a variety of social functions. For an August 1942 picnic, each sponsor was advised to bring enough food for "two hungry soldiers." After the meal, soldiers and civilians spent a pleasant afternoon playing croquet and badminton, and held archery matches. That Christmas, Crawford businessmen contributed cash to provide each soldier at Fort Robinson with a Christmas package. A servicemen's recreation center was opened in town, where local families entertained soldiers. Off-duty troops were often treated to chili feeds, followed by an evening of cards. Volunteers at the center also sent birthday cards to soldiers and provided cookies, rolls, and magazines for their military guests. Dances for servicemen were frequently held in the park pavilion. Soldiers were invited to dances and parties in the nearby communities, and whenever they were in town, Fort Robinson men were cordially welcomed at the Chadron USO.[64]

Soldiers from the post reciprocated the kindness, and helped the town on civic projects. In 1943 a twenty-man detail helped the undermanned city crew with its annual spring park cleanup. Crawford Mayor B. F. Richards complimented the enlisted men, who "rendered willing, whole-hearted, and efficient service." In 1945 several soldiers and K-9 dogs from the post joined neighbors from the Bethel community east of Crawford in the search for a missing two-year-old child, who had wandered off into the timber. After an all-night search, the boy was discovered asleep in a field a mile from home.[65]

Fort Robinson's largest contribution to the civilian community came during the near washout of a dam at the Whitney irrigation reservoir in the spring of 1942. In early May twelve inches of rain fell in seven days, leaving the reservoir dangerously full. The high water, coupled with winds that pushed six-foot waves over the south dam, seriously eroded the dam face. The heavy rains had also washed out roads and bridges, making it nearly impossible for relief workers to reach the reservoir. With the dam's loss imminent, irrigation district officials asked post commander Col. Paul Kendall to send soldiers to bolster the local workers. Less than an hour later, Kendall had a fleet of army trucks on the road loaded with soldiers, equipment, and mules. Additional soldiers arrived, filled thousands of sandbags, and cut and placed hundreds of trees to protect the eroding dam. Throughout the night, soldiers and civilians endured rain and sleet, working in knee-deep mud. Kendall rode up and down the line on horseback, coordinating the civilian-military effort. Late the next after-noon the danger abated, and the tired, muddy troops returned to the post. In gratitude, the chairman of the irrigation district wrote Kendall: "Our local folks decided at that time if all our officers and men in the armed forces were as willing and efficient as these had proven to be, that the outcome of the present world war couldn't remain in doubt."[66]

Fort soldiers were required to have a pass to make off-duty trips to Crawford or other neighboring towns. A Class A pass entitled a soldier to be absent from evening retreat until the next morning's reveille, within a sixty-mile radius. Passes were kept in a box in the orderly room and were picked up when the soldier left, and deposited when he returned. After reveille the next morning, the box was removed. If a soldier was late returning, his pass could not be put in the box, so "it just wasn't there for you the next night." Violation of Class A pass rules brought the issue of a Class B pass, which required the soldier to remain within a three-mile radius of the post. He was also required to be back in the barracks by 11:00 P.M.[67]

Many soldiers drove to Lusk, Wyoming, for the evening, where the congenial residents enjoyed showing the troops a good time. At least one remount soldier met his future wife there. During the war, a number of Fort Robinson soldiers met girls from Crawford and Chadron at social functions, contacts that ended in marriage. Lt. Homer Dye and Phyllis Bolden of Crawford, the secretary to the post commander, were married in the Comanche Hall officers' club.[68]

Other soldiers used passes to attend nearby rodeos. In July 1945 Sgt. Glen Nutter was acclaimed the Champion Buffalo Rider of the World after winning the first annual buffalo riding contest at the Black Hills Roundup. According to one account, "The stands went wild as Nutter skillfully stuck to his perch on his [the bison's] humped back." Other men rode with the post jumping team, giving exhibitions at county fairs and rodeos. The Fort Robinson Army Jumping Team also participated in War Bond drives and was featured at the 1943 dedication of the Alliance Army Air Field.[69]

Another form of recreation was the NCO club, organized in 1940 to "promote and maintain the spirit of comradeship and sociability" among its members. At its peak the club had 150 members with civilians allowed as associate members. The club was in the former officers' mess hall west of the post, which had been built when reserve artillery officers trained there. The club for the enlisted men was the Rathskeller, located in the basement of the east barracks. Beer could be sold on post, but no hard liquor; a bottle club was available for officers.[70]

During the war years, several notable personalities were stationed at the fort. Capt. Stephen Sanford, whose family owned a large carpet manufacturing concern, was an excellent polo player and brought his own horses to the post. Lt. Waldo Sessions was from the Sessions Clock Company family. Lt. Ralph Kercheval was an All-American football player from Kentucky and before arriving at Fort Robinson, played professional football for seven years with the old Brooklyn Dodgers team. On October 22, 1939, he kicked three field goals against Philadelphia when Brooklyn won the first televised NFL game. Kercheval was also an excellent horseman, and was in charge of issuing and processing, in addition to commanding the post exhibition jumping team. Lt. Walter "Butch" Luther arrived at the post with the reserve officers in 1941. Luther, from Cambridge, Nebraska, was an offensive backfield star at the University of Nebraska, and a member of the team that played in the 1941 Rose Bowl. At least one other member of that legendary Nebraska football team, Herman Rohrig, served at the post with Luther.[71]

Several professional jockeys also were assigned to the remount at Fort Robinson. Basil James, rated by many as the top jockey in the United States, Louis Hildebrandt, and Ira and Carl Hanford, all professional jockeys or trainers in civilian life, now handled horses at the post. Ira

"Babe" Hanford won the Kentucky Derby riding Bold Venture in 1936. One of the jockeys once showed a fellow remount soldier a letter he received from the IRS because he still owed taxes on 1941 earnings. The soldier commented that the jockey wasn't earning that much now. The jockey replied, "No, here's what I think," and tore the letter up. "If they want me, they can come and get me."[72] Along with performing regular remount duty, the ex-jockeys occasionally rode in exhibition races on the post's seven-eighths mile track.

In the words of Cpl. George Richmond, who served during this period, "I don't think anyone would challenge the statement that more top horsemen from the ranch to horse show world were congregated in the army at Fort Robinson during World War II than anywhere else in history."[73] A noted remount cowboy/soldier was Sgt. "Turk" Greenough, several times a world champion rodeo bronc rider. While Turk was at Fort Robinson, his wife, Sally Rand, came for a visit. With her reputation as a fan dancer, Sally's visit created quite a sensation. Post officers made sure she received first-class treatment, including a tour of the new war dog center and a ride around the fort in a fringe-topped surrey. Later Rand joined the appreciative remount men for dinner in the mess hall.[74]

Because of criticism that many veterinary officers lacked experience with horses and mules, a veterinary officer replacement pool was organized at the post in July 1943. The pool gave young veterinarians practical instruction in the care and handling of large animals prior to their assignment to active duty. Pool training lasted four weeks, with daily instruction in administration and care of army mounts, which included surgery, dental work, feeding, and field duties. For more than a year, veterinary officers came to the post in groups of two or three for training.[75]

Oddly, in 1944 someone in Army Service Forces headquarters at the Pentagon proposed closing both the Fort Reno and Robinson depots and transferring all remount operations to Fort Riley. When questioned about the feasibility of such a move, chief of remount Col. Frank L. Carr adamantly defended his depots. Carr, who had commanded Fort Robinson from June 1942 to February 1944, thought such a change was out of the question. He explained that both depots had excellent facilities, established at considerable expense, solely for remount work. Animals at Reno and Robinson were maintained in excellent health and condition at a minimum expense, with extremely low personnel costs. He did not consider Fort Riley suitable for remount activities, and "it does not appear logical nor sound business practice to abandon ideal facilities for improvised or make-shift facilities at great expense." Carr declared that if it were "obligatory" that a remount depot be closed, Front Royal, Virginia, should be considered. No more was heard of the idea to transfer or suspend Fort Robinson's remount activities.[76]

Two other vital wartime activities took place at Fort Robinson. In line with remount operations, the Fort Robinson War Dog Reception and Training Center was activated in 1942. In December of that year, word came that a prisoner of war camp was being planned for the post. War dogs and German PWs provide the final chapters in the story of the fort's important role during World War II.

Chapter 5

War Dogs

For centuries man has used dogs in war, where their acute senses, loyalty, speed, and stamina were of great value. The Greeks and Romans trained dogs to attack enemies, and in the Middle Ages, armored dogs defended caravans. Frederick the Great's army employed messenger dogs in the Seven Years' War. In the Napoleonic wars, the French trained dogs to carry ammunition; the Bulgarians used sentry dogs in the 1910 Balkan Wars. During World War I dogs were used by the Germans, French, Belgians, and Russians, Germany alone employing thirty thousand dogs as messengers and for other purposes.[1]

World War II revived interest in the military use of dogs. The Germans had devised a uniform system of war dog training during the 1930s; the British began a war dog program early in 1941. American interest in war dogs began just before Pearl Harbor, when the records of the American Kennel Club revealed that large numbers of registered dogs, of breeds often used in war, had been transferred from German to Japanese registry. Reports were also received that Japan had successfully used dogs in its war against China.[2]

When the U.S. declared war in December 1941, the army had no plans for training or using dogs. It was civilian canine enthusiasts and trainers who promoted the value of dogs to the American military forces. Organizations such as the Long Island Dog Training Club developed training techniques for the military use of dogs. In January 1942 Dogs For Defense, Inc., was established to secure dogs for the military. Founded by leading breeders and trainers, including Mrs. Arlene Erlanger and Harry I. Caesar, the organization served as a national clearinghouse for canine procurement.[3]

In February 1942 the secretary of war authorized the acceptance of donated dogs. Dogs For Defense secured, catalogued, and reported to the government those animals available for service. The dogs would be trained for guard duty at defense plants and military installations. German submarine activity along the East Coast raised concern that saboteurs might land, and dogs could patrol the coasts against infiltrators. Throughout most of the war, such donations supplied all the dogs used by the U.S. military forces. By the time the government began direct procurement in March 1945, Dogs For Defense had provided eighteen thousand dogs for military use.[4]

Thirty-three breeds were accepted for military service, including spaniels, German shepherds, collies, and Dalmatians. The dogs had to be at least twenty inches tall at the shoulder, weigh more than fifty pounds, and be between one and five years old. Experience later proved that crossbred dogs were often superior to purebreds. Siberian huskies and malamutes were accepted for sled and pack training. To donate a dog, the owner contacted a Dogs For Defense office and filled out a questionnaire. The dog was inspected and given a preliminary medical examination; only about forty percent received preliminary acceptance. Dogs that met the minimum requirements were shipped to training centers at government expense for a more thorough inspection.

Employing trained dogs relieved manpower needs in home front defense work. Sentry dogs could reduce the number of men required for patrols. In combat, scout dogs could precede soldiers to discover snipers and ambushes. Messenger dogs could be trained to carry field dispatches in dangerous situations, and sled dogs could be employed in arctic regions. The army quickly ordered its command and theater commanders to explore how dogs could be used in various military roles.[5]

When the canine (K-9) program began, Dogs For Defense provided a few trained guard dogs, but had no uniform plan for sentry and guard dog training. Nor was there an agenda for training dog handlers. To remedy this deficiency all handler training was assigned to the Quartermaster Corps, which also was charged with receiving, conditioning, training, and issuing war dogs. Direct administration of the K-9 program was the job of the remount branch, which had long experience dealing with animals, and maintained strategically located depots capable of accommodating the growing K-9 program. The Front Royal, Virginia, and Fort Robinson remount depots were designated War Dog Reception and Training Centers (WDRTC). Besides being established military installations, the remount depots could supply large quantities of dog food in the form of slaughtered surplus horses and mules.[6]

Because dogs had never been a part of the United States military establishment, the army had to set up an entirely new training apparatus. In July 1942 the quartermaster general broadened the scope of the war dog program beyond training sentry and guard dogs to include scout, messenger, and sled dog training. Under the leadership of Col. Edward M. Daniels, who had left Fort Robinson to become chief of remount, the branch "formulated plans for the procurement of suitable dogs and their training, as well as recruitment of personnel for the latter function."[7]

The quartermaster department hired civilian dog trainers to oversee actual field training of students, and experienced dog trainers already in the service were reassigned to the K-9 Corps. Many enlisted candidates for dog training came from the Fort Warren Quartermaster Replacement Center, where those with an aptitude for dog handling or an interest in dogs were detailed for the K-9 Corps. Some recent inductees with experience working with dogs were sent directly to the WDRTCs without any basic military training, and selected enlisted men from other service branches also were sent to the depots to be trained as sentry dog instructors. When their training was completed, the men returned to their stations with extra dogs to begin training handlers there.[8]

Besides setting up WDRTCs at the Front Royal and Fort Robinson depots, special schools were created at several other locations later in 1942. In the mountains near Helena, Montana, the Rimini center was established as a sled and pack dog school. Cat Island, just off the coast southwest of Biloxi, Mississippi, with its semitropical climate and dense vegetation, was used for jungle training. Across the bay from San Francisco, the San Carlos center was established in 1943 to prepare dogs and men for West Coast duty.[9]

With facility planning underway, effective and uniform training procedures were needed. Once the actual training began, remount chief Daniels instructed his depot commanders to make recommendations to improve the process. Trainers were allowed a great deal of latitude to "bring out the best of ideas."[10] A preliminary training manual was quickly produced, to be replaced in July 1943 by *TM 10-396, Technical Manual, War Dogs,* the Bible for all military dog training during World War II.

On July 27, 1942, Colonel Daniels wrote to Fort Robinson commander Lt. Col. Frank L. Carr alerting him that a dog training center would be established at the post. A maximum of 150 handler-trainees would eventually arrive from the Fort Warren replacement center. Carr was to locate a site large enough to accommodate training activities and forty fixed kennels that were to be built by purchase and hire according to specifications from the quartermaster general's office. Construction at the center was to be supervised by the Corps of Engineers district office in Omaha. The K-9 phase of Fort Robinson's history had begun.[11]

Fort Robinson offered several benefits for the WDRTC. The large reservation included rugged, forested land for training, two major railroad lines in nearby Crawford facilitated rapid transportation, and the fort was centrally located. On the other hand the post had to be made ready to undertake a significant new role. An area for K-9 functions had to be selected that would not interfere with the post's ongoing remount activities, and the new operation would double, and at times, triple the number of enlisted personnel on post and require additional officers.

Carr selected a broad hillside just north of the warehouse area for the K-9 center. Although the area had been heavily used in the past by post quartermaster activities and was once covered with buildings, by 1942 it was largely empty, with only two old sets of quarters, a hay shed, and the post magazine remaining. The fifty-acre site, bounded on the north and west by Highway 20, was quickly enclosed by a high fence topped with barbed wire. About a third of the area was eventually covered with kennels organized in blocks of ninety-six. A separate, fenced quarantine section was established on the south.

By summer's end construction of new K-9 buildings was proceeding under the supervision of Maj. Clinton D. Barrett, detailed from the veterinary section. The first building completed was the canine hospital, just inside the center's main gate. It was a long structure, 20 x 250 feet, which contained eight, ten-unit kennels with outside runs. The south end had a combination examination/operating room, office, laboratory, and grooming/supply room. East of the hospital was the conditioning and isolation building, a T-shaped, ten-unit kennel that adjoined ninety-six outside isolation kennels.[12]

West of the hospital, classroom and training buildings were built. The remount hay shed was converted into a carpenter shop for building kennels and other training necessities. The classroom was a temporary theater-of-operations structure, 20 x 100 feet, for lectures and academic instruction. Center headquarters and administrative offices were located in the two old buildings previously used for employee housing. K-9 personnel joked that the buildings were so old that perhaps George Armstrong Custer had stayed in them, though he had never been at the post. In the northeastern corner of the kennel area, a large training shed, 30 x 208 feet, was built to be used in inclement weather. North of the building area and close to the highway, an obstacle course, nicknamed the "Crazy Horse Run," was laid out. It contained a variety of movable obstructions through which the dog and his handler pursued a moving target man.

In September Carr received plans for the outside kennels, to be built by local civilian contractors. Each was about four feet square, made of a double layer of fiberboard with a hinged roof for cleaning. In cold weather an interior baffle wall was inserted, dividing the kennel into two compartments. Each kennel had a water pan attached to the outside. Because the dogs were secured to the kennels with nine-foot chains, each kennel was staked down to prevent the animal from moving it. Scores of new kennels arrived weekly, and in late October it was estimated that at least one thousand would be needed. By 1943, eighteen hundred kennels had been installed.[13]

Incoming trainees and cadre were first housed in the post's east brick barracks replacing the remount detachment, which moved to the vacant west barracks. Before long it became apparent that more quarters were needed for the increasing K-9 population, and in the winter of 1942–43, work began on three, theater-of-operations-type barracks and a mess hall on the west edge of the school area. The new quarters were 20 x 112 feet, each with a fifty-man capacity. Like other temporary structures, the barracks were frame buildings covered with battened tar paper, heated in the winter with three stoves. An abandoned electrical substation nearby was remodeled as a latrine for the new barracks. The next summer nineteen framed tents and additional latrines were added to accommodate more trainees. By the fall of 1943 the Fort Robinson WDRTC had a capacity of 450 students.

Remount personnel were detailed to organize and prepare the school for operation. Several enlisted men and officers, including Major Barrett, who became chief animal officer and head K-9 veterinarian, were transferred from the post veterinary section. Other veterinary officers, particularly those with canine experience, were brought in. The center was organized into three branches: an administrative branch composed of the officer in charge, kennel attendants, and clerical workers; a basic training branch consisting of head and assistant trainers; and a specialized training branch for advanced sentry and messenger dog work. By 1943 thirteen remount and veterinary officers had been assigned to the K-9 section.[14]

Equipment for the K-9 operations had to be procured. However, quartermaster efficiency decreed that the center would not be furnished with full allowances of supplies until experience established actual needs. Nevertheless a tentative five-month supply list called for three thousand metal feed boxes, six hundred grooming brushes, one thousand muzzles, six hundred dog combs, two thousand choke chain collars, and three thousand five-foot leashes. To meet some of the requirements, the Jefferson QM Depot shipped six hundred Model 1912 horse brushes and two thousand longe (long leash) lines. With the essential facilities, organization, and equipment available, the Fort

Robinson training center was activated on October 3, 1942. On that day the first dogs arrived, followed several days later by eighty trainees.[15]

K-9 training began with reception and processing. Upon arrival the dogs were removed from their shipping crates, collared with a tag containing a serial number, and exercised. The serial number was then permanently tattooed inside the left flank using a Preston brand, the same identification the remount used for their horses and mules. The dogs were then measured and weighed, and a blood smear was taken. Veterinarians gave them shots for rabies and distemper; dogs with mange or defects that would impede their usefulness were rejected. Dogs that passed inspection were put in isolation for two weeks of exercise and observation.[16]

By December 31, 1,070 dogs had been received, and 93 had been trained and shipped for field use elsewhere. Thirty-five had been rejected for a variety of reasons, including excitability when exposed to noise or gunfire. Rejected dogs were offered for return to their owners, but if no response was received in ten days, they were "disposed in a manner deemed to be of interest to the government and donors."[17]

Among the first units to complete training at the new center was a detachment of nineteen marines under command of Capt. Jackson H. Boyd, who arrived from Camp Lejeune, North Carolina, in late November. After five weeks of dog handler training, the detachment returned to Lejeune to train other marines to work with sentry and guard dogs. They did not take dogs from Fort Robinson to Camp Lejune because the Marine Corps had received a donation of Doberman pinschers from the Doberman Club of America. Some of the marines who had trained at Fort Robinson were deployed with dogs to guard Shangri-La (later Camp David), the presidential retreat in Maryland.[18]

Besides the quartermaster personnel assigned to K-9 training from replacement centers, personnel from the army air forces, the military police, and the U.S. Coast Guard also arrived, as did some civilian trainees including security guards from ordnance plants, such as the Ogden Depot in Utah, and personnel from the Tennessee Valley Authority. All the newcomers were told that their tour of duty at Fort Robinson would be brief, "and somewhat of a grind." The trainees were warned to "be neat . . . shower every day, and be military." They followed a rigid daily schedule. First call was at 5:30 A.M., followed by breakfast at 5:45 and policing of the barracks. At 7:00 there was a lecture session, followed by morning training details beginning at 7:30. Dinner was at 11:45. The afternoon began with a lecture at 12:45 P.M. and afternoon training lasted from 1:30 until 4:30. Then, the men were on their own or assigned to special details until 9:30, lights out. Friday night was cleanup night, and a weekly inspection was held on Saturday morning at 10:00.[19]

Experienced instructors carefully matched dogs and handlers because the trainee had to establish himself as the master of the dog or dogs. He needed a friendly attitude toward dogs, along with patience and perseverance. Each trainee was initially assigned to work with four dogs, except for coast guardsmen; two men were trained as a team with one dog.

The trainees were responsible for the care and feeding of their assigned dogs. Dogs were fed once a day, promptly at 4:00 P.M. The daily ration for a typical dog consisted of eight ounces of cooked horse meat, twelve ounces of raw horse meat, eight ounces of cornmeal, and eight ounces of commercial dog food. To provide the rations, three surplus and condemned horses or mules were slaughtered each day. At first the slaughtering was done in the open, but in 1943 a standard military slaughterhouse was built. K-9 details helped prepare food each day, and placed the rations in individual pans for delivery to the kennel area in horse-drawn wagons. With quartermaster efficiency, all the dogs could be fed in ten to fifteen minutes.[20]

Each trainee also was responsible for daily grooming of his animals. Good grooming reflected on the trainee's attitude, and gave him a chance to inspect the dogs' ears, teeth, and feet. Trainees also cleaned the kennel areas; according to the training manual, "a dirty kennel makes a dirty dog." Each man policed his kennels inside and out with bedding straw shaken and replaced as needed. Drainage around each kennel was monitored, the kennel blocks were mowed in the summer, and paths and roadways were cleared during the winter.[21]

Like regular army inductees, both dogs and trainees received basic training. Before the dogs were assigned to them, trainees received two weeks of orientation, including instruction in health care, kennel management, dog psychology, and other subjects relative to K-9 training. After the classroom period, each man began working with dogs. Basic training for the dogs developed patterns of behavior essential in war dogs. The animals became accustomed to wearing a muzzle or gas mask, riding in vehicles, and hearing gunfire. They received close order drill and instruction in basic commands, such as heel, sit, come, and lie. Each animal received forty to forty-five minutes per day of actual training during the basic training period. If a dog failed under one trainee it was assigned to another group. After two weeks of initial work, the dogs were classified for specialized training and each trainee selected two dogs with which to continue.[22]

Specialized or advanced training for a specific mission took four to six weeks. At first sentry/guard dog training was the primary purpose of the school. Sentry dogs were trained for interior guard work and to accompany patrols; they learned to warn their handlers of the presence of a stranger by barking or growling. The dogs were taught to be aggressive, and "agitation" training insured a vocal reaction to all strange noises or persons. Attack dog training was a variation of sentry training in which dogs were taught to detect, and when released, pursue and hold an intruder. Through sentry/attack training, dogs learned trailing, obstacle jumping, negotiating water hazards, and withstanding blows.[23]

Selected animals received other types of tactical training. Silent scout dogs were trained to warn combat troops of the presence of strangers without growling or barking. They needed acute hearing and a keen ability to detect motion. Messenger dogs were trained to carry dispatches and worked with two handlers. Such dogs learned to carry messages long distances without distraction. Pack dogs were prepared for service in arctic regions and were trained to carry packs and negotiate varied terrain.[24]

Sled dogs were also trained at the former CCC camp on the Wood Reserve, aptly christened Little America. Two to three hundred of these dogs were usually at the center. Because few sled dogs were donated, most had to be purchased by the army or bred at other centers. Husky, malamute, and Eskimo sled dogs were trained to work in harness pulling a load. Sled dog training was done year-round, using sleds mounted on wheels when there was no snow. On occasion the soldiers held wheeled dogsled races on the main parade ground. The camp included a well-organized carpenter and harness shop, where enlisted men built most of the sleds, harnesses, and packs used at Fort Robinson and elsewhere.[25]

Visitors to the center were impressed with the training dogs received in a short time. Unfortunately, as the number of dogs arriving increased, so did the attrition rate. More than thirteen hundred dogs were returned to their owners in 1943 alone, and in the first six months of 1943, 661 dogs died or were destroyed for a variety of causes, including 261 from distemper. Losses from distemper at the center were greatly reduced before the end of the war.[26]

Trainees, like their dogs, came from all parts of the country in groups as large as 150. After training was completed, assignments for men and dogs varied. Pvt. Dick Zika arrived from Camp Custer, Michigan, in 1943 for sentry training before going overseas to India. Sgt. "Woody" Woodbury trained sentry dogs at the center in 1942 before returning to Yuma Army Air Field in Arizona to instruct new handlers there. Cpl. Ralph Trickey arrived in 1943 before serving with the Thirty-ninth Scout Dog Platoon in the Pacific Theater. Merlyn Ankrum of the Coast Guard trained at the post and was assigned to Pensacola, Florida, for guard duty. Others remained at the center for the duration. T.Sgt. Don Stuber, from Minnesota, remained at the center as an instructor and supply sergeant. Incoming personnel, regardless of their service branch, had regular duties in addition to K-9 work. They included mundane tasks such as latrine orderly, KP, and guard duty in the K-9 area. Colonel Carr conducted a weekly review of trainees and dogs, and small groups competed in ten-minute drills.[27]

The relationship between the remount detachment and the K-9 soldiers was a bit strained at first. The K-9 personnel were at Fort Robinson only for a short time, making it difficult to form real friendships or associate with men from other service branches. Some K-9 soldiers thought the remount men did not have much use for "dog people." Of course, there was a fundamental tension between the two operations— the horsemen did not particularly appreciate providing their animals to be used as dog food. But it was all part of the war effort, and the remount detachment personnel quickly became used to their new tenants. While the remount soldiers observed the novel training procedures of the K-9 Corps, the K-9 men learned horsemanship.[28]

In 1942 and 1943, U. S. Coast Guard seamen trained at the Fort Robinson WDRTC and sailor uniforms were as common as olive drab and khaki. In 1942 the Coast Guard had decided to use sentry dogs for beach patrol, and that fall seamen began to arrive at the center. Eventually more than three thousand sentry/attack dogs were used on coastal patrol. At first the sight of sailors in northwestern Nebraska "attracted a lot of attention," but like the dogs, they soon became an accepted adjunct of the center's mission. Some sailors referred to themselves as the Nebraska Navy while they were stationed at Fort Robinson.[29]

After the workday, a variety of off-duty diversions were available for the dog soldiers. Both K-9 and remount soldiers benefited when a wealthy New York dog fancier donated an assortment of baseballs, bats, boxing gloves, and horseshoes to the post recreation office. The men played softball and watched regularly-scheduled baseball games between the post team and nearby military and town teams. Movies such as *Mission to Moscow* and *Stage Door Canteen* were shown at the post theater, along with army orientation films. Some K-9 men fished and hiked in the surrounding buttes, and most attended weekly dances in Crawford. A dayroom in the east permanent barracks was furnished by the local American Red Cross chapter, and beer was available at the remount enlisted men's club. On weekends the soldiers went to town to see the sights and hit the local bars. One K-9 veteran recalled an incident when "most of [the] barracks went to [the] village & tried to drink up all the liquor in town."[30] But the troops were not allowed to bring alcohol back to the barracks. In March 1943 the entire K-9 detachment was confined to quarters when empty bottles were found in the barracks. The guilty parties were not identified, and the "most pain caused by confinement was in missing the showing of Walt Disney's new feature at the post theater." Such is war.[31]

Like the other soldiers sent to Fort Robinson, most K-9 personnel enjoyed the post's western lifestyle and relative isolation. Some, however, did not share such feelings and left their sentiments in anonymous poems tacked on barracks bulletin boards. One K-9 bard wrote:

> A shame it is that a man of my knowledge
> Should ever end up in a dog training college. . . .
> I think of our furloughs and rejected pleas
> As I pull out the ticks and stomp on the fleas. . . .
> There are thousands of ways of fighting a war
> But don't let them talk you into the K-9 Corps.[32]

The rigorous training at Fort Robinson was occasionally hazardous. Rattlesnakes were common in the region, but bites were infrequent. In the summer men encountered poison ivy and ticks while training in the rough butte country or along waterways near the post. But the biggest threat proved to be dog bites, a type of injury that usually occurred when the trainee was first assigned his dogs, or while performing agitation training. Sergeant Woodbury was bitten by Sandy the first day he received him. Personnel were ordered to report all dog bites or scratches to the station hospital for treatment, and were to be doubly sure to record the number of the dog that inflicted the injury. A typical agitation training injury was reported in the post newspaper: "Corporal George Henne, 'The Great Agitator,' also found that it does not pay to hold your hand in front of one of the trained dogs too long. He was bitten quite badly on the right hand and arm last week, by a German Shepherd, while engaged in attack work." Henne was bitten several times while serving at Fort Robinson.[33]

Even though the center was surrounded with a high fence, dogs escaped fairly often. When a dog was loose on the main post, expert ropers from the remount veterinary detachment pursued the fugitive on horseback on a "wild chase across the parade grounds, officer quarters lawns, etc." followed by the dog handlers in jeeps. After the dog was roped, the mounted wrangler kept him on a tight line until handlers in protective gear could control the dog and escort him back to the compound. Occasionally, when dogs decided to go AWOL, "Dog Lost" items appeared in Crawford want-ads.[34]

The K-9 Corps' only fatal accident occurred in late February 1943. While Pvt. John L. Smith, a permanent member of the K-9 detachment, was loading refuse in the kennel area, his team of horses bolted. Smith tried to stop them but became entangled in the harness, and was severely injured when the team ran into a telephone pole. He was taken to the post hospital, then flown to Fitzimmons Army Hospital in Denver, where he died.[35]

After training, dogs and men were deployed on a variety of home front and overseas assignments. In early spring 1943 the first overseas deployment was 119 dogs for sentry duty at Pacific stations. In the United States, the army air forces received hundreds of guard dogs for its bases, including the nearby Alliance Army Air Field. Coast Guard men and dogs patrolled such installations as Patuxent Naval Air Station in Maryland and numerous others on the East and West coasts. During 1943 and 1944, army canine deployment sent men and dogs to the China-Burma-India Theater to guard supply installations and to serve with Merrill's Marauders.[36]

Guard dogs were soon assigned to prisoner of war camps; it was recommended that each camp have four sentry dogs, two trail dogs, and two attack dogs. At Fort Robinson, K-9 handlers trained at the nearby PW camp. PW camp commanders appreciated the guard dogs' worth. One asked for more dogs, remarking that the "excellent working efficiency of the dogs we have received from your depot increases our security and minimizes the number of personnel required for this work."[37]

Because civilians were interested in the novelty of the war dog program, a big part of the center's activity dealt with public relations. K-9 demonstrations were presented at open houses, and dog units marched in local parades and celebrations. On one occasion Santa Claus arrived in Crawford via a Fort Robinson dogsled. Signal Corps film crews documented training, and private movie companies, such as Paramount, filmed training sequences for newsreels. Articles about the K-9 Corps appeared in major magazines, including *Life*, *Saturday Evening Post*, and *National Geographic*, and in various special interest publications such as *The North American Veterinarian*. The editor of *Dog World* visited Fort Robinson in 1944. He was also a regional director for Dogs For Defense and a representative of the American Humane Association. The *Omaha World-Herald* published many stories on K-9 activities at the post. A reporter was once sent to check on rumors that dogs were being mistreated. He informed the readers that the dogs were being well cared for and the "rumors can be discounted 100 percent."[38]

Official visitors came at a steady rate, often accompanying remount officials making regular inspection trips. Service command and Army Ground Forces general officers also visited the center and observed the training. In March 1943 two dog trainers from the British army visited for a week to compare training techniques. Visitors were impressed with the efficiency and economy of the operation. One commented, "They had to start from scratch, with very little information . . . today they are turning out a satisfactory finished product."[39]

Meanwhile, the center received hundreds of letters from former owners concerned about their dogs. The clerical staff faithfully answered them, assuring the donor of the dog's good health and sometimes sending a snapshot of the animal in training. One letter from an eleven-year-old asked, "I would like to know if I can put a star in my window because I gave you my dog. When does he get a rating?" Another young donor wrote, "I hope you have been a good dog, and whoever gets this letter will read it to you and let you know how much we miss you."[40] Ezio Pinza, the great Metropolitan Opera basso, donated his two Dalmatians, named Boris and Figaro, to the K-9 Corps. He later sent an album of his recordings to Fort Robinson, explaining the dogs were accustomed to hearing him sing around the house. "If they get lonesome," he added, "play one of these records for them."[41]

By October 1944 Fort Robinson was the nation's leading dog training center, with 3,565 dogs having been trained and issued, and 1,353 dogs on hand. A total of 745 army and 1,033 Coast Guard dog handlers had graduated, not counting others trained for civilian projects. After two years of operation, the center was near the peak of its activity.[42]

By 1944 the need for sentry and guard dogs for U.S. duty was declining, and the army switched much of its emphasis to training scout dogs. With the gradual abatement of the German submarine menace and the lifting of the blackout, coastal patrols and guards at installations in the zone of the interior became a lower priority. While hundreds of sentry/guard dogs were detrained and returned to their owners or surplused, a demand grew for scout dogs for the Pacific Theater.

In the spring of 1943 the War Department had sent a small detachment, consisting of one officer and four army handlers with six scout and two messenger dogs, to the Pacific Theater to test their value under combat conditions. Commanded by Lt. Robert Johnson, who served at the Fort Robinson center in 1942–43, the detachment served with the First Marine Division in the New Britain campaign. The scout dogs soon proved their worth in jungle warfare. On one occasion, detachment member Sgt. Art Tyler and Duke accompanied a marine patrol. The dog alerted Tyler to the presence of unidentified persons, suspected to be Japanese soldiers. An ambush was set up and five of the enemy were killed as they came down the trail toward the marines. For months the men and dogs accompanied patrols, each time returning without suffering casualties. As a result of the dogs' "consistently excellent performances" in the field, the army accelerated its program for tactical use of silent scout dogs.[43]

In the early spring of 1944 the detachment that had taken dogs to New Britain returned to the United States. Sergeants Tyler, Menzo Brown, Herman Boude, and Lieutenant Johnson, were reassigned to the Fort Robinson WDRTC, where they used their experiences in scout dog training. The revised training program eventually consisted of a twelve-week schedule, with the men and dogs working six and one-half days per week. After the two-week basic training period, men and dogs had two weeks of aggression training and work on short patrols. Weeks five through eight (intermediate period) saw the beginning of tactical scout training, with exercises in scouting, patrolling, and cover concealment. The last four-week period (advanced scout dog) consisted of field training on increasingly difficult tactical missions under simulated combat conditions.[44]

In May 1944 Quartermaster War Dog Platoons were organized and began training at San Carlos, California, and Fort Robinson. The units consisted of about twenty enlisted men with eighteen scout dogs and six messenger dogs commanded by a lieutenant. The platoons were intended for deployment with combat infantry units for reconnaissance and security patrols. The messenger dogs were to be used for communication between patrols and command posts. Fifteen such platoons were activated, with the Thirty-seventh, Thirty-eighth, Thirty-ninth, and Forty-fourth platoons coming from Fort Robinson. Fort Robinson-trained personnel also served with war dog platoons activated at other centers. Eventually, seven of the platoons were sent to the European Theater, and eight served in the Pacific.[45]

About this time the army experimented with the use of war dogs for mine detection. In the North Africa campaign the Germans began using nonmetallic land mines, which could not be located by conventional means, and the Quartermaster Corps decided to train dogs at Fort Robinson to detect such mines. Working on a leash, a mine dog was taught to locate buried objects, then alert his handler from a distance of one to four yards. Two mine detection dog units were organized and shipped to North Africa in 1944 for combat testing, where their success in actual detection proved to be fifty percent or less, and mine dog training was discontinued. One unit, the 228th Engineer Mine Detection Company, was reassigned to Fort Robinson and disbanded early in 1945.[46]

As dog training focused on scout dogs and returning surplus dogs to civilian life, all U. S. K-9 training was consolidated at Fort Robinson. In May 1944 the Cat Island center was closed and all equipment, dogs, and most personnel were transferred to Fort Robinson; the Rimini sled dog center was also phased out. San Carlos closed in the fall. In July projections were drawn up for the increased activity at Fort Robinson. A pool of two hundred scout dogs was to be established and maintained, along with an increase in the number of trainees. With the offensive in Europe drawing all available army manpower, nonquartermaster personnel began to be incorporated into the K-9 training program. Soldiers from the WAC detachment, which had been recently assigned to the post, were called on to serve as hidden enemies in scout training exercises. In the latter part of the war, up to eighty-five German prisoners of war worked in the K-9 area, helping in kennel management and maintenance.[47]

The experience of the quartermaster platoons in the Pacific indicated that the dogs had not been adequately prepared for exposure to rifle and artillery fire. Colonel Daniels, who had returned from Washington in February to replace Carr as post commander, organized a series of tactical exercises to better train the war dog platoons. The revised scout dog training program, held in the rugged Wood Reserve area, required that both men and dogs be prepared for combat. Participants were advised, "these field exercises are not being conducted for amusement but are staged as part of necessary training for deadly purpose."[48] Because the training involved day and night marches, bivouacs, simulated combat, scouting, patrolling, and physical conditioning, the maneuvers required much coordination. To get the maximum benefit from the new program, each session lasted several weeks.

Training platoons were transported by truck to a base camp in the Wood Reserve by a long, circuitous route, which helped accustom the dogs to vehicle travel. In the field, dogs and handlers were sent on patrols, which were frequently ambushed by "aggressor" forces. To simulate combat, four 75mm cannons, three .30-caliber machine guns, pyrotechnics, and parachute flares were used, and an amplifying audio system provided additional battle noises. C-47 transports from Alliance Army Air Field flew overhead, serving as strafing aircraft. To add more realism, live ammunition was occasionally used. Before one exercise, a directive from Daniels warned, "Live ammunition, real bullets, so conduct yourselves accordingly."[49]

All aspects of the maneuvers were critiqued to determine their value. Between major training sessions small patrols were continually sent out in the hills near the post to test the scout and messenger skills of men and dogs. In spite of the rugged conditions, Daniels ordered his dog soldiers to maintain proper military appearance, and "only under exceptional circumstances will men be allowed to go without shaving."[50]

One of the problems affecting the quartermaster scout dog platoons was that most quartermaster personnel were not trained for combat. In the fall of 1944, the army authorized the creation of Infantry Scout Dog Platoons to replace the quartermaster scout units. Army Ground Forces troops, trained in infantry tactics and scouting and given advanced instruction with infantry units, were sent to Fort Robinson for training with scout dogs. The public, always interested in how their dogs were being used, were duly informed, "The education of scout dogs is not new to the center, but the training of infantry scouts to handle these dogs in war . . . is new. At Fort Robinson platoons of trained infantry scouts are being taught the tactics and techniques of leading reconnaissance and combat patrols with scout dogs."[51] A new phase of K-9 training was about to begin.

After experience proved that scout dogs could not be used effectively in the more open European war zones, the War Department decided in early 1945 that scout dogs would be deployed only in the Pacific. As scout training began, the increasing number of dogs at the center brought a shortage of kennel space. One problem was that returning sentry/guard dogs were not being surplused fast enough. To reduce the numbers, the center's war dog survey board was urged to expedite the disposal of excess dogs. About this time an improved type of kennel was being built in a new area north of the main kennels. The new doghouses were on raised platforms and were easier for the attendants to clean. The old style kennels sat directly on the ground, where rats burrowed beneath them. The older units were to be replaced with the improved models as soon as possible.[52]

With the emphasis now on receiving and training scout dogs, the K-9 center was restructured. All K-9 officers were relieved of any noncanine duties or assignments, enabling them to concentrate solely on their work. Formerly the commander of the post and depot had overseen K-9 operations, but a field grade officer was sent to become permanent officer-in-charge of the reorganized center. In May Lt. Col. Irvin A. Hirschy, from the quartermaster school at Camp Lee, Virginia, arrived to take command of the WDRTC. Under supervision, management improved and even more attention was given to Army Ground Forces combat training methods. With the army mobilizing for the final effort to end the war, Hirschy and his staff were charged with assuring "the successful accomplishment of the training of personnel and animals constituting the War Dog Platoons."[53]

The army was convinced that scout platoons were "a capable and valuable adjunct when properly trained and used." By the summer of 1945, Army Ground Forces command estimated that at least sixteen hundred scout dogs would be needed in the Pacific war. More men arrived, and on June 11, six platoons were organized and activated at Fort Robinson to begin an intensified period of infantry scout dog training. With the war in Europe over, some trainees realized the scout dog units were training at Fort Robinson for one purpose—the invasion of Japan.[54]

The new platoons were similar to the quartermaster dog units, except the messenger dogs had been eliminated. Each platoon consisted of three, six-man squads commanded by a lieutenant, with a technical sergeant for his assistant. Each unit had twenty-seven dogs and a veterinary technician to care for them. The men were trained and qualified with the .30-caliber M-1 carbine, and instructed in mines, booby-traps, and demolition.[55]

During the twelve-week training period, the men and dogs received at least 180 hours of intense instruction, much of the work centering on reconnaissance patrols, where the silent scout dogs had already proven themselves. The handler worked with his dog on a leash, usually at the point or alongside a patrol, depending on the wind. Scout dogs also were trained to detect the approach of an enemy or attempted infiltration of an outpost. In this role the dogs were especially valuable for night guard, because they could give the handler silent warning of the enemy long before humans were aware of any danger.[56] By August the six platoons neared completion of their training, and an elaborate graduation ceremony was planned. Then atomic bombs were dropped on Japan and the war was over.

On August 18 graduation ceremonies were held for the Forty-sixth, Forty-seventh, Forty-eighth, Forty-ninth, and Fifty-first Infantry Scout Dog platoons, and the Fiftieth Overseas Replacement Platoon. The ceremony was unique; these soldiers were the first Army Ground Forces troops trained in handling dogs in combat. A special guest was Arlene Erlanger, a founder of Dogs for Defense, who delivered remarks on behalf of the secretary of war and the quartermaster general. Then followed a scout dog obedience demonstration narrated by Colonel Hirschy. Brig. Gen. Paul X. English, acting commanding general of the Seventh Service Command, presented the diplomas. As the men stepped up to receive their certificates, each was accompanied by his dog. The three-hour program ended with a review of the graduating platoons.

After the ceremony the day was occupied by dog demonstrations and jumping and other mounted contests for remount personnel. The close order drills executed by the scout platoons brought "cries of admiration" from the crowd. Then sled dogs from the Little America camp were exhibited, including a team of pups pulling a jeep. When a team of older huskies pulled a bus carrying two soldiers and a WAC around the parade field, General English reportedly exclaimed, "Now I've seen everything!"

The day's events were capped by a special half-mile horse race dubbed The Erlanger Star Handicap, featuring the remount's star jockeys, Privates Hildebrandt, Hanford, and James.[57]

The end of the war brought a halt to all overseas K-9 deployment and in one case, relief to the family of a new scout dog handler. Just before they were to graduate, several soldiers had been transferred into the Fiftieth Platoon, which had expected to be sent to the Philippines immediately after graduation. One of the men, Pvt. Lester Gertsch, wrote of this plan to his family in Lincoln, Nebraska, and they began to save their gas ration stamps for the long trip to see him before he left Fort Robinson. After V-J Day, the overseas orders were canceled and the seven recent transferees were reassigned, not to graduate as originally planned. The parents, who did not receive the letter telling of the change of plans, arrived for the scheduled graduation ceremony. Nevertheless, according to Gertsch, they enjoyed their visit to Fort Robinson and "were not disappointed that I did not graduate on that day."[58]

Chapter 6

Prisoners of War

In the spring of 1943 Hitler's once powerful army in North Africa collapsed. After the surrender, tens of thousands of German and Italian prisoners were herded into temporary prisoner of war camps, large, open pens surrounded by barbed wire that held between ten and thirty thousand men. Allied victory in the North African campaigns netted about 250,000 prisoners.[1]

The responsibility for those prisoners of war (PWs) fell on the British army, which by 1942 found itself with multitudes of captured enemy soldiers to feed and maintain. The British government began to pressure the United States to take some of the prisoners, and in the fall of 1942 the U.S. Army agreed, and began a crash program of building prisoner of war camps in the United States. In 1943 scores of internment camps sprang up throughout the countryside, as troop and supply ships arrived with German and Italian PWs. January 1943 saw a mere 2,400 PWs in the United States; that number had swelled to 168,000 by the end of October and to 425,875 by war's end. Of that total 371,683 were Germans; the rest were mostly Italians with a few Japanese.[2]

One reason prisoners were brought here in such numbers was a shortage of labor that became an increasing problem as this country became more involved in the war. The United States and Germany had both signed the 1929 agreement on the treatment of war prisoners, commonly known as the Geneva Convention, and Article 31 of that accord allowed war prisoners to perform "any work outside of the combat zone not involving the manufacture or transportation of arms or munitions."[3] Administrative control of the prisoner of war program fell to the Provost Marshal General's Office, which quickly planned and established a functional apparatus for PW camp operations.

Existing sites, such as former CCC camps, were preferred for prisoner of war camps, as were military installations, including the army's remount depots. In late November 1942 the army engineers' office was instructed to provide plans for one-thousand-man internment camps at the Fort Reno, Oklahoma, and Fort Robinson quartermaster depots. With its rail connections, potential work projects, and isolated location, Fort Robinson was an excellent choice. Work for prisoners at the camp would be of two types: Class I labor involved prisoners working within the PW stockade for maintenance and administration; Class II projects used PW labor for jobs on the main post. With a large number of remount animals at the fort, work would be available for at least a thousand prisoners.[4]

On December 4 remount officers met with a team from the Corps of Engineers and selected a site for the camp, about halfway between the post and Crawford, in a pasture area just south of the old Red Cloud Agency site. The site was large enough to provide the required thirty-foot spacing between buildings, and if necessary, permit construction of an additional one-thousand-man compound. The camp plan, a standard layout with minor adjustments, was submitted for approval on December 12. Instead of building hospital facilities at the camp, medical care for prisoners would be provided by the post hospital.[5]

The military was tightlipped about construction of war-related projects, and even more so in the case of internment camps. Many Americans were worried about the prospect of Nazis coming to the United States, and consequently, the army provided specifics about the PW program only on a "need-to-know" basis. Several weeks after the planning began, Nebraska Congressman Harry B. Coffee contacted the provost marshal general for information about the Robinson camp and another camp to be established near Scottsbluff. The provost marshal general asked Coffee to keep the nature of the installations confidential. Before releasing any information on such projects in his district, Coffee was to contact the army Bureau of Public Relations office.[6]

When the plans and specifications were ready, contractors were selected, and construction began in late December 1942. Busboom & Rauh of Salina, Kansas, and Southard Engineering of Springfield, Missouri, built the camp under the close supervision of the Corps of Engineers district office in Omaha. Initial planning called for the completion of all buildings by June 1. Although rumors about the PW camp had circulated locally for several weeks, no official word appeared in the Crawford newspaper until December 18. Residents were advised, and perhaps reassured, by the statement that "it will be quite a while before any prisoners will be coming in."[7]

During a mild winter, construction progressed rapidly. Due to a shortage of nearby housing, workers stayed in camp buildings as they were completed. Although not scheduled for completion until June 30, the camp was finished on February 28. Compared to other war projects, the total cost was small, about half a million dollars. The camp contained more than sixty buildings in the prison compound itself and a garrison area for the American personnel. With the exception of fences and guard towers, the camp was similar to other temporary military posts housing American servicemen.[8]

The buildings were of theater-of-operations-type construction, basically frame structures erected on concrete piers, with sidewalls and roofs covered with battened tar paper. Barracks for PWs and GIs alike were 20 x 100 feet, heated with three coal-burning stoves, and designed to hold twenty-five bunk beds. The prison compound was surrounded by a double fence of hog wire with a barbed wire overhang. Twenty feet inside the perimeter fence was the "dead line," a single-strand wire. Prisoners crossing the dead line were ordered to halt twice by the guards; if the order was disobeyed, the guards were authorized to fire. Spaced around the perimeter fence were several guard towers, each with searchlights, a siren, and a .30-caliber machine gun.

The buildings in the compound were arranged in four individual company units, with each company area containing five barracks, a mess hall, and a latrine for 250 men. The compound also had a canteen, a recreation building, and an infirmary. In the southeast corner of the barracks area was a segregated complex to house thirty officer prisoners, although officer PWs were never held at the camp. The theater-of-operations construction soon proved unsuitable for northwestern Nebraska's windy and often harsh weather. By April high winds had badly damaged the battened tar paper roofs, and exposed doors were constantly in need of repair.[9]

On the main post, a PW hospital complex was built just south of the station hospital with five temporary wards and other support buildings to accommodate 118 patients. Like buildings at the prison compound, the hospital buildings were surrounded by wire fences topped with barbed wire, overlooked by guard towers. Although spartan, the facilities at Fort Robinson were far superior to the enclosures that held the prisoners in North Africa. The barracks were described as "spacious and well-ventilated," and the latrines as "modern and clean . . . with mirrors in the wash rooms."[10]

With camp buildings completed, the administrative staff and two Military Police Escort Guard (MPEG) companies, the 331st and 635th, arrived for duty. Each company comprised two or three officers and 135 enlisted men. The 1765th Service Unit, with nineteen officers and seventy-five enlisted men, was organized to administer the camp. Although most of the 1765th's manpower had to be brought in, several soldiers transferred from the main post. Men of the new unit were assigned to headquarters and intelligence staffs, and served as clerks, interpreters, cooks, and chauffeurs.[11]

The guards at PW camps were criticized for being unprepared and unqualified for this often sensitive duty, but the army's first priority was fighting the war, and prison camp duty was secondary. Although the monotonous nature of guard duty frequently led to low morale, one inspector rated the morale of the Fort Robinson guards as "fair, perhaps even good."[12] Another problem affecting camp efficiency was that few guards spoke or understood German. Later in the war, German-language lessons were organized for guards so "that more ears can be created."[13]

Several camp officers had health problems or disabilities that kept them from overseas assignments, and unsubstantiated rumors surfaced that some had deliberately "goofed up" in order to avoid combat duty.[14] Such criticisms aside, most camp officers were dedicated and performed their difficult and trying duties admirably. Col. Arthur C. Blain, described as rugged yet courteous, was typical of the camp commanders.[15] Intelligence officer Lt. Clarence L. Duell was "a high type of man with vision and imagination."[16] During his tour as assistant executive officer, Capt. Jason R. Silverman displayed unusual initiative and won the confidence of the German PWs. "Prisoners constantly come to him for advice and requests, the fact that he is Jewish notwithstanding."[17] The capable enlisted men and officers in key camp positions were responsible for the successful operation of the Fort Robinson camp and its reputation as an outstanding facility.

By May 1943 the camp was staffed and stood ready to receive prisoners. On May 4, however, camp commander Lt. Col. Lester Vocke prepared a memorandum that delayed the PWs arrival. Vocke's report suggested that there was enough work at the camp and on the post to sustain three thousand prisoners, and the army decided to enlarge the camp by adding two compounds. On June 4 authorization came to expand the camp to hold three thousand men, with a corresponding increase in housing for American military personnel. Because an officers' club was required in a camp of that size, a large building was added in the garrison section.[18]

Work began in early summer on the new compounds east and west of the original compound. All the buildings in the new compounds (except latrines) were arranged along a single street that ran through the center of each compound area. Each of the compounds was separately fenced, restricting the internees to their assigned areas. The new barracks and other buildings were covered with a tan sanded building board, a substantial improvement over battened tar paper.[19] Guard towers were erected at each corner of the expanded area, and the original towers were retained at the main north and south gates. Sentry houses were located for additional security outside the fence between the towers. By fall 1943 the camp was ready for prisoners.

As the soldiers manning the camp awaited their charges, work projects occupied their time. In the camp administration echelon and garrison area, they laid out walkways and planted shrubs. A carpentry and woodworking shop was set up, managed by an ingenious sergeant, where GIs built furniture for the new officers' club and other offices. The sentry houses around the perimeter fence were also built by GI labor. The soldier in charge of the shop, Sgt. Royal Draime, praised the effort: "You can see that the Americans did a very credible job while working in and out of the shop."[20] For off-duty diversion, the Windy Flats Enlisted Men's Club was organized to provide entertainment and recreation for members, their families, and guests.[21]

Meanwhile, at the fort the remount soldiers observed the activities at the new installation with interest. Although the PW camp was almost independent of depot operations, its existence could not be overlooked. In July the post newspaper informed fort residents that Axis prisoners of war were to be interned at the camp for the duration. In compliance with the Geneva Convention, post personnel were advised, "The camp was not located here for the convenience of the Sunday afternoon curiosity seeker, and they will not be allowed to use this camp in that manner." Soldiers and civilian employees were further warned, "DON'T try to go there on a sight seeing tour."[22]

Many soldiers thought they would be guarding Italian PWs. Before he arrived at Fort Robinson, Sgt. Samuel Mitchell was told he would be working with Italian prisoners, and attended an Italian-language course. Preparations were made to paint camp building signs in Italian, and a few men who could speak Italian were brought in as interpreters. Finally, on November 19, 1943, the first prisoners arrived, and they were Germans.[23]

The first internees at the Fort Robinson camp were members of the Tenth Panzer Division, who became prisoners with the surrender of Rommel's Afrika Korps the previous May. The Tenth Panzer was a composite division, made up of units from various parts of Germany, with Stuttgart as its home station. The division fought well in Poland, and in 1941 was heavily engaged in the central sector of the Russian front. It remained in Russia until 1942, when "there was nothing left of our division." After being sent to France to rest and refit, the division was transferred to Tunisia in late 1942. For those men, the war was over by May 13, 1943.[24]

The journey to the United States was an enlightening experience for PWs. Although German propaganda had led them to believe German U-boats had cleared the Atlantic of allied ships, "we noticed there were [too] many allied boats on the water to count."[25] The Germans were also amazed by the lack of bomb damage at American ports and that there was no blackout. For many, the realization came, "This war is lost for us!"[26]

After disembarking, usually at Virginia ports, the PWs were loaded on trains for the long trip to camps in the interior. Another surprise came when they found they would be traveling in passenger cars rather than boxcars. Before his repatriation after the war, one PW bard reflected on this trip:

> Now begins the Myst'ry Journey,
> Pullman Cars, how elegant,
> Cushioned seats and a Black Waiter,
> Boy, oh brother, what a land.[27]

To gather information in case he might escape, PW Dietrich Kohl recorded each town the train passed through. His four-page list began at Newport News, Virginia, and ended, "Chadron, Whitney, Crawford" in Nebraska. He never used the list.[28]

The first prisoners arrived late on the afternoon of November 19; about 680 enlisted men and noncommissioned officers. The PWs unloaded along the Chicago & North Western tracks about half a mile north of the camp and marched in, escorted by mounted and dismounted MP guards. Kohl recalled, "We marched a short distance, [and] entered a great installation of barracks bound by barbed wire and guard towers, our new home for months or years to come."[29]

The reception process at the camp was well organized. The PWs first disrobed for a contraband search—one prisoner was found with a Chihuahua dog in his overcoat pocket. All personal effects were inventoried, and any money was taken to be kept for the prisoners while they were at the camp. Many PWs still had Tunisian, Italian, and French currency and coins in their possession. The prisoners were given medical examinations, and some were immediately sent to the post hospital for care or observation. The PWs were interviewed and individual records were created. Then they showered, were issued work clothes, and assigned to a company and quarters. PW companies were lettered A, B,

C, D, four companies per compound. Each company was supposed to have 250 men, but some were not completely filled. After the first group of prisoners was processed, reliable PWs assisted the Americans in processing subsequent groups.[30]

Sergeant Mitchell, who was watching the first PWs detrain, reported an unusual incident. The first prisoner off the train looked at a lieutenant from one of the MPEG companies and shouted his first name. The German had lived next door to the officer in Yonkers, New York, before the war. Several days later, the PW told the sergeant that he was planning to write his former congressman for help getting out of the camp. Needless to say, the congressman did not intervene.[31]

The same prisoner poet who commented on the luxurious railroad accommodations later commemorated the arrival and processing of the first Afrika Korps prisoners at Fort Robinson with a certain degree of levity:

> Soon arrived in old Nebraska,
> Quickly moved into Hotel,
> Where the Desk Clerk said quite friendly
> "Get undressed, and Mache Schnell!"
> Single rooms sold out already,
> Sorry, Sir, and by the way,
> Only 50-Bed Suites left now,
> Here're the Keys, Enjoy your Stay![32]

After PWs were established in the camps, the German Red Cross informed their families where they were interned. In April 1944 Hans Wallendorf's wife received word that her husband was at "Camp Ft. Robinson, Arkansas" (there was a Camp Robinson Prisoner of War Camp near Little Rock, Arkansas). Four months later the Red Cross correctly notified her that he was at Fort Robinson, Nebraska.[33]

The arriving PWs settled into the daily camp routine. First call was at 6:00 A.M. with breakfast at 6:45. Roll calls were at 6:30 A.M. and 5:15 P.M., and each day there was barracks inspection at 10:00 A.M. Lights out was called at 9:00 P.M. in the barracks, and 11:00 P.M. in the dayrooms. All PWs were required to bathe and shave twice a week.[34]

Every aspect of camp life was rigidly controlled by the Geneva Convention. With the full knowledge that American prisoners were being held in Germany, the army followed the agreement to the letter. Rules on housing, food, and work were strictly observed, and representatives of the International Red Cross made periodic inspections. Swiss representatives, usually accompanied by a member of the Special War Problems Division of the State Department, were granted full access to American camps. In 1944 one inspector reported, "I was given every opportunity to find out things by myself . . . with absolute freedom to move about."[35]

Throughout their confinement, prisoners were allowed to receive mail and send two, twenty-four-line letters and two postcards each month. The Afrika Korps PWs complained that they were not receiving their mail. The Americans were probably not entirely to blame; by January 1944 about seventy percent of the PWs had received no mail for a year, which included several months before their surrender. By July the Swiss representative reported that the camp received an average of sixty letters a day, "which seemed very satisfactory in view of the small number of prisoners."[36]

The German and International Red Cross sent German-language books and musical scores to the camp. Commissions arrived to inspect PW medical care, and to consider the repatriation of seriously injured or sick prisoners. Red Cross representatives also certified German protected personnel, who were exempt from work under the convention.[37] Through the Red Cross, the PWs received information and instructions from the German government. One communiqué urged all noncommissioned officers, in addition to enlisted men, to work while at the internment camps. The German government also sent funds for the PWs to rent movies and purchase athletic supplies, and in 1944, money for a Christmas fund. The PW barracks at the camp were decorated with reproductions of paintings provided by the German Red Cross.[38]

As at other camps, the prisoners at Fort Robinson were allowed visits from relatives living in the United States. PWs wrote home for addresses of relatives, and could also apply to the American Red Cross for help in locating them. A woman from Chicago, who came to visit her brother, left "with the happy thought that he was not being mistreated." The occasional family visits were monitored by German-speaking members of the camp intelligence staff.[39]

With approval, brothers, sons, and fathers could be transferred to the same camp. Such transfers could be made only if the prisoners agreed to pay the transportation costs, which included an accompanying MP guard. In November 1944 a German corporal was transferred to Camp Robinson, Arkansas, to be with his brother. In another case, the transfer of a PW to Camp Hearne, Texas, was denied because his brother there was considered uncooperative and "very arrogant in his attitude." One prisoner tried to stretch the family relation rules; he wanted to be transferred to a camp near Chicago so an aunt "could have more opportunity to visit me." Although the aunt agreed to pay transportation expenses, the transfer was denied because the request did not fall into an approved category.[40]

Among the first prisoners to arrive at Fort Robinson were members of the German Forty-seventh Infantry Regiment Band. Band members had been permitted to retain their instruments and remain together, and the bandsmen, considered protected personnel, spent their time practicing and presenting concerts and other entertainment. Both prisoners and American personnel fondly remembered the outdoor "Great Tattoo" presented by the band just before Christmas in 1943. With the prisoners assembled and holding torches, the band serenaded the Americans with impressive ceremony.[41]

While most of the band was held at Fort Robinson, three members had been sent to camps in Texas and Arkansas, and early in 1944 the band leader requested that these men be transferred to Fort Robinson. The provost marshal approved this "non-relative" transfer on the condition that band members pay the transportation costs, about three hundred dollars. The bandsmen quickly raised the funds through a camp subscription, and the three men joined their comrades at Robinson. Nevertheless, there was some dissension between the musicians and other PWs. At one weekly concert, where refreshments were served, the audience stayed only long enough to eat and drink. The band members, described as "prima donnas" by the camp administrators, resented this attitude, and requested a transfer to a larger camp, where their talents would be more appreciated. In June the Forty-seventh Regiment Band was sent to Camp Concordia, Kansas.[42]

Because all prisoners received the same rations as the GIs, PWs had to accept changes in their diet. Few had ever eaten white bread, which they thought was cake. Obliging American quartermasters managed to obtain rye flour so the Germans could bake the more familiar dark bread. Nor were German prisoners used to corn-on-the-cob and sweet potatoes, which they claimed were fed only to hogs in Germany. GI and German cooks traded certain foods between their respective messes. One surprise to the Germans was corn flakes, "dry cereal, a real American breakfast."[43] Eventually, to the culinary delight of the remount soldiers, German cooks were assigned to post mess halls.

In the restricted world of the prisoner of war camp, the most important PW position was that of camp spokesman, the key intermediary between the American command and the prisoners, who had free access to visiting Red Cross representatives. At Fort Robinson, the PWs chose Stabsfeldwebel (S. Sgt.) Harry Huenmoerder as spokesman. Huenmoerder, a veteran of twelve years in the German army, was the highest ranking PW at the camp. He also had an excellent command of English and some U.S. camp officers felt his character was beyond question.[44]

At first, soldiers and civilians at Fort Robinson were apprehensive about German PWs. After all, they were the enemy, and everyone at the post had friends or relatives involved in the war; distrust, fear, or even hatred would be justifiable reactions. One GI working in the post hospital taunted PW patients with magazine pictures of bomb damage in Germany. Gradually, as PW labor was integrated into the post routine, some attitudes changed. Post soldiers found most Germans were reliable workers and easy to get along with. Sgt. Herman Wulf recalled, "There were an awful lot of good young boys just like we were, and they appreciated being in a place like this." A stable foreman, whose son was with Patton's Third Army, was unhappy when PWs were assigned as replacements when his stablemen went on furlough. But the Germans worked so hard the foreman didn't want his regular men to come back.[45]

German PWs were extremely curious about their new home. Most had read books and seen movies about cowboys and Indians, and now here they were in the great American West. To satisfy their curiosity, the camp intelligence staff translated and distributed a mimeographed edition of a small booklet on the history of Fort Robinson. Some PWs enjoyed the post's beautiful setting, and commented how the buttes reminded them of castles along the Rhine. PW Wolfgang Loesche later recalled how the area reminded him of the steppes of Russia. While some thought the climate was extremely cold and windy, the Russian front veteran replied, "I have been to Russia at minus fifty-six degrees Celsius and to Africa at forty degrees Celsius. This was comfortable."[46]

Besides Germans, prisoners from other countries who had been drafted or impressed into the German army, were brought to the camp. Upon reaching the United States, some of these PWs had voiced their disdain for the Nazis. Several Austrians, who arrived at Fort Robinson in 1944, wanted total segregation from the Germans. They had no interest in the Fatherland, and had been forced into fighting for Germany. Belgian and Czech PWs also spoke out against Germany, precipitating occasional violence between the various PW groups. Once, when processing a group of new prisoners, the Americans encountered three PWs who did not understand German. They were Italians serving in the German army "because Mussolini told us."[47]

As is typical in situations when people are incarcerated, the prisoners began to file complaints, mostly petty, against their captors. There was no ice cream cooler in their canteen, or the compound recreation area was not level enough for soccer games. A German doctor assigned to the post hospital once complained that his liberty on the post was restricted; he could not leave the PW hospital compound as frequently as he wished.

Investigations proved his complaint was unfounded—he had as much freedom as did other PWs working on the post. Another PW lost a tooth while on a work detail and wanted it replaced. His request was refused; under similar circumstances, American soldiers were not provided with missing teeth.[48]

The Americans tried to maintain strict discipline among the internees. Common problems were prisoners refusing to work, or attempting to steal government property. Because Fort Robinson was a well-run camp, there were fewer than thirty cases of punishment for those infractions between February and June 1944. Even with its record of good prisoner deportment, Col. Arthur Blain ordered a shakedown inspection of the compounds just after assuming command of the camp on February 14, 1944. PWs had rarely been searched after returning from work details, and the search turned up an "almost unbelievable number of improvised knives, nippers and other articles made from metal," which were duly confiscated by the MPs.[49] Although the prisoners strongly objected to the search, the commanding officer was within his rights. By 1945 discipline at the camp was reported as "strict but fair."[50]

Because one of the primary reasons for bringing PWs to the United States was to supplement the depleted American workforce, prisoners at the Fort Robinson camp were put to work immediately after their arrival. They were issued khaki or old GI denim clothing, marked with the letters "PW" in white paint. All prisoners were allowed to retain their uniforms, which they wore on special occasions or when off-duty. In accordance with the Geneva Convention, working prisoners were paid eighty cents per day, which approximated the base pay of a private. All prisoners, working and nonworking, received a ten-cents-per-day allowance for canteen items, paid in canteen coupons that could be used for personal items or saved.

Supervisors were instructed not to talk to prisoners except in the line of duty, and were to make sure they worked the full period assigned. Box lunches were prepared at the camp for noon meals, and at the end of the day, prisoners were assembled at the loading area and WAC truck drivers returned them to the camp. Americans working with PWs were sternly warned, "Do not ever believe a PW likes you; he does not," and "Do not think a PW will not escape if he can. He will." With such warnings in mind, post personnel integrated PW labor into regular operations.[51]

At the camp itself, prisoner work crews hauled coal and trash, and worked in the supply warehouse, operated mess halls, and served as firemen. In the garrison area, they laid out a baseball diamond, built a volleyball court, three horseshoe courts, and a softball pitching court complete with backstop, all for the GIs.[52] Work on the main post and reservation area included unloading lumber, delivering fuel, repairing roads, and working in yards. Other men cared for horses and mules, worked on feed bunks, hauled hay, cleaned stables and feed traps, hauled manure, maintained fences, and did conservation work on the Wood Reserve and reservation. By January 1944 about two-thirds of all the Fort Robinson prisoners were employed.[53]

One objectionable job was working in the post slaughterhouse, where condemned horses and mules were killed and butchered for dog food. Some prisoners claimed they became ill and could not eat after working there, so crews at the slaughterhouse were frequently rotated. Prisoners also tilled and irrigated a thirty-acre Victory garden on the post to supplement mess hall rations.[54]

By 1944 many post veterinary soldiers were being transferred to other assignments, and PWs were used as replacements. With detachment strength shrinking, supplemental labor was welcome, and prisoners soon worked in the operating room, served as teamsters, and cleaned and policed veterinary stables and corrals. By 1945 thirty PWs were working in the veterinary section, and reports noted, "German PW labor made it possible for the unit to continue to function."[55]

Although most Germans appreciated the opportunity to work and followed orders, a few proved difficult. In March 1945 fencing foreman Roscoe Craig asked that PW Rudolf Fleischfresser be removed from his work detail. According to Craig, the prisoner was frequently uncooperative, and attempted sabotage by "throwing nails in the path of vehicles, turning on the switch of the vehicle, and at one time [he] grabbed the gear shift when I was trying to drive." All in all, PW workers at Fort Robinson performed satisfactorily, and disobedient types like Fleischfresser were the exception.[56]

By 1944 all available prisoners were being used for Class II labor at Fort Robinson, leaving none for off-reservation civilian projects. In mid-1944 Whitney area farmers applied for PW labor to help with sugar beets and other agricultural work. In addition to the shortage of PW laborers, there were not enough guards to supervise working parties outside the post. As the war progressed, the camp guard staff was further reduced, ruling out any off-post labor until the war ended.[57]

To occupy PWs nonworking hours, various diversions were available. Soccer was the most popular outdoor sport, and the recreation area south of the middle compound offered a 1,600-by-500-foot playing field. By February 1944 nine soccer teams had been organized, using balls and other sporting equipment provided by the YMCA and the American and

German governments. During one Red Cross inspection, the representative brought a welcome present: "Pleased as I was, and so were they, that I had two first-quality balls to use in their championship game."[58] Handball and volleyball were also popular. Most of the PWs participated in some outdoor activity, a "contributing factor to the robust and healthy appearance of so many of the men."[59] The camp special services officer, assisted by two PW sports leaders, was in charge of athletics and all other recreation. At one time thirty-two PWs were enrolled in a refresher course for sports officiating. Indoor activities included chess, checkers, Ping-Pong, and cards.

Educational courses were offered at the Fort Robinson camp for those wanting to enrich their minds as well as occupy their time. Under the supervision of the American camp chaplain, classes in American history, geography, music, and basic architecture (including drafting, plumbing, and carpentry), were initiated. The University of Nebraska was asked to provide correspondence courses at high school and college levels. English classes were popular, and classes in chemistry and physics were offered. By early 1944 half the Germans at the camp were attending some sort of class.[60] In July 1944 the prisoners organized an engineering school, with enrollees exempt from work four afternoons a week. American camp staff translated and reproduced textbooks and lessons, and also taught English and classes on American government. As the camp population increased in 1944–45, so did school enrollment; by January 1945 about two thousand PWs were taking classes.[61]

Religious services were provided both for Protestants and Catholics and a 250-seat chapel was built during the May 1943 expansion. Sunday services and evening Bible study were scheduled, with special events for Easter and Christmas. The camp Lutheran chaplain was assisted by Father Albert Albel, who came from Crawford to minister to Catholic prisoners. Later, two PW Catholic priests arrived at the camp and assumed Albel's duties.

Chaplains were often discouraged by church attendance that sometimes dipped as low as twenty-five. But they provided an important service by "keeping up the tone of the camp, not by camp politics and internal maneuvering,[but] by their day-in and day-out presence."[62] When the camp population increased, so did church attendance, once averaging as high as 170, causing "the pastors [to] rejoice in their work and the response of the men."[63]

Arts and crafts were also popular pastimes in the compounds. Several PWs were skilled artists, who taught classes and painted portraits for camp officers. Many men engaged in woodcarving and competitions were held to judge their handiwork. PWs often fashioned ships in bottles and carved wooden plaques that were traded or given to Americans at the camp or on the post. One day Major Kercheval noticed the tails on some horses in a particular feed trap appeared to have been bobbed. Upon investigation, he found that PWs were using the horse hair to make brushes. The practice was quickly stopped.[64]

Each compound had a canteen that provided a modest assortment of items that PWs could purchase with the canteen coupons they earned while working. Merchandise included candy, cigarettes, watches, clothing, and toiletries. They were also allowed to buy two bottles of beer per day. Similar to practice at the post exchange, dividends from canteen sales went to a fund that was used for PW benefit. The daily beer ration did not always appease some prisoners' desire for alcohol. One day guards smelled alcohol on prisoners' breath, and suspected there was a still in the compound. After a thorough search, the MPs located the illicit distillery in a barracks attic; the Germans had used raisins and dried prunes to make their home brew. Copper tubing from a refrigeration unit in an unused compound had been appropriated for the still. The MPs quickly confiscated and destroyed it.[65]

Some of the Germans organized a theater troupe that regularly presented variety entertainment. Some members had been performing artists in prewar Germany, including Willi Schwind, a former professional clown, trapeze artist, and humorist, who "freely and untiringly shared with all his abilities."[66] The group took the name Varista, a contraction for Variete im Stacheldraht, literally, Variety (Vaudeville) in Barbed Wire. In January 1945 the troupe presented *Die Fledermaus* and a variety show that included eleven comedy, musical, and juggling numbers. A new show was presented every ten weeks. With limited seating in the Varista Hall, it was necessary to give eighteen performances of each show to provide each PW an opportunity to attend. An orchestra and band were organized with the PW director of music receiving ten dollars per month through prisoner donations. Costumes were ingeniously made up in the PW tailor shop, including white dinner jackets for the orchestra musicians made from bleached mattress covers.[67]

Profits from canteen sales were used to purchase a projector, and movies for PWs were rented from commercial sources. Eventually one full-length film and two short features were shown every five days. Although films were selected by the camp spokesman, the choices were sometimes criticized by other PWs for "low quality of content."[68] The camp chaplains were disturbed by the selections, seventy-five percent of which they considered "trash."[69]

A camp library was established with books received from the German Red Cross. In addition to German-language books and newspapers, the library received contemporary American newspapers and magazines. The German government sent numerous Soldatenbriefes (Soldier Briefs) for the prisoners. By July 1944 the library contained one thousand titles, excluding religious books and textbooks.[70]

German prisoners' attitudes toward their confinement and captors varied. Most were happy to be out of the war and glad to be at Fort Robinson, "the best place for us to regenerate after war and heat in Africa."[71] Some agreed they had never had it so good, with three meals a day and hot and cold running water. Although officially prohibited, soldiers at the fort frequently conversed with the PWs while on work details. Pfc. Carl Still was particularly amazed at the PWs' continued belief in German victory: "Talk to them prisoners, they really believed they were going to win . . . Boy, them people was bull headed. Damn. Talk till you were blue in the face, they wouldn't believe me."[72] But most PWs were pleased with their treatment and living conditions. PW Kurt Kohler wrote home, "Otherwise I am still well off since I have, all things considered, a good life also here in Nebraska."[73]

Allied success on the battlefield was directly reflected in the number of prisoners held at U.S. camps. By the spring of 1944, all the German and Italian PWs from North Africa had been distributed and for several months no additional prisoners arrived at Fort Robinson. The number of prisoners there dropped below five hundred. Correspondingly, the guard component was reduced, to a low of 119 men. Although by July 1944 the camp population had declined to the size of a large branch camp, the Fort Robinson camp had "acquired a settled quality" not always found in prisoner of war camps.[74] The situation changed after the D-Day invasion, when the Allies captured German prisoners at the rate of 100,000 a month. Once again large numbers of German prisoners were shipped to camps in the United States. By October the PW population at Fort Robinson had grown to nearly one thousand, and by January 1945, it was 2,980; the camp had finally reached full capacity.[75]

With an increased number of prisoners and a limited guard staff, two-way radios and binoculars were used to aid in the supervision of work parties. The remount depot provided horses for perimeter patrol. To supplement camp security, guard dogs were deployed, handled by men selected from the unit that had trained at the K-9 center. With many more PWs at the camp than were needed for the work available, many prisoners were merely held until they could be transferred to other camps.[76]

Combating Nazi influence and control over prisoners was the biggest problem faced by American camp personnel. According to the Geneva Convention, captors were prohibited from attempting to change or subvert the political beliefs of prisoners of war. Nazism followed the prisoners into American camps; ten percent of the PWs were considered fanatic Nazis, and thirty percent were sympathetic. At camps across the country, there were violent clashes between Nazi PWs and those who expressed anti-Nazi sentiments. Fort Robinson was no exception, and beginning in 1944 several prisoners were beaten or threatened. Prisoners soon learned to keep their political opinions to themselves.[77]

The camp intelligence staff suspected that spokesman Huenmoerder was pro-Nazi. He had protested the placement of certain American magazines and newspapers in PW dayrooms, arguing that these periodicals would create dissension among the prisoners. He also recommended transfer of certain anti-Nazi prisoners, "in interest to good order and discipline among the German Soldiers in this camp." Another clue was his selection of movies, some of which were violent, and showed American life in the worst possible light.[78]

Prisoners were allowed to display Nazi flags and pictures of Hitler in their barracks, and observe German national holidays, including the Fuehrer's birthday. The most visible sign of Nazism was the use of the Nazi salute. In 1944 prisoners received orders from Germany to begin using it instead of the traditional army salute. A German sergeant apologized for giving the Nazi salute to an American officer whom he knew was Jewish. The officer told the sergeant he should not feel bad, because it was his duty to use the prescribed salute.[79]

Nationwide, the problem of Nazism at the camps became more apparent to the U.S. Army and the public. By April 1944 at least seven politically-related murders, numerous beatings and assaults, and a disturbingly high number of suicides had occurred. As victory over Germany began to seem inevitable, the War Department decided to root out Nazi influence in the camps. It initiated a special program to expose prisoners "to the facts of American history, workings of democracy, and the contributions made to America by peoples of all national origins." The program's overall goal was not to Americanize the PWs, but to instill respect for the quality and potency of American institutions.[80]

Selected enlisted men and officers from the camp intelligence staff were sent to special training seminars to prepare them for re-educating the prisoners. Through what became known as intellectual diversion, Americans sought to reframe the political thinking of German PWs. The re-education process had a modest beginning with the removal of pro-Nazi books from the compound library, and the substitution of books

Troop B, 252nd Quartermaster Squadron, marching in the 1941 Memorial Day parade in Crawford. RG1517:53-5

Lt. Charles Lumley (left), **Maj. Paul Kendall, and Lt. Donald Melton** (right) **gather around a hitching post at post headquarters, 1941.** Courtesy Robert McCaffree, RG1517:115-1

Post commander Lt. Col. E. M. Daniels (left) and his executive officer, Maj. Paul Kendall, relax at the officers' club, 1942. Courtesy Robert McCaffree, RG 1517:115-3

A social gathering at the officers' club. Dr. Richard Ivins (civilian dress) was the post contract surgeon for many years. Courtesy Robert McCaffree, RG1517:115-2

Horse herd in the Cherry Creek feed area, 1941. RG4896:2-5

Riding the feed traps, 1942. Left to right: **Pvt. Martin Weber, Lt. Robert McCaffree, Maj. William Ranck, and Lt. Kenneth Sadler.** Courtesy Robert McCaffree, RG1517:115-6

Changing the guard at the post water towers after the attack on Pearl Harbor.
Courtesy Robert McCaffree, RG1517:115-4

Col. Joseph M. Tully, Fourth Cavalry, salutes his regiment at its final horse-mounted review, April 9, 1942. RG2731:10-8

Surplus horse sale at the condition and issue stable, 1943. The prisoner of war hospital complex is in the background. RG1517:45-48

Unloading a shipment of hay at the warehouse siding. RG1517:45-47

Pack mule training, 1943.
RG1517:45-38

Pack mule trainees return from a hike below Saddle Rock. RG1517:24-3

Basic training close-order drill. RG1517:6-4

Fort Robinson troops on the firing range during basic training. RG1517:6-3

Instruction in hand-to-hand combat was part of the spring 1943 basic training program.
RG1517:45-19

Interior of the post chapel, today Bethlehem Lutheran Church in Crawford.
RG1517:95-8

Wrecked glider at the site of the August 1943 airborne maneuvers west of the main post. RG1517:88-5

"Fan Dancer" Sally Rand with post commander Lt. Col. Frank Carr, New Year's Day, 1943. RG2721:1-2

WAC detachment at Fort Robinson, 1944. Courtesy Mrs. Roland Pinson,

Cpl. Mike Jasmann and Pfc. Weldon Harold ride in a pairs jumping class at a 1944 horse show. RG1517: 44-7

Incoming dogs received an initial medical examination at the War Dog Reception and Training Center hospital.
RG1517:52-38

Hospital attendants take a blood sample from a K-9 candidate. RG1517:52-46

Attack dogs were trained to attack from the rear. RG1517:52-35

Close-order drill accustomed the dogs to sudden movements by their handlers and to working in a group. RG2731:6-13

Agitation training, an essential and often dangerous aspect of the training regimen, was designed to teach the dog to be aggressive while remaining under his handler's control. RG1517:52-40

A wintertime view of the sprawling Fort Robinson kennel area. RG1517:52-36

K-9 attendants gather food pans after a feeding in the kennel area.
RG2731:2-12

Officers make a final examination of a trained dog, part of the first group to be deployed from the center, 1942. RG1517:52-45

Coast Guard trainees and their dogs form the "V for Victory." RG2731:6-31

Mrs. Arlene Erlanger, one of the founders of Dogs for Defense, with Lt. Robert Robertson (left) **and Lt. Robert Johnson** (right) **during a visit to Fort Robinson in 1945.** Courtesy Robert Johnson

German prisoners of war arrive at the Fort Robinson internment camp, October 1944. RG2725-14

A 1943 photograph of German prisoner of war Karl Schlager.
Courtesy Wolfgang Dorschel, RG3997-19

Fritz Eisenwein, Company C, Fort Robinson internment camp, 1943–46.
Courtesy Wolfgang Dorschel RG1882-1

Headquarters of the prisoner of war camp, April 1945. The flag flies at half-staff following the death of President Franklin D. Roosevelt. RG4889;1-5

Unteroffizier Wolfgang Dorschel, prisoner of war camp spokesman, 1945–46. Courtesy Wolfgang Dorschel, RG3897-7

Varista Hall, the prisoner of war theater and recreation center. RG2725-16

Interior of the guard company barracks at the prisoner of war camp. T5 John
C. McGaillard (right) was an interpreter. RG4001-51

German cooks on duty in a compound kitchen. RG4001-52

A German prisoner of war on a work detail. Note the "P" and "W" marked on his coat, and the Seventh Service Command insignia on the truck door. RG1517:59-6

Flagpole at the prisoner of war camp, 1944. Major buildings in the garrison area included (left to right) the officers' club, mess hall, and quarters. RG1517:115-5

Capt. Lee O. Hill, the last commanding officer at Fort Robinson. RG2411-2395

U.S. Department of Agriculture beef research headquarters was located in Comanche Hall. RG1517:114-7

Beef research feedlot in the old cavalry corral area, about 1960. RG1517:114-8

Surplus bull sale at the former broodmare stable complex. RG1517:114-9

with more democratic themes. Henceforth, the camp assistant executive officer, not a PW, chose movies for PW viewing. After attending an intellectual diversion orientation program in New York, one Fort Robinson staff member purchased *The Defeat of Germany* and *Why We Fight* at Macy's for screening at the camp. To reinforce the idea of freedom of speech and the press, in 1945 prisoners at all U.S. camps were allowed to publish camp newspapers. At Fort Robinson, reliable prisoners wrote and edited a mimeographed paper appropriately titled the *Neuer Horizont* (*New Horizon*), where "one could find treatises on all nature of subjects, political, social, historical, cultural and technical."[81]

According to a provost marshal directive issued in 1945, no pro-Nazis were to be retained as camp spokesmen. At Fort Robinson Huenmoerder was immediately removed from the position and transferred to another camp. He was replaced by a progressive non-Nazi NCO, Unteroffizier (Sgt.) Wolfgang Dorschel, a veteran of the Tenth Panzer Division. Dorschel, who entered the army in June 1940, fought in Russia and North Africa as part of a motorcycle reconnaissance unit. After his capture on May 13, he arrived with the first Afrika Korps prisoners at Fort Robinson in late 1943. The American intelligence staff considered Huenmoerder's replacement by Dorschel as its most important accomplishment, a change that added to the success of future reorientation.[82]

Slowly, the PW camp mission changed from that of only holding prisoners, to one of reforming their political thought. Perhaps the most successful mechanism for this reformation was the Arbeitsgemeinschaft zur Pflege der Politischen Aufkläerung (Working Association for Political Enlightenment), a sanctioned camp organization formed by progressive, anti-Nazi prisoners. In compound-wide meetings, democratic-thinking prisoners presented lectures to fellow inmates on political and social thought and current events, and speculated about what the future held for Germany and the world. As Nazi influence slowly waned, membership in the organization grew; by war's end, more than ninety percent of the PWs in the camp signed statements swearing to break forever with national socialism. One American boasted, "Our biggest difficulty is in getting space enough to handle the audience."[83]

In February 1945 the Fort Robinson camp was designated as a camp for enlisted sailors of the German navy, and almost all the army PWs were moved to other camps in the Seventh Service Command. Excluded from transfer were several hundred men of the original Afrika Korps contingent. Because of their work experience, the "Africans" were a valuable asset to post operations, and "the relief of those trained men at this time would work a considerable hardship on the post."[84]

With the changeover from army to navy prisoners, camp population dropped to twenty-one hundred, a number maintained until midsummer. To provide additional work for inmates, side camps were organized. In the fall of 1944 a branch camp had been established at Fort Meade, South Dakota, where Fort Robinson PWs were sent to work converting that recently abandoned post into a Veterans Administration hospital. In May 1945 a detail of twenty PWs with several GI enlisted men was sent to fence a former CCC camp near Fort Meade for an additional camp. A third work site was soon established at another old CCC camp at Belle Fouche, South Dakota. Prisoners housed at the latter two sites worked sugar beet fields in the Belle Fouche Irrigation District. By the fall of 1945 nearly five hundred Fort Robinson PWs had been assigned to the South Dakota side camps.[85]

By May 1945 the European phase of the war was rapidly drawing to a close. On May 7 the assembled PWs were informed that all German military resistance had ended, and they were no longer duty bound to the German government, but were responsible only to American laws and regulations. All prisoners of war were still expected to conduct themselves in a military manner. A May 8 (V-E Day) proclamation encouraged the PWs to face the future with "faith, courage, a clear heart, and open mind."[86]

Most of the Germans were relieved that the war was finally over. Many broke into tears, hoping they soon would be going home. A few die-hards, however, were distraught. One man wanted to commit suicide, and tried to get some poison from a PW medical assistant. He sincerely believed "No Fuehrer, no Fatherland!" Camp spokesman Dorschel convinced the man to relent, arguing "life would go on."[87]

With the end of the war in Europe, the Americans could maintain stricter control over the PWs. All references to Nazism were strictly forbidden, swastikas were removed from uniforms and insignia, and the Nazi hand salute was banned. Prisoners in all camps were required to watch films of the horrors found at recently liberated Nazi death camps. As further punishment for Nazi crimes, all prisoners were put on half rations for several weeks. The ration cut bothered staff GIs, who had worked hard to gain the confidence of the prisoners. Sgt. Alfred Thompson wrote home in disgust, "It is hard to convince the German Prisoner of War of the honesty of the American government, of the respect we hold for international agreement when we make [an] open breech [*sic*] of such agreements."[88]

By midsummer 1945 full rations had been restored, and camp life continued much as before the German capitulation. PW labor was made available for farmers in the Whitney Irrigation District for beet work. On May 25 Colonel Blain and the local farm labor corporation contracted for sufficient numbers of workers until "available labor hits the market."[89] By this time it was noted that Fort Robinson prisoners had donated nearly five thousand dollars to welfare organizations, including the International Red Cross, War Prisoners Aid of the YMCA, and the American Red Cross.[90]

Germany's surrender also brought the only recorded successful escape from the Fort Robinson camp. On May 15 Siegfried Boestel made off from a work detail and hopped on an eastbound Burlington freight train in Crawford. For the first time, the long-prepared camp escape procedures were implemented. After notification of local authorities, the camp was secured and PWs restricted while a thorough search was made for the escapee.

Several days later, a very hungry Boestel entered a tavern named Buddy's Place in York, Nebraska, about four hundred miles southeast of the fort. He walked to the rear of the room, took a seat at the far end of the bar, and began gesturing wildly and talking to the waitress in "a language I could not understand."[91] After giving him a beer and something to eat, the owner called the York police, who apprehended the fugitive. According to witnesses, Boestel seemed relieved and grinned rather foolishly. He told his captors he was a German sailor, and was heading to St. Paul, Minnesota, with hopes of making it to Canada. In his pockets were hand-drawn maps of the West Coast, the Colorado River, and other points. His sightseeing trip over, Boestel was returned under escort to the Fort Robinson camp.[92]

Chapter 7

Abandonment, Transfer to the USDA

On August 14, 1945, word reached Fort Robinson that Japan had accepted the Allies' unconditional surrender terms—World War II was over. After hearing the news on the radio, many soldiers rushed to town to get supplies for celebrating. A formation was ordered at the fort, and a formal announcement of the surrender was read. Two 75mm artillery pieces used in K-9 training fired several salutes. Although the MPs had closed the post to prevent men from going into Crawford, "plenty of celebrations" took place in the barracks. Evidently the garrison made good use of the "supplies" picked up earlier in town. By direction of the president, all civilian workers were given a two-day holiday on August 15 and 16.[1]

During the war more than ten thousand pack mules were processed and issued from Fort Robinson; 4,339 in 1944 alone. Besides shipments to various ports of embarkation for overseas service, thousands were sent to units in the United States, and mule teams were trained and shipped to numerous military installations. As with the horses and dogs, the end of the war brought a reduction in the mule population at Fort Robinson.

During the last months of the war, mule shipments to the Fort Robinson depot had gradually declined. April 1945 saw the last of the large monthly receipts, when more than eight hundred pack mules arrived from remount purchasing officers. In July 1945 the final shipment of riding horses from the dismounted cavalry regiments was received, 750 horses from Fort Riley to be held until they were sold. At the time of the Japanese surrender, more than thirty-three hundred horses and six thousand mules remained at Fort Robinson.[2]

In the spring of 1945 plans were made to move the remount veterinary research center from the Front Royal depot to Fort Robinson. Because there were more animals at Robinson, remount officers felt the post provided a "broad opportunity" for disease research exceeding that available at the Virginia depot. The first brick stable on the row was remodeled to house virology, biochemistry, bacteriology, and other laboratories, with a large autopsy room and isolation stalls in the rear. By the fall of 1945 the laboratory began work on prevention and control of equine diseases. Although its establishment hinted at the continued use of the old post, the conversion of the stable proved to be the army's last major construction project at Fort Robinson.[3]

During the winter of 1945–46, thousands of mules were prepared for sale. In October alone, depot personnel processed 2,380 animals. The animal section trimmed the feet of 560 mules, while veterinarians gave tetanus toxoid shots to 1,160 horses and mules, and malleined (tested for glanders) a total of 890 animals. Hundreds of mules were shipped for War Assets Administration sales, with more than four thousand eventually being sold to the Reconstruction Finance Corporation. By mid-1946 the number of animals at Fort Robinson had returned to prewar levels.[4]

The postwar phase-out of animal operations brought a corresponding reduction in the number of enlisted men in the remount detachment. The peak had been reached in June 1945, when more than five hundred men were on duty. By October the remount component was 265. Throughout most of 1946, fewer than one hundred remount soldiers were at the post; by 1947 the number dropped into the thirties.[5] With a similar reduction in the number of officers at the post, noncommissioned officers were once again allowed to move into vacant quarters on officers' row. The remaining officers occupied the large brick quarters on the west end. The post complement was reorganized into two units for operation and administration; the 9171st Technical Service Unit-Quartermaster Corps Remount Detachment and the 5023rd Army Service Unit Station Complement Detachment. As enlisted men were steadily discharged, civilian workers were hired to replace them. Civil service truck drivers and heavy equipment operators were hired in addition to clerks, carpenters, and laborers.

Although the army had become mechanized, the remount occasionally issued military animals. Riding horses were prepared and issued to ordnance depots, including the Black Hills Ordnance Depot at Igloo, South Dakota, and the huge Dugway Proving Grounds in Utah, for perimeter and interior patrol. Horse and mule teams were sent to national cemeteries and army posts such as Fort Belvoir, Virginia, where they were used in maintenance work. Mules and tons of excess hay were transferred to Camp Carson, Colorado, where infantry pack units trained. Despite the decrease, Fort Robinson was still the acknowledged center of remount activity. In December 1946 four veterinary officers from the Nationalist Chinese army arrived at the post for thirty days training in handling and processing mules. The Nationalists, once again fighting the Communists, had retained the mules shipped to China during the war, including hundreds trained at Fort Robinson.[6]

Remount service operations continued as usual, but never again approached prewar levels. The depot continued to receive and ship stallions to agents in the upper Plains states. In the animal section, work with depot-raised animals went on, producing twenty-seven foals by May 1946. Yearlings were taught to stand tied and saddle broken; three-year-olds were ridden daily. Depot veterinarians inspected and vaccinated all stallions in the depot's remount area. In 1947 headquarters for the North Central Remount Area was moved from Sheridan, Wyoming, to Fort Robinson, adding several new states to its agent area. At that time some 130 issue animals from the depot remained in the hands of civilian agents.

The fort's jumping team kept busy providing exhibitions for local fairs and celebrations. In August 1947 the team performed at horse shows and rodeos in Sidney, Stuart, Kimball, and Mitchell, Nebraska, and at Lusk, Wyoming. The traditional Quartermaster Day and new Army Day programs presented displays of depot breeding stock, war dogs, and demonstrations. In July 1946 the post hosted a benefit horse show with the proceeds going to "destitute people in war ravaged areas."[7]

The postwar years also saw the end of the Fort Robinson Prisoner of War Camp, though repatriation did not take place as rapidly as many prisoners hoped. The immediate return of thousands of former PWs was the last thing the Allies wanted during the reconstruction of Germany, and the repatriation process was delayed as long as possible.

In September 1945 the army announced that the PW camp at Fort Robinson was to be gradually deactivated, and most of the prisoners and guard staff were transferred to other camps in the Seventh Service Command area. The Fort Robinson camp was designated as a branch camp of the Scottsbluff prisoner of war camp. In late November Alfred Thompson, one of the remaining GIs, wrote a recently discharged buddy about the changes:

> As of today we have 660 PWs and 27 EM [enlisted men]. Compounds II & III are completely closed and gradually being dismantled. They have not as yet begun on the buildings but the telephone lines, lights, kitchens, etc. have been dismantled. Jim is busy disconnecting water and painting

stoves. The five men in the [carpenter] shop are nailing slats over windows and doors to prevent them from blowing off. ... We have closed all the buildings outside the fence outside of the officers barracks where the EM live, the labor office, which is now headquarters, the library where I work, the club, and [Capt. Lawrence W.] Tabbert's quarters.[8]

Most of the remaining PWs were members of the original contingent of Afrika Korps prisoners, who had spent their entire internment at Fort Robinson. Because of the semipermanent nature of its buildings, the Fort Robinson camp was used longer than those elsewhere. In December 1945 prisoners from the South Dakota side camps returned when those camps were closed. By that time the guards "number only a dozen or so, most of whom are new." On January 31, 1946, the 1765th Service Command Unit was discontinued after nearly three years of effective camp management.[9]

In the first months of 1946 repatriation began in earnest. To prepare reliable PWs for roles in the reconstruction of Germany, the Special Projects division organized a crash course in democratic thinking and politics. In March and April more than twenty thousand selected prisoners were sent to Fort Eustis, Virginia, to attend the six-day program, including one-fourth of the remaining Fort Robinson PWs, a large ratio for any camp. In May 1946 the last sixty prisoners left the camp; that summer the vacant buildings were surplused. Due to the wartime shortage of lumber, the public quickly purchased the camp buildings offered for sale by a Minneapolis lumber supply company.[10] By late fall, all the buildings, except one warehouse, had been demolished or moved.

A similar phase-out came for the Fort Robinson War Dog Reception and Training Center. During the fall of 1945 training continued for several scout dog platoons still in the cycle when the war ended. With no further need for dogs in combat, the training schedule was relaxed. In late August one platoon was sent to Cheyenne to march in the annual Frontier Days parade. On other occasions, men and dogs were detailed to give demonstrations at various dog shows and other patriotic events around the country. By October the army had decided that there was no need to train additional dogs for occupation duty, and the center was ordered to begin curtailing training. On October 16 four final provisional Infantry Scout Dog platoons were graduated. Although some of the scout dogs were to be held in the army's strategic reserve, the other dogs at the center, more than a thousand, were to be disposed of. Besides ending K-9 training, post commander Col. Brisbane Brown was also advised to "take steps without delay to terminate the activities of the WDRTC."[11] Thereafter, only dogs to be detrained and surplused were sent to Fort Robinson.

Even before the end of the war, hundreds of sentry and guard dogs had been shipped back to the training centers. By 1945 the remount gave high priority to processing these dogs for return to their owners or for sale. Seventy percent of the dogs on active service were returned to Fort Robinson; those east of the Mississippi River were sent to Aleshire Depot (Front Royal). No dog was released until it passed a demilitarization or detraining process. First, a dog's record was studied to determine the proper approach to detraining. Then the handlers attempted to convince the dog that every human was a friend—men talked to, played with, and constantly petted the animal, and different men were assigned to care for it. The dogs were exposed to various noises and stimuli to see how they would react. Finally, they were taken into Crawford to reacquaint them with the normal sounds they would encounter at home.[12]

Beyond a doubt the army made every effort to ensure that war dogs could return to civilian life. Having kept meticulous records, the army contacted donors, and scores of detrained dogs were shipped home directly from the center every week. Some civilian donors, understanding the strong bond that wartime training had developed, allowed the dog's handler to keep their former pets. Owners who received their dogs back were provided with information on how to maintain the obedience skills taught by the army, and were given a copy of the K-9 manual. At the completion of their military service, dogs were issued Honorable Discharge certificates. If, however, a surplus dog was determined to be vicious, it was destroyed. K-9 personnel were keenly aware that many dogs, particularly those trained for attack roles, could never be returned to civilian life. When a dog died or had to be destroyed while in the service, the owners were promptly notified with a letter thanking them for their contribution. The letters reassured the donor that the dog had been euthanized "mercifully and without pain," and that it had "performed its duties like a good soldier."[13]

As detraining activity gradually decreased, K-9 personnel were discharged or transferred, including Colonel Hirschy, who left for Fort Warren in late September. Some of the men went to the few K-9 units being retained in service. Most, however, took their discharges and returned to civilian life. On November 1 all training, except that for scout and sled dogs in process, was terminated. That month the K-9 section held a party and dance, advertising "this is probably the last K-9 party and it's bound to be a beaut." By December 31, 1945, the Fort Robinson WDRTC had received 11,437 dogs for training. Of that number, 4,889 were successfully trained and issued, while 5,300 had been rejected or discharged and returned to their owners. Only 640 dogs and 77 enlisted men remained at the center.[14]

As the dogs and men disappeared, so did the massive kennel area and the barracks, mess hall, and other temporary buildings built in 1942–43. On June 30, 1946, the war dog training center was officially deactivated—but not all the dogs had left Fort Robinson. Seventy-five sled dogs remained at the post. After the war, dog teams and men from Fort Robinson were called on to participate in several rescue missions in the mountains of Colorado and Wyoming, including the recovery of eleven bodies from a fatal United Airlines crash near Elk Mountain, Wyoming. In August 1946 sixty sled dogs were transferred to Fort Richardson, Alaska, for duty with a combat intelligence platoon. The other dogs were offered to the Air Transport Command and the Alaskan Department, neither of which accepted them. Finally, in June 1947 the last fifteen government-owned dogs at Fort Robinson were sold to Stuart Mace, a former sled dog training officer at the post. Later that summer a War Assets Administration sale disposed of the remaining feed boxes, dog blankets, muzzles, leash sets, and even dog gas masks. The Fort Robinson War Dog Reception and Training Center, the largest single dog training installation in the annals of the U.S. Army, passed into history.[15]

The post-World-War-II period brought reorganization and realignment, as the army experienced peacetime reduction. Just as mechanization had marked the end for the horse cavalry, modernization brought an end to many of the older posts, when the army consolidated its forces in newer, large-scale installations. Older posts, including Fort Meade, Robinson's neighbor to the north, were declared obsolete and abandoned. Once home to Comanche, the old Seventh Cavalry regiment, and the long-time station of the Fourth Cavalry, Fort Meade was abandoned in 1944. At war's end, some area residents feared that Fort Robinson would also be abandoned. With the end of the horse cavalry, it seemed reasonable that the end was near for quartermaster remount operations and depots.[16] Many in civilian circles doubted the future necessity of army remount operations, and some looked on Fort Robinson as a white elephant and as a "race horse activity . . . only of interest in these artificial circles."[17]

The handwriting was already on the wall for the remount branch, and for the army's continued use of Fort Robinson. Under the army reorganization, the secretary of the army ordered the remount service "disbanded and all horses disposed."[18] Rather than break up its remount branch, the army decided to turn it over to the other government agency that held a keen interest in horse production, the United States Department of Agriculture. For many years the USDA had been a strong advocate of improved domestic horse production, and it was only natural for that agency to assume the role traditionally held by the army. Transfer of remount operations included turning over control of the four depots, Fort Reno, Aleshire (Front Royal), Pomona, and Fort Robinson, to the Department of Agriculture. Representative Francis Case of South Dakota publicly announced the proposed transfer in April 1946. In addition to the depots, the USDA would receive all the army's breeding stock. In its twenty-eight years of operation, the army breeding plan placed more than seven hundred stallions across the country, which produced 230,000 foals. The program "resulted in immeasurable improvement in the horse stocks of the country and added untold wealth to its economy."[19]

Under the USDA Fort Robinson was to be operated as part of the Agriculture Remount Service, continuing the breeding program established by the army. The production of light horses for civilian agriculture would be ensured, because all efforts of the new remount service would be "directed toward the development of horses for utilitarian purposes on the farms and ranches of the country."[20] The army remount service apparatus was to remain in place; the secretary of agriculture assured stockmen that "all activities of the Remount Service will be continued."[21]

Naturally, area residents were keenly interested in the army's plans for the fort. Immediately after Case's announcement, post commander Col. Thomas E. Whitehead told the Crawford Chamber of Commerce he had not received orders for army abandonment or transfer, but he thought the depot, "lock, stock, and barrel," eventually would be turned over to the USDA.[22] However, legislative action was needed before the army could move out. With the fort's future in limbo, some feared the army would merely abandon Fort Robinson and the land would be returned to the tax rolls. Until a transfer could be finalized, the army agreed to provide funding to continue the remount service.[23]

Officials assumed the transfer from army to USDA control could be executed upon the signing of an executive order by President Harry S Truman, but on February 24, 1947, the attorney general declared an executive transfer illegal; congressional action was required.[24] Case and other congressmen (including Nebraska Senators Hugh Butler and Kenneth S. Wherry and Representative A. L. Miller) began work on the legislation. Regardless of technicalities, Whitehead had already announced to the community that Fort Robinson would be turned over to the USDA. The Crawford newspaper echoed the sentiments of many residents, stating that the fort was one of the town's greatest assets, and "so it is with a feeling of regret that we announce that it will no longer be a military post, and it is hoped that the new department will prove successful."[25]

On May 15, 1947, Representative Case introduced HR 3484 to transfer the remount service and its depots from War Department to Department of Agriculture control, effective July 1, 1947. The bill authorized the secretary of agriculture to "administer it [the remount program] in such manner as he deems will best advance the livestock and agricultural interests of the United States." The bill reiterated the goal of "improvement in the breeding of horses," in effect continuing the army's remount program. To help the USDA assume the program, army remount personnel were to be detailed to the agriculture department until June 30, 1948.[26]

In May 1947 chief of remount Col. Ralph E. Ireland and Henry W. Marston, investigator from the USDA Research Administration Office, inspected the fort in preparation for the transfer of the army's breeding program. At that time Ireland reaffirmed that the army was getting out of the horse and mule business entirely. Reflecting on the decision, Col. "Pink" Hardy later lamented, "It is one of the big mistakes of our Government that they did not keep at least a small Remount Service so as to continue the excellent work that has been accomplished from World War I to World War II."[27]

While in Crawford, Marston addressed the Chamber of Commerce and again stressed that the agriculture department would continue remount operations. He added that the USDA expected to take over the fort, along with the remount program, on July 1. As that day approached, the soldiers planned to lower the flag for the last time at Fort Robinson as an army post. The flag was to be lowered by Sgt. Weino Frantsi, a twenty-five-year veteran in charge of the post military police. By July 1, however, the transfer bill had not passed the Senate, and the legislative session ended. Several weeks later, with the flag still flying, post commander Col. Edward W. " Tommy" Sawyer was notified that the post would continue under army control, at least until Congress convened in 1948. Meanwhile, others jumped on the transfer bandwagon, including Senator Elmer Thomas of Oklahoma (where the Fort Reno depot was located), who stated he would insist on action in the next session of Congress.[28]

While awaiting final legislative action, the post staff began procedures to effect the transfer.[29] Military auditors and inspectors made frequent visits, and records were inventoried for transfer or disposal. Sawyer's staff prepared detailed cost studies to aid future agricultural remount budgets, including an analysis of all post buildings, utilities, and facilities. In the interim there were several sales of surplus government equipment and horses. One sale bill advised that the horses were "being disposed of only because they are excess to the needs of the army."[30] At several sales discharged soldiers returned to buy a particular animal—"they wanted to own him, they came to buy them if they could."[31] In late 1946 forty surplus horses were sold to the New York Police Department. Equipment sales disposed of tools, furniture, generators, harness, and miscellaneous maintenance materials, all at cut-rate prices. The WAC compound and PW hospital complex buildings also were sold and removed.

It became painfully evident that future USDA operations would not require the same level of manpower previously employed by the army. The Chamber of Commerce was informed that appropriations for the new agricultural station would be smaller than the army had received to operate the depot in the postwar period. Naturally, this meant fewer jobs for the local work force. With a bleak outlook for local employment at the post, chamber members urged the USDA to increase the budget for station operations. Meanwhile, as military operations at Fort Robinson were being phased out, the civilian work force gradually decreased as civil service employees were separated or transferred to other military installations. A few went to the Sioux Ordnance Depot near Sidney, Nebraska, and the Black Hills Ordnance Depot. A few veteran civilian employees were to be retained for the USDA.[32]

During the last week of April 1947, the Chicago & North Western Railroad closed its Fort Robinson depot. In continuous use since 1886, the peak year was 1944, when the railroad did half a million dollars of business at the post. At the time of its closing, the army was the depot's only customer and the closure received War Department approval.[33]

In July graves in the post cemetery were moved to Fort McPherson National Cemetery at Maxwell, Nebraska. By that time the cemetery contained 258 burials of soldiers, dependents, civilian employees, and others who died at or near the post. Among those removed were the graves of eleven soldiers killed in the 1879 Cheyenne Outbreak, the only soldiers killed at the fort in combat with Plains Indians. Unfortunately, fifteen graves yielded no remains. Included in this group was the grave of Moses Milner, or "California Joe," the famous scout and frontiersman who was killed at Camp Robinson in 1876.[34]

Also in July 1947 crews exhumed the remains of eleven German prisoners of war, who had died of disease, natural causes, or injury, and had been buried in the PW cemetery located on a small rise south of the compounds. Five of the burials were PWs from Fort Robinson while the others were from Scottsbluff and Wyoming branch camps. One soldier died on a PW troop train while it passed through Cherry County near Valentine; his death came from a gunshot wound to the head he had received in combat months earlier. Two of the men died of injuries sustained in a beet truck accident near Veteran, Wyoming, in November 1945. The German remains were shipped to Camp Butler National Cemetery near Springfield, Illinois, for reburial with other World War II prisoners.[35]

Some fort business continued as usual; a large horse show was held September 24 to 27, 1947, attracting ten thousand visitors to the exhibits and mounted competitions, and to purchase sale horses. The gala event drew breeders, buyers, and the public, attracted by cash prizes and awards valued at more than fifteen hundred dollars donated by Crawford businesses. The first day featured horses and colts exhibited by breeders from various parts of the north-central remount district. On the afternoon of the second day, Crawford businesses and schools closed and a crowd of five thousand arrived to view exhibits and watch horse races. The races ended tragically; a rider from Mitchell was instantly killed when his horse left the track and bolted into a tree. The jockey had won two previous races and was "well on his way to win the race."[36]

Friday's program included shows of various halter classes, riding contests, and variety races. A feature of the afternoon show was the "triumph" of Mary Bell Cooksley, the wife of remount detachment commander Maj. Leo Cooksley, in the cattle cutting class. Riding her own horse, Sparta, she beat a field of well-known local horsemen in a difficult exhibition of horsemanship and cattle-moving skills. A horse and colt auction on Saturday disposed of more than two hundred government horses and sixty-three privately owned animals. Despite the fatal accident, the show was called "one of the best of its kind."[37]

One of the last true military horse issues of the remount period occurred on December 6, 1947, when twenty-one riding horses were shipped to the Atomic Energy Commission at Los Alamos, New Mexico, for perimeter guard use. Along with the dawn of the atomic age, this issue symbolized the changes that came to the army and Fort Robinson in the postwar years.[38]

The spring of 1948 brought the last army-sponsored public events at the fort. On April 6 the final Army Day open house was held, with showings of the remaining stallions, brood mares and younger horses at the stables. On June 14–16 the remount hosted a final horse show and sale. The program presented halter classes, children's horsemanship, and novice jumping, as well as stock horse classes and contests for other horses. June 15 was designated "Crawford Day," with a special appearance of the Panhandle Patrol, a well-known mounted drill team from Alliance. As usual, a variety of races and jumping competitions completed the day's activities. A sale of privately owned horses the next day brought an end to the popular remount shows held at the fort for many years.[39]

On April 9, 1948, the Quartermaster General's Office notified all depot commanders that Senate passage of the transfer bill was assured, and they were to plan accordingly. Public Law 494, transferring the remount service to the USDA, was approved on April 21. The law placed Fort Robinson, selected property, and designated civilian personnel under Department of Agriculture control effective July 1, 1948. Military personnel were detailed to the USDA for a period not to exceed one year; transferred civilian employees included horse trainers Ed Nyberg, Leon Humbert, and Bud Parker. On June 1 a board of quartermaster remount officers made a final inspection to determine the post's "condition and fitness for transfer to Department of Agriculture." After the transfer date, the post was officially designated Agriculture Remount Service, Robinson Remount Depot. [40]

The press heralded the transfer as the end of an era that for "many an old soldier" brought a "twinge of sorrow." Beyond its role in western history, the fort was described as one of the finest places in the world to raise horses and as a last refuge for horse-loving army men. With the end of seventy-four years of army occupation, one newspaper lamented the transfer as "a sad change to contemplate for a proud frontier outpost which played a great part in the winning of the west." A new era in Fort Robinson history had begun. [41]

For several years a steady stream of officials from the USDA and the University of Nebraska made inspection and planning visits to the post. Early emphasis centered on "agricultural remount," and agriculture department officials repeatedly reassured area residents the station would be maintained and that "good horse flesh" would remain available for any potential need. Fort Robinson was to be the largest unit in the USDA plan to continue the four remount depots. The new program would employ 250 men, 360 horses, and cost $590,000 annually. However, others saw a different future for Fort Robinson. [42]

The true course of the USDA's involvement with Fort Robinson was likely formulated in the Research and Marketing Act of 1946. This act initiated beef cattle breeding research, and authorized funds to states and the USDA for cooperative research. Because Public Law 494 transferred the army's remount facilities to the USDA to further the "livestock and agricultural interests" of the country, it opened the door for animal research in areas other than horse breeding. Cattle interests quickly realized Fort Robinson was well-suited for beef research, and, in fact, the Nebraska Legislature petitioned Congress to make Fort Robinson available to the USDA specifically for that purpose. [43]

In reality, the USDA had planned to get out of the remount business almost immediately. Late in 1948 it announced that the University of Nebraska might receive nine thousand acres of the former reservation for research purposes. The department reported that appropriations to operate the four depots fell well short of requirements, and quickly decided to drop the Front Royal and Pomona depots from further remount-type use. Earlier in 1948 the agricultural remount had been designated as a sub-appropriation of the Bureau of Animal Industry, and not as a separate unit of the Agricultural Research Administration. This enabled the remount to be absorbed by the bureau, reducing its importance in USDA priorities. Officials blamed this change of policy on budget bureau examiners, and claimed it would not affect support for the remount in the Department of Agriculture. Nonetheless, in the words of one Nebraska newspaper, the "wind is blowing away from Fort Robinson" along with hopes for continued remount activities there. Remaining stocks of army horses were classified surplus by the USDA and sent to Fort Reno for sale under sealed bid; other horses were sold at Fort Robinson in 1949.[44]

Supporters of continued remount operations at Fort Robinson expressed their dismay and concern. They believed horse breeders "should be entitled to help from the Government in a manner similar to [that] which is provided in other phases of agriculture."[45] Despite the assurances of agriculture officials, western horsemen were not optimistic about the continuation of the remount program, either under army or civilian control. One Panhandle rancher spoke for all the horse interests declaring, "Unless the Government retains these fine stallions and brood mares, there is no chance for the small breeder and rancher in this part of the country to improve the blood line of his horses." Regardless of protests, the USDA joined with the University of Nebraska Agricultural Experiment Station to use Fort Robinson for cattle research, not horse breeding activities. The fort had a "million-dollar" veterinary laboratory that could be used for research on bovine diseases. In April 1949 the university and the Bureau of Animal Industry signed a memorandum of understanding for cooperative investigations at Fort Robinson.[46]

For the dwindling number of military remount people still at the post, the last months were both melancholy and filled with hard duty. Sadness about the end of the army remount briefly subsided when the Blizzard of 1949 blew in. The storm was reminiscent of the harsh winter conditions the soldiers faced when they first came to White River back in 1874. Capt. Lee Hill, the army's last post commander, recalled:

> Mother nature offered the military one last chance to be of service to our civilian neighbors in Crawford and the ranch-ers and farmers surrounding the fort. That reason was the terrible blizzard of January 1949 which left the area covered

with 41 inches of snow on the ground, all area roads completely closed and with temperatures that dropped 30 degrees below zero at times. On 3 January all heavy equipment
available at the fort was placed into operation and until 23
February most units were operated on a 24 hour basis, many
roads had to be reopened a number of times due to drifting
snow. I might add that the equipment operators were officers
(including myself), enlisted men and civilian employees of
the fort working 12 hour shifts. We received many kind
words of thanks for our efforts.

During the height of the storm one soldier headed to work and made it
thirty feet from his quarters before fear of losing his way caused him to
return, "so that's one time I did not report for duty." For others the blizzard
delayed transfer to other stations for weeks.[47]

By April 1949 only thirteen military personnel remained at Fort
Robinson: three officers, nine sergeants, and one corporal. In early May
the troops shipped Dakota and Renzo, the last two Olympic jumping
horses at Robinson, to Fort Riley, Kansas, for retirement. Later that month
remount soldiers prepared several riding horses for transfer to the Forest
Service in Colorado. At a final sale on June 9, 126 brood mares, stallions,
and colts were sold, realizing a total of $91,425. About eight hundred
buyers and spectators attended, including Colonel Ireland and Col. James
"Jumping Jimmy" Adamson, post commander in the prewar years.[48]

By July the soldiers at Fort Robinson were gone. As the last representative of the army, Hill was responsible for closing military operations and
the final transfer of the post to the USDA. Hill did all he could to cooperate
with the new occupants, and even "disced land for grass seeding to
increase our grazing area." Hill departed in December and effectively
"closed the gate" for the army remount. The beef research phase of Fort
Robinson's history had begun.[49]

Much of the early USDA effort was centered on the conversion of the
remount depot to a research station. The facility formally became known
as the Fort Robinson Beef Cattle Research Station with Russell L. Davis the
first superintendent. Initial research concentrated on the genetic improvement of beef cattle; eventually the work expanded into research on
reproductive problems and nutrition management studies. All efforts at
the station had an ultimate goal of improving range beef production. As
the 1950s began, Crawford citizens were optimistic and were "interested
in seeing old Fort Robinson put to a useful purpose in assisting the beef
cattle industry of Nebraska."[50]

The USDA furnished the facility and necessary coordination, and the university provided the livestock. Both agencies contributed scientific staff, labor, supplies, and equipment. The research program was part of the North Central-1, Improvement of Beef Cattle through Breeding Methods project (NC-1), a cooperative project of twelve north-central state experiment stations and the Department of Agriculture. One scientist described Fort Robinson as a research laboratory "where scientists and technicians are more likely to be found wearing blue jeans than white frocks and handling cattle instead of test tubes."[51]

Research cattle, eventually nearly two thousand head, came from various sources. Midwestern ranchers donated purebred bulls and heifers to the university, and various foundations provided outright and matching grants for livestock purchases. Some stock was leased from local breeders to increase the station herd. To hold the growing numbers, the reservation was divided into more than thirty pastures to control the breeding groups. The former stable area was converted into feedlots for nutrition studies.[52]

The beef research program required substantially fewer employees than did quartermaster remount operations. Cattle did not need the level of care and training provided to thoroughbred horses. The station staff normally consisted of six scientists and technical personnel, plus twelve other workers. Most of the employees moved into quarters on officers' row. During much of Davis's superintendency, work proceeded on the development of beef lines suitable for both range and Corn Belt conditions. Cows were separated into groups of twenty or thirty with two or more bulls; about one-quarter of the herd was Angus and the remainder Herefords. In the early days, the Fort Robinson herd comprised one-fourth of the total number of cattle used for experimental breeding in the NC-1 project. By 1961 Fort Robinson was touted as the world's largest research station devoted exclusively to the improvement of beef cattle through breeding.[53]

Most of the operational costs of the program were reimbursed from sales of surplus cattle raised at the station. With the cattle being furnished by the state, sales income could be returned to a revolving fund to defray the cost of their production. If the federal government owned and sold the cattle, then the proceeds would have to be deposited in the U.S. Treasury and operating funds provided by appropriation. Another benefit of stock sales was that they returned superior blooded bulls to area herds. The Animal Research Administration felt it was obligated to make this stock available to local ranchers to improve their production.[54]

All in all, it was a wise and effective policy, but one that met with considerable opposition. Some local ranchers criticized the USDA and university for raising "tax-free beef." Purebred breeders opposed station sales, claiming the practice represented unfair competition with private enterprise. One particularly opinionated rancher held a dim view of the "real values" of the station, declaring it was "carrying on self-perpetuating operations in direct competition" to purebred producers in the area. Opposition also came from operators of the Crawford sale barn. Nevertheless, surplus sales continued to generate a major portion of the station's total operating budget.[55]

A popular educational service of the beef research program was its annual Cattlemen's Roundup field day. Beginning in the early 1950s roundups featured special speakers, demonstrations, and tours to explain procedures and results gained through the research process. Each year hundreds of ranchers attended and received "reports on problems of breeding and management that affects beef production." Practical demonstrations on farm and ranch safety and sessions on conservation were also presented. One program featured a demonstration to show how farm tractors could upset when they were driven too fast on rough terrain or were improperly hitched. The special tractor was driven by "Jughead," a dummy who "will give his head that others may learn."[56]

In the mid-1950s the Soil Conservation Service established a training center at the Fort Robinson station. The center provided selected SCS personnel with a better understanding of the principles of soil and water conservation, as well as advanced training to veteran employees and education on public speaking. One of five operated by the SCS nation-wide, the center was housed in Comanche Hall, where classrooms, a dormitory area, and dining facilities were available for western states trainees. Groups of twenty-four students in agriculture from Turkey, Indonesia, Rhodesia, and other countries attended four-week sessions at the center to study soil conservation and instructional methods. Range management conferences were also held periodically.[57]

After the beef research program had been firmly established at Fort Robinson, one superintendent proudly welcomed a group of visiting dignitaries with the assurance, "History has been recorded at Fort Robinson for three-quarters of a century. However, we are no longer fighting Indians or settling the West. Today and tomorrow Fort Robinson is dedicated to recording history in another area through research to serve the Nation."[58] The beef research program at the fort had its own agenda, carefully guarded by officials of the USDA and the University of Nebraska. To them, the historical significance of Fort Robinson's past was a mere footnote for the future. But a new era of Fort Robinson history was at hand that began with what a former research administrator deemed "The Battle of Fort

Robinson." The battle lines were drawn early in 1950 with the release of the first surplus building list.

When the army left Fort Robinson, the USDA inherited some two hundred buildings and structures on the military reservation and Wood Reserve. More than 150 were in the main post area, including sixteen sets of officers' quarters, two troop barracks, thirteen noncommissioned officers' quarters, thirteen stables, eighteen garages, and a vast array of other support buildings including kennels, hay sheds, magazines, and chicken coops. There were far more living and working facilities than the beef research operation could ever hope to utilize.[59]

In April 1950 the USDA announced that several buildings would soon be declared surplus. Late the next year, ninety-four buildings, including both of the brick barracks and the post hospital, were in fact surplused for subsequent removal. Only the living quarters to be occupied by staff members would be retained. Because the buildings were government property, they were turned over to the General Services Administration for disposal. Beef research administrator Marvel Baker explained the dilemma:

> [T]here are a number of other buildings which properly may be considered surplus. These buildings generally are in such disrepair or of such obsolete design that it is doubtful if their renovation for most uses would be economical.[60]

One evident and pressing problem was that most of the buildings sat empty and neglected. There was no further need for a post bakery, commissary, hospital, guardhouse, or barracks for hundreds of soldiers. Frugal appropriations for operation of the experiment station at Fort Robinson made no allowances for maintenance of the buildings actually being used, much less those standing vacant; consequently, many buildings deteriorated. Station supervisor Davis urged their removal, declaring the excess buildings a king-size financial headache, unnecessary to the beef breeding project, and "a fire hazard as long as they remain standing." University Chancellor R. G. Gustavson and other agriculture officials supported Davis's views, declaring the empty and neglected buildings added to "the difficulty of keeping the place presentable."[61]

A public outcry over what some considered senseless demolition of valuable government property surfaced shortly after the surplus list was announced. Some felt that surplusing the buildings would benefit only a few salvage contractors. Others, including Congressman Miller, were upset at the idea of the USDA destroying buildings that could still be used.

In particular, the proposed destruction of the two brick barracks and the substantial post hospital was seen as a needless waste. One of the more vocal opponents was Gene Kemper, publisher of the *Alliance Daily Times-Herald*. His January 1952 editorial, "The Crime of Fort Robinson," fueled the fires of the growing opposition. He wrote, "It is regrettable that the federal government, which has joined the University of Nebraska in making use of the fort's lands for a beef experimental station, couldn't have found some better use for the buildings than leaving them idle."[62]

Despite such protests, the GSA announced the surplus buildings would be put up for bid on March 28. Opposition leaders and the Western Nebraska United Chambers of Commerce (WNUCC) quickly organized a tour to examine the "worthless" buildings slated for demolition. Sixty Panhandle residents made the tour, and afterward voted to "go all the way to Washington" to prevent the buildings' destruction.[63] With urging from the Nebraska congressional delegation, the GSA granted a sixty-day reprieve on the sale and also reduced the number of buildings on the list to eighty-five. One month later both the USDA and GSA agreed to postpone the sale for one year until the state could find alternative uses for the surplus structures. Proponents of saving fort buildings hailed the news as the "best we've heard in months." The race began to find some feasible, alternative use for the buildings before the beef research administration managed to dispose of them.[64]

Another outspoken critic of USDA demolition was Harold Cook, son of the famous frontiersman, Captain James Cook. The younger Cook had served at the fort as a CCC work supervisor in the 1930s. Like a number of area ranchers, he was bitterly opposed to the beef research activities at the historic fort, but Cook also supported other uses of fort facilities that would keep it intact. He asked his state senator with particular vitriol, "WHY, in Heaven's name, should we NOW permit BONEHEADS,—with NO VISION, [to] wantonly DESTROY all this,—as those now in charge there seem determined to accomplish."[65] Besides individuals, statewide groups such as the Nebraska Jaycees and the Nebraska Federation of Women's Clubs voiced opposition to the demolition.

A driving force in the movement to save the fort was Crawford businessman W. Lloyd Pipher. Pipher also had a personal attachment to the post, having worked there from 1939 to 1947 as the civil service property clerk. As president of the Crawford Chamber of Commerce and the WNUCC, Pipher mobilized the press and public in an attempt to halt the "complete devastation of the fort complex and lands." On the local level, Pipher, Cook, Kemper, and State Senator Monroe Bixler joined forces with others to find some use for the surplus post buildings.[66]

There were obvious sentimental reasons for preserving fort buildings, but there were other considerations as well. The popular movement to save the fort followed an agenda deeply rooted in the traditional Crawford/Fort Robinson relationship. The local economy still suffered from the loss of the military income that area citizens had grown used to. Finding an alternative use for fort facilities would doubtless boost the local economy. The prospect of employee salaries and the increased need for goods and services of an additional entity at the fort besides the USDA recalled the old "post town" days, when the citizens always called for more troops. The destruction of buildings at Fort Robinson would certainly limit potential for alternative uses and their related economic benefits for the local community.

The alternative uses suggested for the vacant fort buildings were varied, both in application and practicality. In 1950 rumors reached Nebraska that the Quartermaster Corps was looking for a site for a new research center. Although Governor Val Peterson urged the army to consider the fort's ample facilities, nothing came of it.[67] For a while consideration was given to using the barracks and hospital as a home for "seniles" that were overcrowding eastern Nebraska state mental hospitals. Kemper made short work of the proposal, urging that the west could do better than "furnish landscape for their castoffs."[68] Bixler favored a two-year agriculture school, somewhat naively declaring that "all that would be needed would be to move in a faculty."[69] The American Legion suggested a home for veterans. In a throwback to another age, it was suggested that a National Guard training center could be established at the fort. In fact, since the early 1950s the Nebraska guard had leased and periodically used the old rifle range for target practice.

There was even some hope for a partial return of the regular army to Fort Robinson. The Korean conflict brought interest in a revitalized army K-9 training program. In August 1950 Captain Hill visited the fort on an official tour of dormant army posts, inspecting their suitability for emergency dog training, and also for possible pack mule training and distribution. Hill stressed his visit was no indication such a program would be set up at the fort, but he did think K-9 activity could be resumed without disturbing USDA operations. Two years later the army again investigated Fort Robinson for a possible return of the K-9 Corps. Although the subject was a hot topic in 1952 and other army inspectors scouted the fort, nothing came of the idea.[70]

In a change of strategy, western Nebraska state legislators introduced a resolution urging the fort property be transferred to the state of Nebraska. By this means the state could control the surplus buildings and use them for any purpose designated by the legislature. In May 1953 the resolution passed by a 40-0 vote. Earlier a bill to transfer the fort to the state had been introduced in the U.S. House of Representatives by Congressman A. L. Miller, but in November Miller reported to his constituents that he doubted sufficient support could be mustered to gain the bill's passage. Apparently Nebraska Senator Hugh Butler did not support the transfer. Reportedly, he called the chairman of the Agriculture Committee and said, "I want that damned bill put on the bottom of the pile and kept there." Butler is, however, remembered for his strong support of the beef research program.[71]

While this was going on, the beef research staff was solidly opposed to any outside use of their facility, in particular any use of the surplus buildings that would interfere with the research program. Superintendent Davis bluntly told the Chamber of Commerce group touring the buildings that USDA "has no idea" of turning over the ownership of the property to anyone else.[72] The USDA believed its opposition to outside use was fully justified—research by dedicated scientists could not be conducted in an atmosphere where outside activity might interfere. Marvel Baker, associate director for the university experiment station wrote, "You can imagine what would happen to the breeding project if the gate were left open and a bull from another group were to get into the pen. That would simply mean an entire year's work was lost."[73]

Beef research officials were adamant about resisting any transfer of Fort Robinson property from federal to state ownership. University staff feared that under state control, their operation would lose the considerable funding provided by the USDA. Congressman Miller refuted their claim, stating he had been assured that the agriculture department would continue its funding whether or not the fort was under state or federal ownership. In the spring of 1953 the transfer issue brought spirited debate in Nebraska state government.[74]

Throughout the controversy, interest grew in allowing some historical and recreational activities on part of the old post. When the fort was transferred to the Department of Agriculture, some thought that land along Soldier Creek should be turned over to the state as a recreational fishing area. Several years later Bixler visited with Nebraska Game, Forestation, and Parks Commission secretary Paul Gilbert about the feasibility of converting the fort area into a national park. He stressed the scenic beauty and historical significance of Fort Robinson—for the first time the idea of preserving the fort because of its history came into play. Citing the best of both worlds, one reporter commented, "Fort Robinson's buildings stand today a solid reminder of the past and a present challenge to the imagination."[75] Harold Cook was quick to make comparisons between what might be developed at Fort Robinson and the highly successful Custer State Park in the Black Hills of South Dakota. He thoughtfully noted that taxpayers already had paid for everything at Fort Robinson.[76]

In April 1953 Governor Robert Crosby appointed representatives of the Nebraska State Historical Society and the Nebraska Game, Forestation, and Parks Commission to a special committee on Fort Robinson. The committee was to study the possibility of combining the beef research use of the area with recreational and historical uses. Predictably, the committee report supported additional public use of Fort Robinson. A supplemental report by James C. Olson, director of the society, recommended an immediate halt to any further plans to dispose of surplus buildings, and urged that efforts be made to maintain as much of the historical integrity of the fort as possible. In support of the committee's findings, a western Nebraska newspaper editorialized on joint usage of the fort:

> It is a decision that must be made now, or within a few months, not 50 years hence when perhaps an older, more mature state might wish there had been the vision 50 years earlier to take full advantage of the opportunity to preserve a site which possesses such magnificent recreational possibilities.[77]

Cook stood firmly behind the proposal, exalting the opportunity to preserve and develop the fort's historical and recreational possibilities along practical lines. However, some game commission commissioners, including one from the Panhandle, openly opposed state park activities at Fort Robinson, believing the state already had more parks than it could support.[78] Although the beef research program remained, and even grew more possessive, support for joint usage gained momentum.

At this time the surplus sale threat reappeared. Even though an August meeting between Pipher, Davis, and Dr. T. C. Byerly, chief of the Bureau of Animal Husbandry, brought agreement that no brick buildings, housing, or buildings of historical value would be declared surplus, the GSA proceeded with the sale.[79] In November the Kansas City office of the GSA received only a single bid of $10,863 for the surplus buildings. The bid was rejected as "hopelessly inadequate" and the buildings were readvertised after a sixty-day delay. In January 1954, under pressure from Representative Miller, the GSA agreed to delay the sale.[80]

Beginning in 1954 the university changed its attitude toward outside use of its Fort Robinson station. Until then, university officials had frowned on the idea of having tourists visit the fort, contending that "people and controlled experiments with animals don't mix."[81] Credit for this change of policy is due to Clifford Hardin, who replaced Gustavson as chancellor. Hardin recommended that the state historical society be permitted to develop and operate a museum on the fort grounds to interpret its history, the same idea suggested by the governor's 1953 committee report. His recommendation became a reality on November 2, 1955, when the society was granted a revocable permit for museum operations. The western press praised Hardin for his intervention in a difficult situation. Monroe Bixler hailed the change in policy, declaring, "with the appointment of University Chancellor Clifford Hardin, the major problems have resolved themselves . . . he has aided us a lot in the solution of the Fort Robinson problem."[82]

Also in 1954 Dr. Robert Koch replaced Russell Davis as station superintendent. Koch, who "possesses excellent human qualities," was also a talented and capable animal scientist. As superintendent, he advanced the technical work of the station and also managed to improve relations between the warring parties over fort usage.[83]

In addition to a museum, plans were developed to use some of the surplus quarters for park facilities. The historical society and game commission asked the legislature for $130,644 to develop a "multipurpose tourist center" at Fort Robinson. To some state senators this was a hefty sum to expend on what might be seen as nonessential state projects; Senator Hal Bridenbaugh, chairman of the budget committee, thought the matter needed more study and warned, "the state must be careful how it sets precedents in developing such a park."[84] But in the late spring of 1955, LB 545 passed, granting the society $36,644 to establish a western branch museum at the fort, and $94,000 to the game commission to begin park operations. Cook wrote his longtime friend, Col. Edwin Hardy, that the old fort was saved "from the VANDALS who were bent on wrecking and destroying it" without consideration for other uses.[85]

Initially, the historical society explored the idea of using the post hospital to house its museum. But society officials feared the large building would be too expensive to operate and it was in a poor location on the far west end of the main post area.[86] About this time the USDA decided to move its administrative offices from the former post headquarters building to Comanche Hall, and the historical society agreed to take over the headquarters building for its museum. In addition to being smaller than the hospital, the headquarters building was centrally located, and the new museum would be situated next to the highway on a site that would keep visiting tourists away from research areas of the post. Roger T.

Grange, recently on the staff of the Chicago Natural History Museum, was appointed museum curator and immediately began work with the society's Lincoln staff to prepare exhibits.

The USDA agreed to allow the game commission to use the row of original 1874–75 officers' quarters for tourist cabins, and the commission also received the east brick barracks to be remodeled into hotel-type accommodations. By allowing the commission the use of those buildings for visitor lodging, tourist activities would again be centered on the more publicly-accessible part of the station. Several years later, the University of Nebraska State Museum opened a natural history museum in the old post gymnasium on the highway through the fort.[87]

By 1956 work progressed on the headquarters building museum and on renovating the old officers' quarters. The beef research administration had fulfilled their obligations to make concessions for other uses, which grew to include fishing and hiking in certain areas. At the same time the USDA succeeded in protecting its sensitive research operations. To the apparent satisfaction of both sides, the Battle of Fort Robinson was over. The issue of joint usage had been resolved, and preservation assured for some of the fort buildings on the surplus list.

By late spring the Fort Robinson museum was ready for visitors. To celebrate its opening the Crawford Chamber of Commerce planned a large celebration, with appropriate ceremonies and a free barbecue. Several hundred area residents cleaned up the grounds, removed dead trees, and in the words of Superintendent Koch, really "made the debris fly." The opening of the museum was heralded as yet another new era in the history of the old post.[88]

As many as ten thousand visitors attended the June 3 dedication, several thousand more than anticipated. Dignitaries included Governor Victor Anderson and James H. Red Cloud, second cousin of the original Chief Red Cloud. A band played, speeches were made, and several of the officers' quarters, then being converted to tourist cabins, were opened for public inspection. Governor Anderson told the crowd, "I assure you I want to make this one of the best historical and tourist attractions of Nebraska." At the same time, however, posted notices on the west barracks and hospital informed visitors that those buildings would soon be salvaged.[89]

In the end a new regulation permitted surplus property, including buildings, to be transferred from General Services Administration back to the originating agency for disposal. Control over the surplus fort buildings reverted to the USDA, and in April, the department placed seventy-one buildings, including "seven brick and concrete buildings," up for sale.

Western Development Disposal Corporation, owned by Clive Short of Chadron, bid $3,000 for salvage rights; on June 30 his bid was accepted. Immediately after the museum dedication celebration, Short began demolition of the west barracks, spurring a last-ditch effort to save the imposing, but doomed brick hospital building. He offered to sell the hospital if the WNUCC and others could come up with $1,500. Just as efforts got underway to raise the money, the USDA announced its refusal to break Short's demolition contract. Ruling that Short had an irrevocable contract, the USDA dashed any further hopes of saving the hospital or other surplus buildings.[90]

By the end of 1956 the west barracks, hospital, and many of the other seventy-one buildings were gone, including all six of the 1891 officers' quarters, the colt and two-year- old stables, the post guardhouse, and the elaborate depot stallion stable. The beef research administration were finally free of what they considered an unnecessary burden, and also a threat to their control of the research station. Ultimately, the demolition caused bitter feelings on the part of many local residents and returning veterans who had served at Fort Robinson.

Park operations at Fort Robinson opened in September 1957. The USDA's system of issuing revocable permits to the game commission and historical society gave the beef research program firm control over the fort. Years later Bob Koch recalled the difficulties of joint usage, a period of fort history when "there seemed to be quite a difference of opinion as to the extent of activities that should be involved." Simply put, "Two people can't run the same operation." Nevertheless, the course leading to Fort Robinson's ultimate destiny had been set.[91]

By the early 1960s Fort Robinson was described as one of the best equipped and staffed agricultural experiment stations in the country. In spite of what the USDA saw as a continual barrage of "unreasonable and sometimes dishonest harassment," their work provided the beef cattle industry with a steady stream of useful information. On the other hand, those who had opposed the demolition of fort buildings viewed the beef research occupation of Fort Robinson in a different light. A full decade after the Battle of Fort Robinson broke out, Kemper still accused the USDA of being "a selfish neighbor, a terrible housekeeper, a bumbling merchant and an unworthy caretaker of the hallowed ground that is Fort Robinson."[92]

The removal of fort buildings was controversial, but one that needs to be viewed in context. In retrospect, several points overlooked by opponents were key to the removal decision. The beef research agencies never had enough funding to maintain buildings surplus to their needs, and demolition opponents were less than realistic about which surplus buildings were really usable. Many of the demolished buildings would have been considered incidental to any plan for preserving and using the post area for historical and tourism purposes. Demolished buildings that would have been significant in future interpretive efforts, such as the 1892 guardhouse and 1906 bakery, were never mentioned as part of the "preserving the fort" issue. What were considered the two major building losses, the hospital and west barracks, had not been requested by the state agencies wanting joint usage with the USDA. Even though many buildings were lost, structures from every period of the fort survived. In the mid-1950s there was no possibility of obtaining funds to preserve the entire fort complex, a goal that might be impossible to achieve even today.

Throughout its history Fort Robinson's changing roles determined its physical layout and the facilities it required. The demolition of old, unneeded buildings was really nothing new. The cycle of building removal dates from the early 1900s, when the army demolished almost all of the original Indian wars-era post, including the guardhouse where Crazy Horse was killed in 1877. The process continued in 1930–32, when some twenty-five buildings were salvaged. After World War II several war period buildings that were once important to fort operations were declared surplus and removed. Fort Robinson was a dynamic institution, with a physical appearance that evolved over time as it faced new missions and challenges.

Chapter 8

The Evolution of a State Park

The 1956 museum dedication ushered in a new period of preservation and public recreational use for Fort Robinson. With beef research firmly established, and fledgling park and museum operations in place, all the parties appeared satisfied. Even though concerns relating to joint usage had apparently been resolved, another period of "warfare" at Fort Robinson soon broke out between its long-term occupants and the new tenants.

At this critical juncture, the onsite administrators for the university beef research station and the game and parks commission were both "aggressive gentlemen," equally devoted to their respective missions. Station superintendent James E. Ingalls, a dedicated stockman, joined the beef research staff at Fort Robinson in February 1956 and replaced Koch as superintendent in 1957. The same year, John C. Kurtz was appointed the first superintendent of Fort Robinson State Park, and enjoyed the strong support of game commission director Melvin O. Steen. Ingalls was intent on building a cattle breeding and research operation; Kurtz pursued recreational and tourist development with determined enthusiasm. That problems would arise between the superintendents was, in the words of one observer, "perhaps inevitable."[1]

Clashes over use of Fort Robinson soon surfaced. Although the disputes with Kurtz were relatively minor, Ingalls believed they could seriously disrupt the beef research program. Disagreements over fishing access, animals (Ingalls did not want riding horses kept in the stable areas), hunting, trespassing, and nonapproved remodeling of buildings led some university officials to question the limits of park development. If further concessions were made, the beef research staff feared the game and parks commission would "inch by inch, get the University out," a strategy Kurtz seemed to be pursuing.[2]

Since 1955 the game commission had held revocable permits to use the 1874–75 officers' row, east barracks, swimming pool, and tennis courts, along with access to the butte area for trail rides. After receiving complaints from university staff, the USDA decided to revoke the permit. On July 1, 1959, the USDA advised Steen that park operations had been unsatisfactory and the permit would be revoked in ninety days. At the end of that period, Steen was to meet with Ingalls to discuss how recreational activities could be conducted at Fort Robinson in a "fully satisfactory manner." Only then would the Animal Research Service consider granting the new permit. Some university agriculture officials thought another option was to remove park superintendent Kurtz, "a must if we are to have any peace," but Kurtz remained.[3]

The controversy drew responses from across the state. Those interested in park development saw the USDA charges as phony and easily refuted. On the other hand, the beef research staff maintained that if the game commission wanted to remain at the fort, it must abide by the terms of the permit. Stock growers supported beef research, voicing concern that recreation would interfere with USDA efforts. People wanting outdoor recreation could go to Chadron State Park or the Black Hills. Recreational interests formed the Fort Robinson Association to show support for the park, preservation of fort buildings, and enlargement of park facilities.

Park development at Fort Robinson drew strong support from the Nebraska Legislature's Committee on Outdoor Recreation, which had been created to study and make recommendations on projects throughout the state and specifically explore the potential for future recreation opportunities at Fort Robinson. In November 1959 the committee heard testimony from both sides, and concluded there was a definite lack of cooperation between the parties. Predictably, committee members also felt that the USDA should give more consideration to state interests.[4]

The legislative committee's report evidently spurred reconciliation between park and beef research officials. In late November 1959 the USDA reinstated the ninety-day permit and later extended it indefinitely. In a further show of cooperation, beef research administrators declared they would impose no unusual conditions on park use and would make every effort to solve problems. Park interests saw the permit renewal as a sign that the public wanted expanded park and museum activities at the fort. But the outdoor recreation committee was apprehensive about spending money on tourist and museum projects as long as the use permits could be revoked. One solution was to ask the USDA to transfer the buildings used by the game commission and historical society, and their adjoining tracts of land, to state control.[5]

The revocable use permits enabled the beef research program to maintain physical control of the fort and made it clear the state was a guest. But for various reasons the time seemed right for an important concession to park development. In a December 1960 meeting at the fort, T. C. Byerly, chief of the Bureau of Animal Husbandry, agreed to the transfer of the buildings then under revocable permit, and recommended that the Department of Agriculture not oppose the transfer. In March 1962 Governor Frank B. Morrison asked the Department of the Interior to transfer seventy-seven acres of land adjoining the state-use buildings, including the 1874 parade ground and the Red Cloud Agency site, to Nebraska for park purposes. In due time the transaction was executed under the Federal Property and Administrative Services Act of 1949, and the land was deeded to the state in fee title. There was an underlying reason why such a change in philosophy had even been considered. Unbeknownst to some of the concerned parties, a Pentagon decision several years earlier ultimately resolved the conflicts over the use of Fort Robinson.[6]

In 1959 the Department of Defense announced the abandonment of the sprawling Naval Ammunition Depot at Hastings in south-central Nebraska. With thousands of acres of surplus land and facilities soon to be available, the USDA had considered establishing an animal research center there. Due to a lack of funding the plan fell through. In November 1962 Nebraska officials went to Washington to encourage the government to proceed with building the new center. Although it was to be a federal project, the university agriculture staff agreed to fully support and participate in the endeavor. By 1963 the Animal Research Service had been authorized to proceed with planning for the project. On June 16, 1964, Secretary of Agriculture Orville Freeman officially announced the establishment of the Meat Animal Research Center to be located near Clay Center, Nebraska, on the eastern edge of the depot.[7]

The Clay Center site would enable the beef research program to consolidate and strengthen its work on beef cattle and expand research to include swine and sheep, bringing scattered activities together. The area around Hastings included both crop and grazing land and afforded "endless permutations and combinations" for agricultural research.[8] University officials quickly realized that the USDA would not support two major animal experiment stations in the same state, and that government support would certainly go to the Clay Center project. More programs could be pursued there than at Fort Robinson. The days of the beef research station at Fort Robinson appeared to be numbered.

Naturally, the decision was opposed by many western cattlemen. At a public meeting in Crawford on February 16, 1963, university officials announced the proposed center and explained that the research station at Robinson would eventually be closed. Ranchers who had quietly supported beef research at the fort suddenly came to life. Some felt the proposed move was a political sellout and that closing the station and turning over the fort to the game and parks commission was a result of "dirty politics." Others were skeptical that a program at Clay Center could replace the Fort Robinson operation and wanted it continued even without USDA support. Several animal husbandry staff from the University of Nebraska were equally distressed over the termination of a fifteen-year research program. One warned, "If Fort Robinson is allowed to disappear from the inventory of research facilities now and suitable range research is not developed elsewhere, the University may have to live with this unfavorable image for a long while."[9]

Nor did the possibility of turning the entire fort into a state park meet with universal approval. Ranchers wanted the reservation lands returned to private ownership and put back on the tax rolls. Some Chadron residents, fearing for their own state park, did not favor having two large state parks in the same county, only twenty-five miles apart. They worried that both parks would suffer from inadequate funding.[10]

Even with the eventual departure of the beef research program on the horizon, the wars at Fort Robinson continued. Soon after park operations began in 1957, articles began to appear in state newspapers and regional publications advocating recreational use of the fort, and the petty bickering between superintendents and agencies also made its way into the press. Small skirmishes that should have been settled locally drew statewide attention. Disagreements about roads, livestock, tree removal flag ceremonies, and flagpoles marked the 1960s at Fort Robinson. The pressure for increased recreational use mounted as the USDA phase-out moved closer to reality.

In August 1965 Secretary Freeman met with Governor Frank B. Morrison and state senators to find a means to "de-accelerate the war at Fort Robinson." The outgrowth of the meeting was the formation of the Fort Robinson Advisory Committee to include representatives of the USDA, the university, the game and parks commission, and the governor's office. The committee met periodically to hear grievances and make recommendations. In 1966 the committee chair wrote to the USDA, stating that most of the problems at the fort were due to the "childish manner" of handling disputes between superintendents. In response, the USDA suggested transferring Kurtz and Ingalls to other assignments. As a result of these recommendations, Ingalls left in September; Kurtz, however, remained.[11]

In 1967 R. Dean Humphrey was appointed superintendent of the beef research station. As the USDA gradually moved out, controversy between the fiesty park superintendent and beef research staff continued. This round of infighting drew in several hundred local ranchers, dissatisfied with game commission policies, who threatened to close their lands to public hunting if Kurtz were not replaced. In September 1968, John Kurtz, who had supervised park operations with the "zeal of [an] Evangelist," was reassigned, to be replaced by Vince Rotherham, transferred from Niobrara State Park.[12]

During the transition, the issue of who would control the ten-thousand-acre Wood Reserve was settled. Park supporters had long advocated having the former military reserve turned over to the state for recreation. In 1959 the game commission bluntly told state legislators that the beef research station was not making good use of the reserve and the land should be turned over to the commission. By 1965 plans were being made to transfer the land to the U.S. Forest Service. Early in 1967 an agreement with the Forest Service allowed access and grazing rights for beef research as long as needed. Even though the game and parks commission did not gain control of the land, it was now available for public use.

Although the game commission was anxious to get possession of the entire fort, the USDA was deliberate in its withdrawl of beef research operations. The move to Clay Center was projected to be completed by early 1966, but appropriations had to be secured and facilities prepared for the new operation. The year 1966, however, did see the beginning of the first of many shipments of cattle from Fort Robinson to Clay Center. A 1970 departure date was announced, but delayed again, ostensibly because of the conflict in Vietnam. According to one beef research observer, as "time rolled along, it seemed that pressure against Beef Research accelerated in tune with progress at the new Hastings [*sic*] site."[13] As beef research operations were gradually phased out, the USDA turned over fort buildings to state agencies. The brick officers quarters and part of the 1887 row were made available to the state, and in 1970 more buildings excess to station needs were transferred.

The last surplus bull sale was held October 29, 1971, conducted by former station superintendent Bob Koch; fifty-one Hereford bulls were sold. On December 28 the last of the research cattle were moved to Clay Center. In early 1972 Governor J. James Exon signed the permit for transfer of the Fort Robinson property to the state of Nebraska. By this time superintendent Dean Humphrey was the only beef research employee at the fort, and he was immediately released to move to Clay Center. After twenty-four years, the era of beef research activity had come to a close.

Fort Robinson provided the USDA and the university College of Agriculture with an opportunity to conduct important research and they made the most of it. Their work at Fort Robinson continues to influence the beef industry today. In the words of a credible observer, "No experimental station has contributed more to the improvement of the economy of beef production in a comparable period of time for such a low investment of tax funds."[14] But there were other benefits as well. The USDA years provided a viable public use for an abandoned military installation, the fort reservation remained intact, and a beneficial rangeland feed base was established. Finally, the USDA furnished an important link in the unbroken chain of Fort Robinson occupation.

Epilogue

On November 16, 1972, the Fort Robinson Military Reservation was officially transferred to the state of Nebraska for public park and recreational purposes. Because the reservation had mostly remained intact over the years, several fort and Red Cloud Agency historic sites had been preserved and were now made accessible to the public. Once again the mission of Fort Robinson changed. With full state park status finally achieved, the fort's value transcended its significance to northwestern Nebraska. The door was open for full recreational use of the property, and also for those who wanted to visit a site where dramatic historical events took place.

When it became increasingly evident that Nebraska would inherit Fort Robinson, park planning began in earnest. Enthusiastic park supporters predicted that the park was "on the brink of becoming one of the greatest recreation and historical areas in the West."[1] To explore those possibilities and opportunities, outdoor recreation students under Arthur T. Wilcox at Colorado State University worked for several years on a park development plan. Their final report, commonly called "The Wilcox Plan," was submitted to the game and parks commission in 1969. Although the report contained several controversial suggestions, such as moving the brick blacksmith and harness repair shops to a location closer to the parade ground, some of its proposals are reflected in present park activities and operations. Today, visitors to the park can stay in the old officers' quarters and east brick barracks, and participate in a full schedule of summer activities, while during the rest of the year the post serves as a base for outdoorsmen. As a state park administered by the Nebraska Game and Parks Commission, Fort Robinson continues to provide economic benefits to the local community, but not to the extent it did in the old army days, when hundreds of men were quartered there.

Since the beginning of its involvement at Fort Robinson in the 1950s, the Nebraska State Historical Society has always maintained that the fort is a resource to be preserved and protected. The society's Fort Robinson Museum actively collects artifacts and materials to document the fort's role in American history. In addition to the museum established in 1956, significant fort buildings not needed by the beef research station were transferred to the historical society for preservation and use as exhibit buildings. In 1957 the blacksmith and harness repair shops, which had remained virtually intact, were opened. Soon afterward, the wheelwright shop, then thought to be the oldest remaining frame building on the post, left USDA control. Beef research staff reductions made available one of the 1887 adobe officers' quarters for restoration. Several other buildings, including the 1908 veterinary hospital, were later turned over to the society for exhibits or preservation.

In other ways the Nebraska State Historical Society has sought to preserve and interpret the fort. The society initiated a program of interpretive markers throughout the building complex. Beginning in the late 1950s, the museum staff designated certain buildings and historic sites with wooden signs, later replaced with more durable metal markers. In 1958 the society began a series of archeological projects, the first identifying building sites at the Red Cloud Agency. Work on the old parade ground in 1966 and 1967 led to the reconstruction of the guardhouse and adjutant's office, two key structures involved in the death of Crazy Horse in 1877. In 1987–89 staff archeologists and volunteers excavated the site of the 1874 cavalry barracks where the Cheyenne Outbreak took place. The archeology has enabled the reconstruction of some of the most significant structures from Fort Robinson's past.

The transfer of the former military reservation lands to the state enabled the historical society to interpret other important sites away from the main post area, including the post cemetery and prisoner of war camp. Research collections at the Fort Robinson Museum have been used by numerous historians working on topics of military and Native American history spanning the fort's long period of use. Recognition of Fort Robinson's historical significance came in 1963 when the Department of the Interior designated it as a Registered National Historic Landmark, a designation that came too late to save many key post buildings.

On July 4, 1963, the first of many Fort Robinson veterans' reunions was held. The reunions were initially organized by local veterans Sgt. Steve Haseke, former remount soldier Ed Bieganski, and legendary horseman Bud Parker. Other early instigators were Jim Stratton, a remount trooper from Lance Creek, Wyoming, and Larry Norgard, who grew up at the post. The purpose of the "old soldiers' reunion" was to keep alive the spirit of Fort Robinson, a goal accomplished for more than thirty years. Reunions brought together former soldiers, civilian employees, and dependents from across the country, on one occasion including the former PW camp spokesman, Wolfgang Dorschel, who came from Germany.[2]

Of all the groups associated with Fort Robinson, military veterans perhaps have the most sentimental attachment. For many soldiers, Fort Robinson was their first duty station and the first time they had been away from home. Some, such as Homer Blank, Doug Topham, and Bieganski, joined the army and began long military careers at the post. Soldiers were married there and their children were born in the post hospital. While most twentieth-century military posts have been abandoned, veterans can return to Fort Robinson and leisurely revisit their old haunts. Many returning veterans maintain friendships with townspeople and have pleasant memories of the Crawford community.

Members of veterans' organizations have periodically returned to visit the post, including veterans of the Casual Dog Detachment sent into the China-Burma-India Theater. Many of these men initially received their K-9 training at the fort in 1943. Recently CCC veterans, prisoner of war camp staff and former PWs, and beef research personnel, have returned to commemorate their respective roles.

Area residents also have maintained a strong sentimental attachment to the fort, which was northwest Nebraska's oldest public institution, predating every town. Fort Robinson played a vital role in the settlement and development of the region and for generations of local citizens, it had always been there. Older residents fondly recall going to the fort for horse shows, polo matches, Quartermaster Day celebrations, and to visit military friends and dependents. They have vivid memories of vast horse herds, barking dogs, and the soldiers themselves, the last vestiges of the army on the upper Plains.

Crawford residents and neighboring civilians had more than just a sentimental attachment to the old fort. Fort Robinson made a huge impact on the town's economy, providing a source of steady income for merchants and welcomed employment for local workers. It provided security, entertainment, and education for the civilian population, and was a point of local pride for the recognition it brought the town. A Crawford editor summed it up when he wrote in the last army days, "Fort Robinson . . . has been looked upon by Crawford, as one of her greatest assets."[3]

As one looks across the vacant parade ground today, Bud Parker no longer takes jumps on Oliver, nor Sergeant Blank on Diamond Jim. The hillside once housing hundreds of dog kennels and the stable areas are quiet, devoid of the activity marking what was claimed to be the world's largest remount depot. The extensive feeding areas and scattered feed traps are commemorated only by crumbling concrete watering tanks and mounds that once were animal manure. Like Red Cloud, Crazy Horse, and the old army, much of the physical evidence of Fort Robinson's role has disappeared. But the contributions of those who served there during America's century live on.

Appendix A

Commanding Officers at Fort Robinson, 1900–1948

Compiled from Monthly Post Returns, Remount Depot Annual Reports,
and Monthly Information Letters.

Interims in italics

Jan. 1, 1900–Mar. 5, 1900	1st Lt. Edmund S. Wright, First Cavalry
Mar. 5, 1900–June 10, 1900	Capt. Peter S. Bomus, First Cavalry
May 15–30, 1900	*1st Lt. Edmund S. Wright*
June 10, 1900–July 21, 1900	1st Lt. Edmund S. Wright
July 21, 1900–Mar. 15, 1901	Capt. Harry E. Wilkins, Tenth Infantry
Aug. 1900	*1st Lt. George J. Holden, Tenth Infantry*
Mar. 15, 1901–Jan. 7, 1902	Maj. Ralph W. Hoyt, Tenth Infantry
Jan. 7, 1902–Apr. 20, 1902	Lt. Col. Earl D. Thomas, Thirteenth Cavalry
Apr. 20, 1902–May 10, 1902	Maj. Richard T. Yeatman, Twenty-second Infantry
May 10, 1902–June 10, 1902	Capt. Carter P. Johnson, Tenth Cavalry
June 10, 1902–Oct.14, 1902	Capt. Charles H. Grierson, Tenth Cavalry
Oct.14, 1902–Aug. 20, 1903	Col. Jacob A. Augur, Tenth Cavalry
Aug. 20, 1903–Nov. 10, 1903	Lt. Col. Otto L. Hein, Tenth Cavalry
Nov. 10, 1903–July 20, 1904	Col. Jacob A. Augur
Apr. 16–27, 1904	*Capt. Henry C. Whitehead, Tenth Cavalry*
July 20, 1904–Aug. 24, 1904	Capt. Charles H. Grierson
Sept. 24, 1904–Aug. 5, 1905	Col. Jacob A. Augur
Sept. 24–30, 1904	*Lt. Col. Otto L. Hein*
Aug. 5, 1905–Oct. 5, 1905	Maj. Charles H. Grierson
Oct. 5, 1905–July 16, 1906	Col. Jacob A. Augur
July 16, 1906–Sept. 23, 1906	Capt. Henry C. Whitehead
Sept. 23, 1906–Oct. 29, 1906	Capt. Harry L. Cavenaugh, Tenth Cavalry
Oct. 29, 1906–Nov. 15, 1906	Capt. Eugene P. Jervey, Jr., Tenth Cavalry
Nov. 15, 1906–Feb. 28, 1907	Col. Jacob A. Augur
Feb. 28, 1907–Mar. 28, 1907	Capt. Robert J. Fleming, Tenth Cavalry
Mar. 28, 1907–Apr. 19, 1907	Capt. Ellwood W. Evans, Eighth Cavalry
April 19, 1907–May 17, 1907	Lt. Col. Charles M. O'Connor, Eighth Cavalry

May 17, 1907–June 17, 1907	Capt. Robert J. Duff, Adj., Eighth Cavalry
June 17, 1907–July 13, 1908	Col. Henry P. Kingsbury, Eighth Cavalry
Aug. 20–Sept. 9, 1907	*1st Lt. Lawrence T. Carson, Eighth Cavalry*
May 4–June 11, 1908	*Lt. Col. Charles M. O'Connor*
July 19, 1908–Aug. 11, 1908	Capt. Thomas Q. Donaldson, Eighth Cavalry
Aug. 11, 1908–Sept. 2, 1908	Capt. Charles W. Farber, Eighth Cavalry
Sept. 2, 1908–June 30, 1910	Col. Henry P. Kingsbury
June 30, 1910–Aug. 16, 1910	Maj. Henry D. Ripley, Eighth Cavalry
Aug. 16, 1910–Oct. 31, 1910	Col. Henry P. Kingsbury
Oct. 31, 1910–Feb. 18, 1911	Capt. George E. Stockle, Eighth Cavalry
Feb. 18, 1911–Sept. 30, 1911	Col. George A. Dodd, Twelfth Cavalry
Apr. 9–May 12, 1911	*Lt.Col. Henry J. Goldman, Unassigned*
Sept. 30, 1911–Oct 7, 1911	Lt. Col. Henry J. Goldman
Oct. 7, 1911–Feb. 27, 1913	Col. Cunliffe H. Murray, Twelfth Cavalry
Feb. 27, 1913–April 16, 1913	Capt. Charles J. Symmonds, Twelfth Cavalry
April 16, 1913–Mar. 14, 1916	Col. Horatio G. Sickel, Twelfth Cavalry
Aug. 15–Sept. 16, 1914	*Capt. Lewis W. Case, Adj., Twelfth Cavalry*
March 14, 1916–Dec. 12, 1916	Maj. Carter P. Johnson, Eighth Cavalry, Ret.
Dec. 12, 1916–Mar. 24, 1919	Capt. Frank Nickerson, QMC, Ret.
Mar. 24, 1919–June 16, 1919	Capt. A. A. Merritt, QMC.

Fort Robinson/Robinson Quartermaster Depot

June 16, 1919–Oct. 13, 1919	Capt. Oliver L. Overmyer, QMC.
Oct. 13, 1919–Apr. 1, 1923	Lt. Col. Edward Calvert, QMC.
Apr. 1, 1923–Feb. 10, 1928	Capt. John T. Sallee, QMC.
Feb. 10, 1928–May 24, 1928	Maj. Sumner M. Williams, QMC.
May 24, 1928– Jan. 1, 1929	Lt. Col. William F. Morrison, Fourth Field Artillery
Jan. 1, 1929–Mar. 24, 1931	Lt. Col. Laurin L. Lawson, Fourth Field Artillery
Mar. 24, 1931–Oct. 10, 1931	Maj. Orville M. Moore, Fourth Field Artillery
Oct. 10, 1931–June 24, 1932	Maj. Sumner M. Williams
June 25, 1932– July 1, 1937	Lt. Col. Edwin N. Hardy, QMC.
July 1, 1937–Aug. 1, 1941	Maj. James M. Adamson, QMC.
Aug. 1, 1941–Mar. 1, 1942	Lt. Col. Edward M. Daniels, QMC.
Mar. 1, 1942–June 29, 1942	Lt. Col. Paul G. Kendall, QMC.

June 29, 1942 - Feb. 13, 1944	Lt. Col. Frank L. Carr, QMC
Feb. 13–25, 1944	*Maj. Walter Clayton, QMC.*
Feb. 25, 1944–Nov. 20, 1944	Col. Edward M. Daniels
Nov. 22, 1944–May 10, 1945	Maj. Ralph G. Kercheval, QMC.
May 10–20, 1945	Col. John L. Hornor, QMC.
May 20, 1945–Nov. 18, 1945	Col. Brisbane H. Brown, QMC.
Nov. 24, 1945–Feb. 22, 1947	Col. Thomas E. Whitehead, QMC.
Mar. 1–31, 1946	*Capt. Warren McKinney, QMC*
Feb. 22, 1947–May 22, 1947	Maj. Leo C. Cooksley, QMC.
May 23, 1947–July 1, 1948	Col. Edward W. Sawyer, QMC.

Agriculture Remount Service, Robinson Remount Depot

July 1, 1948–Aug. 26, 1948	Col. Edward W. Sawyer
Aug. 26, 1948–July 1, 1949	Capt. Lee O. Hill, QMC. (Loaned to USDA, July 1–Dec. 12, 1949)

Appendix B

Units Stationed at Fort Robinson, January 1900–December 1916

Compiled from Monthly Post Returns.

FS&B signifies "Field, Staff, and Band." F&S signifies "Field and Staff."
MGP signifies "Machine Gun Platoon." HQ TP signifies "Headquarters Troop."
Other letters are company or troop letters within the regiments.
Number is total monthly aggregate figure reported.

1900

January	A, C, L, First Cavalry	300
February	A, C, L, First Cavalry	308
March	A, C, L, First Cavalry	305
April	A, C, L, First Cavalry	299
May	A, C, L, First Cavalry	314
June	A, C, First Cavalry	219
July	M, Tenth Infantry	112
August	M, Tenth Infantry	117
September	M, Tenth Infantry	113
October	M, Tenth Infantry	113
November	M, Tenth Infantry	114
December	M, Tenth Infantry	114

1901

January	M, Tenth Infantry	113
February	M, Tenth Infantry	127
March	F, Tenth Infantry	78
April	F, Tenth Infantry	75
May	F, Tenth Infantry	75
June	F, Tenth Infantry	74
July	F, Tenth Infantry; B, D, Thirteenth Cavalry	242
August	F, Tenth Infantry; B, D, Thirteenth Cavalry	234
September	F, Tenth Infantry; B, D, Thirteenth Cavalry	226
October	F, Tenth Infantry; B, D, Thirteenth Cavalry	246
November	F, Tenth Infantry; B, D, Thirteenth Cavalry	224
December	F, Tenth Infantry; B, D, Thirteenth Cavalry; Twentieth Battery, Field Artillery	369

1902

January	B, D, Thirteenth Cavalry; Twentieth Battery, Field Artillery	296
February	B, D, Thirteenth Cavalry; Twentieth Battery, Field Artillery	292
March	B, D, Thirteenth Cavalry; Twentieth Battery, Field Artillery; A, D, Twenty-second Infantry	432
April	A, D, Twenty-second Infantry	126
May	A, B, C, D, I, K, L, M, FS&B, Tenth Cavalry	641
June	A, B, C, D, I, K, L, M, FS&B, Tenth Cavalry	667
July	A, B, C, D, I, K, L, M, FS&B, Tenth Cavalry	677
August	A, B, C, D, I, K, L, M, FS&B, Tenth Cavalry	679
September	A, B, C, D, I, K, L, M, FS&B, Tenth Cavalry	684
October	A, B, C, D, I, K, L, M, FS&B, Tenth Cavalry	675
November	A, B, C, D, I, K, L, M, FS&B, Tenth Cavalry	605
December	A, B, C, D, I, K, L, M, FS&B, Tenth Cavalry	605

1903

January	A, B, C, D, I, K, L, M, FS&B, Tenth Cavalry	601
February	A, B, C, D, I, K, L, M, FS&B, Tenth Cavalry	596
March	A, B, C, D, I, K, L, M, FS&B, Tenth Cavalry	603
April	A, B, C, D, I, K, L, M, FS&B, Tenth Cavalry	606
May	A, B, C, D, I, K, L, M, FS&B, Tenth Cavalry	604
June	A, B, C, D, I, K, L, M, FS&B, Tenth Cavalry	601
July	A, B, C, D, I, K, L, M, FS&B, Tenth Cavalry	600
August	A, B, C, D, I, K, L, M, FS&B, Tenth Cavalry	602
September	A, B, C, D, I, K, L, M, FS&B, Tenth Cavalry	574
October	A, B, C, D, I, K, L, M, FS&B, Tenth Cavalry	592
November	A, B, C, D, I, K, L, M, FS&B, Tenth Cavalry	589
December	A, B, C, D, I, K, L, M, FS&B, Tenth Cavalry	587

1904

January	A, B, C, D, I, K, L, M, FS&B, Tenth Cavalry	589
February	A, B, C, D, I, K, L, M, FS&B, Tenth Cavalry	595
March	A, B, C, D, I, K, L, M, FS&B, Tenth Cavalry	585
April	A, B, C, D, I, K, L, M, FS&B, Tenth Cavalry	574
May	A, B, C, D, I, K, L, M, FS&B, Tenth Cavalry	581
June	A, B, C, D, I, K, L, M, FS&B, Tenth Cavalry	585

July	A, B, C, D, I, K, L, M, FS&B, Tenth Cavalry	602
August	A, B, C, D, I, K, L, M, FS&B, Tenth Cavalry	601
September	A, B, C, D, I, K, L, M, FS&B, Tenth Cavalry	604
October	A, B, C, D, I, K, L, M, FS&B, Tenth Cavalry	601
November	A, B, C, D, I, K, L, M, FS&B, Tenth Cavalry	602
December	A, B, C, D, I, K, L, M, FS&B, Tenth Cavalry	592

1905

January	A, B, C, D, I, K, L, M, FS&B, Tenth Cavalry	590
February	A, B, C, D, I, K, L, M, FS&B, Tenth Cavalry	562
March	A, B, C, D, I, K, L, M, FS&B, Tenth Cavalry	557
April	A, B, C, D, I, K, L, M, FS&B, Tenth Cavalry	528
May	A, B, C, D, I, K, L, M, FS&B, Tenth Cavalry	537
June	A, B, C, D, I, K, L, M, FS&B, Tenth Cavalry	562
July	A, B, C, D, I, K, L, M, FS&B, Tenth Cavalry	598
August	A, B, C, D, I, K, L, M, FS&B, Tenth Cavalry	603
September	A, B, C, D, I, K, L, M, FS&B, Tenth Cavalry	603
October	A, B, C, D, I, K, L, M, FS&B, Tenth Cavalry	595
November	A, B, C, D, I, K, L, M, FS&B, Tenth Cavalry	597
December	A, B, C, D, I, K, L, M, FS&B, Tenth Cavalry	596

1906

January	A, B, C, D, I, K, L, M, FS&B, Tenth Cavalry	604
February	A, B, C, D, I, K, L, M, FS&B, Tenth Cavalry	597
March	A, B, C, D, I, K, L, M, FS&B, Tenth Cavalry	589
April	A, B, C, D, I, K, L, M, FS&B, Tenth Cavalry	591
May	A, B, C, D, I, K, L, M, FS&B, Tenth Cavalry	586
June	A, B, C, D, I, K, L, M, FS&B, Tenth Cavalry	580
July	A, B, C, D, I, K, L, M, FS&B, Tenth Cavalry	584
August	A, B, C, D, I, K, L, M, FS&B, Tenth Cavalry	584
September	A, B, C, D, I, K, L, M, FS&B, Tenth Cavalry	570
October	A, B, C, D, I, K, L, M, FS&B, Tenth Cavalry	566
November	A, B, C, D, I, K, L, M, FS&B, Tenth Cavalry	569
December	A, B, C, D, I, K, L, M, FS&B, Tenth Cavalry	568

1907

January	A, B, C, D, I, K, L, M, FS&B, Tenth Cavalry	587
February	B, I, M, Tenth Cavalry	188
March	B, I, M, Tenth Cavalry	197
April	B, I, M, Tenth Cavalry	208
May	A, B, C, D, I, K, L, M, FS&B, Eighth Cavalry	409
June	A, B, C, D, I, K, L, M, FS&B, Eighth Cavalry	415
July	A, B, C, D, I, K, L, M, FS&B, Eighth Cavalry	402
August	A, B, C, D, I, K, L, M, FS&B, Eighth Cavalry	376
September	A, B, C, D, I, K, L, M, FS&B, Eighth Cavalry	373
October	A, B, C, D, I, K, L, FS&B, Eighth Cavalry	338
November	A, B, C, D, I, K, L, FS&B, Eighth Cavalry	359
December	A, B, C, D, I, K, L, FS&B, Eighth Cavalry	470

1908

January	A, B, C, D, I, K, L, FS&B, Eighth Cavalry	471
February	A, B, C, D, I, K, L, FS&B, Eighth Cavalry	393
March	A, B, C, D, I, K, L, FS&B, Eighth Cavalry	446
April	A, B, C, D, I, K, L, FS&B, Eighth Cavalry	450
May	A, B, C, D, I, K, L, FS&B, Eighth Cavalry	450
June	A, B, C, D, I, K, L, FS&B, Eighth Cavalry	543
July	A, B, C, D, I, K, L, FS&B, Eighth Cavalry	539
August	A, B, C, D, I, K, L, FS&B, Eighth Cavalry	513
September	A, B, C, D, I, K, L, FS&B, Eighth Cavalry	530
October	A, B, C, D, I, K, L, FS&B, Eighth Cavalry	560
November	A, B, C, D, I, K, L, FS&B, Eighth Cavalry	670
December	A, B, C, D, I, K, L, FS&B, Eighth Cavalry	643

1909

January	A, B, C, D, I, K, L, FS&B, Eighth Cavalry	635
February	A, B, C, D, I, K, L, FS&B, Eighth Cavalry	626
March	A, B, C, D, I, K, L, FS&B, Eighth Cavalry	616
April	A, B, C, D, I, K, L, FS&B, Eighth Cavalry	596
May	A, B, C, D, I, K, L, FS&B, Eighth Cavalry	583
June	A, B, C, D, I, K, L, M, FS&B, Eighth Cavalry	634
July	A, B, C, D, I, K, L, M, FS&B, Eighth Cavalry	609

August	A, B, C, D, I, K, L, M, FS&B, Eighth Cavalry	620
September	A, B, C, D, I, K, L, M, FS&B, Eighth Cavalry	630
October	A, B, C, D, I, K, L, M, FS&B, Eighth Cavalry	625
November	A, B, C, D, I, K, L, M, FS&B, Eighth Cavalry	636
December	A, B, C, D, I, K, L, M, FS&B, Eighth Cavalry	624

1910

January	A, B, C, D, I, K, L, M, FS&B, Eighth Cavalry	631
February	A, B, C, D, I, K, L, M, FS&B, Eighth Cavalry	623
March	A, B, C, D, I, K, L, M, FS&B, Eighth Cavalry	614
April	A, B, C, D, I, K, L, M, FS&B, Eighth Cavalry	611
May	A, B, C, D, I, K, L, M, FS&B, Eighth Cavalry	605
June	A, B, C, D, I, K, L, M, FS&B, Eighth Cavalry	599
July	A, B, C, D, I, K, L, M, FS&B, Eighth Cavalry	589
August	A, B, C, D, I, K, L, M, FS&B, Eighth Cavalry	586
September	A, B, C, D, I, K, L, M, FS&B, Eighth Cavalry	574
October	A, B, C, D, I, K, L, M, FS&B, Eighth Cavalry	572
November	D, I, Eighth Cavalry	193
December	D, I, Eighth Cavalry	172

1911

January	D, I, Eighth Cavalry	146
February	A, B, C, D, E, F, G, H, FS&B, MGP, Twelfth Cavalry	367
March	A, B, C, D, E, F, G, H, FS&B, MGP, Twelfth Cavalry	532
April	A, B, C, D, E, F, G, H, FS&B, MGP, Twelfth Cavalry	578
May	A, B, C, D, E, F, G, H, FS&B, MGP, Twelfth Cavalry	562
June	A, B, C, D, E, F, G, H, FS&B, MGP, Twelfth Cavalry	571
July	A, B, C, D, E, F, G, H, FS&B, MGP, Twelfth Cavalry	561
August	A, B, C, D, E, F, G, H, FS&B, MGP, Twelfth Cavalry	576
September	A, B, C, D, E, F, G, H, FS&B, MGP, Twelfth Cavalry	568
October	A, B, C, D, E, F, G, H, FS&B, MGP, Twelfth Cavalry	559
November	A, B, C, D, E, F, G, H, FS&B, MGP, Twelfth Cavalry	626
December	A, B, C, D, E, F, G, H, FS&B, MGP, Twelfth Cavalry	605

1912

January	A, B, C, D, E, F, G, H, FS&B, MGP, Twelfth Cavalry	626

February	A, B, C, D, E, F, G, H, FS&B, MGP, Twelfth Cavalry	622
March	A, B, C, D, E, F, G, H, FS&B, MGP, Twelfth Cavalry	637
April	A, B, C, D, E, F, G, H, FS&B, MGP, Twelfth Cavalry	623
May	A, B, C, D, E, F, G, H, FS&B, MGP, Twelfth Cavalry	617
June	A, B, C, D, E, F, G, H, FS&B, MGP, Twelfth Cavalry	599
July	A, B, C, D, E, F, G, H, FS&B, MGP, Twelfth Cavalry	587
August	A, B, C, D, E, F, G, H, FS&B, MGP, Twelfth Cavalry	669
September	A, B, C, D, E, F, G, H, FS&B, MGP, Twelfth Cavalry	662
October	A, B, C, D, E, F, G, H, FS&B, MGP, Twelfth Cavalry	654
November	A, B, C, D, E, F, G, H, FS&B, MGP, Twelfth Cavalry	633
December	A, B, C, D, E, F, G, H, FS&B, MGP, Twelfth Cavalry	632

1913

January	A, B, C, D, E, F, G, H, FS&B, MGP, Twelfth Cavalry	628
February	A, B, C, D, E, F, G, H, FS&B, MGP, Twelfth Cavalry	720
March	A, B, C, D, E, F, G, H, FS&B, MGP, Twelfth Cavalry	720
April	A, B, C, D, E, F, G, H, FS&B, MGP, Twelfth Cavalry	710
May	A, B, C, D, E, F, G, H, FS&B, MGP, Twelfth Cavalry	704
June	A, B, C, D, E, F, G, H, FS&B, MGP, Twelfth Cavalry	686
July	A, B, C, D, E, F, G, H, FS&B, MGP, Twelfth Cavalry	673
August	A, B, C, D, E, F, G, H, FS&B, MGP, Twelfth Cavalry	725
September	A, B, C, D, E, F, G, H, F&SB, MGP, Twelfth Cavalry	713
October	A, B, C, D, E, F, G, H, FS&B, MGP, Twelfth Cavalry	703
November	A, B, C, D, E, F, G, H, FS&B, MGP, Twelfth Cavalry	683
December	A, B, C, D, E, F, G, H, FS&B, MGP, Twelfth Cavalry	641

1914

January	A, B, C, D, E, F, G, H, FS&B, MGP, Twelfth Cavalry	605
February	A, B, C, D, E, F, G, H, FS&B, MGP, Twelfth Cavalry	672
March	A, B, C, D, E, F, G, H, FS&B, MGP, Twelfth Cavalry	745
April	A, B, C, D, E, F, G, H, FS&B, MGP, Twelfth Cavalry	738
May	A, B, C, D, E, F, G, H, FS&B, MGP, Twelfth Cavalry	735
June	A, B, C, D, E, F, G, H, FS&B, MGP, Twelfth Cavalry	727
July	A, B, C, D, E, F, G, H, FS&B, MGP, Twelfth Cavalry	747
August	A, B, C, D, E, F, G, H, FS&B, MGP, Twelfth Cavalry	736

September	A, B, C, D, E, F, G, H, FS&B, MGP, Twelfth Cavalry	698
October	A, B, C, D, E, F, G, H, FS&B, MGP, Twelfth Cavalry	704
November	A, B, C, D, F, G, FS&B, MGP, Twelfth Cavalry	589
December	F, G, FS, MGP, Twelfth Cavalry	300
1915		
January	F, G, FS, MGP, Twelfth Cavalry	293
February	F, G, FS, HQ TP, MGP, Twelfth Cavalry	315
March	F, G, FS, HQ TP, MGP, Twelfth Cavalry	310
April	F, G, FS, HQ TP, MGP, Twelfth Cavalry	309
May	F, G, FS, HQ TP, MGP, Twelfth Cavalry	307
June	F, G, FS, HQ TP, MGP, Twelfth Cavalry	285
July	F, G, FS, HQ TP, MGP, Twelfth Cavalry	276
August	F, G, FS, HQ TP, MGP, Twelfth Cavalry	313
September	F, G, FS, HQ TP, MGP, Twelfth Cavalry	313
October	F, G, FS, HQ TP, MGP, Twelfth Cavalry	311
November	F, G, FS, HQ TP, MGP, Twelfth Cavalry	252
December	F, G, FS, HQ TP, MGP, Twelfth Cavalry	316
1916		
January	F, G, FS, HQ TP, MGP, Twelfth Cavalry	290
February	F, G, FS, HQ TP, MGP, Twelfth Cavalry	281
March	Detachment, QM Corps	43
April	Detachment, QM Corps	22
May	Detachment, QM Corps	20
June	Detachment, QM Corps	18
July	Detachment, QM Corps	18
August	Detachment, QM Corps	17
September	Detachment, QM Corps	17
October	Detachment, QM Corps	18
November	Detachment, QM Corps	20
December	Detachment, QM Corps	20

Appendix C

Remount Enlisted Component, 1944–1949

Compiled from Monthly Information Letter, Jan. 1, 1944, to June 1, 1949.

	1944	1945	1946	1947	1948	1949
January	312	479	159	60	45	*
February	318	470	119	59	45	40
March	312	470	159	56	45	13
April	323	435	125	54	44	13
May	288	448	125	49	47	13
June	373	526	101	43	52	13
July	418	462	84	39	*	
August	386	412	83	33	*	
September	347	355	82	35	*	
October	381	265	73	47	*	
November	513	216	72	50	43	
December	485	189	68	47	*	

*Report not available.

Appendix D

Fort Robinson Prisoner of War Camp Populations

Compiled from Provost Marshal General monthly reports and
Red Cross individual camp inspection reports from RG 389,
Records of the Office of the Provost Marshal General, National Archives.

1943

Dec. 19	677

1944

Jan. 30	669
Feb. 21	659
June 21	447
July 19	447
Oct. 1	984
Dec. 1	2,746

1945

Jan. 1	2,980
Feb. 1	3,044
Feb. 15	1,300
Mar. 1	2,127
Apr. 1	2,131
May 1	2,127
July 1	1,247
September (Fort Robinson becomes branch camp of Scottsbluff PW Camp)	
Oct. 1	1,305
Dec. 1	659
Dec. 15	792

1946

Jan. 15	745
Feb. 1	305
Mar. 1	303
Apr. 1	218
May 1 (Camp closed May 15)	72

Appendix E

Post Population, 1945

"Report of Veterinary Meat & Dairy Hygiene and Forage Inspection"
Robinson QM Depot, Fort Robinson

(Average strength of command during the period covered by this report.)

1945	Military[1]	Civilian[2]	PW [3]	Total
January	1010.89	230	3101.49	4342.38
February	1006.94	230	1834.10	3071.04
March	1002.70	230	2131.55	3364.25
April	888.50	230	2130.06	3248.56
May	916.71	230	2127.07	3273.78
June	1063.50	230	1876.81	3170.31
July	1106.34	230	1870.71	3207.05
August	728.57	230	1853.14	2811.71
September	974.67	230	1566.20	2770.87
October	666.24	230		896.24
November	465.24	230		695.24
December	390.84	230		620.84

[1] Average monthly population figures, including all military detachments assigned to post (remount, veterinary, medical, supply, military police, and K-9 personnel and trainees).

[2] Includes military families living on post.

[3] Monthly population average reported of German prisoners ends after September, when the camp was under the authority of the Scottsbluff PW Camp.

Appendix F

Average Large Animal Strength, 1939–1945

Compiled from "History of the Veterinary Service at the Robinson
Quartermaster Depot (Remount), Fort Robinson, Nebraska,"
reports from Sept. 8, 1939, to Dec. 31, 1945.

Sept. 8, 1939–Dec. 31, 1939	1,323.58
Jan. 1, 1940–June 30, 1940	982.91
July 1, 1940–Dec. 31, 1940[1]	2,605.92
Jan. 1, 1941–June 30, 1941	3,333.80
July 1, 1941–Dec. 7, 1941	3,747.13
Dec. 8, 1941–June 30, 1942	3,781.17
July 1, 1942 - Dec. 31, 1942[2]	9,684.88
Jan. 1, 1943–June 30, 1943	11, 402.67
July 1, 1943 –Dec. 31, 1943	10,913.07
Jan. 1, 1944–June 30, 1944	8,102.90
July 1, 1944–Dec. 31, 1944	8,667.95
Jan. 1, 1945–Sept. 3, 1945	9,443.77
Sept. 4, 1945–Dec. 31, 1945	8,458.74

[1] During this period animal strength increased from 672 to 5,790.

[2] Number of large animals on hand Dec. 31 was 9,974.

Appendix G

Monthly Dog Strength, January 1944–May 1947

Compiled from Monthly Information Letter, January 1, 1944–May 1947.

	1944	1945	1946	1947
January	1,670	1,767	*	17
February	*	1,719	409	17
March	1,313	*	*	17
April	1,227	*	193	17
May	1,335	*	*	17[1]
June	1,367	1,340	*	
July	1,317	1,660	90	
August	1,335	1,456	15	
September	1,353	1,281	13	
October	1.593	1,092	13	
November	1,780	920	11	
December	1,721	621	18	

* Report not available.

[1] The last remaining dogs were sold as surplus in June 1947.

Appendix H

Dogs Received, Issued, and Returned to Owners

Compiled from "History of the Veterinary Service at the Robinson
Quartermaster Depot (Remount), Fort Robinson, Nebraska,"
reports from Dec. 31, 1942, to Dec. 31, 1945.

	Average	Received	Issued	Returned
1942				
July 1–Dec. 31	No breakdown available. 879 dogs present on Dec. 31.			
1943				
Jan. 1–June 30	No report available.			
July 1–Dec. 31	1,433	3,333	1,640	813
1944				
Jan. 1–June 30	1,394	1,641	442	614
July 1–Dec. 30	1,516	1,783	443	699
1945				
Jan. 1–Sept. 3	1,525	2,771	459	1,595
July 1-Dec. 30	978.5	759	84	1,024

Appendix I

Superintendents, Fort Robinson Beef Cattle Research Station

July 1, 1948–Nov. 16, 1954	Russell L. Davis
Nov. 16, 1954–July 1, 1957	Robert M. Koch
July 1, 1957–Sept. 30, 1966	James E. Ingalls
1966–1967	John Rothlisberger (acting)
1967–Feb. 1972	R. Dean Humphrey

Superintendents, Fort Robinson State Park

July 9, 1957–Sept. 10, 1968	John C. Kurtz
Sept. 10, 1968–Mar. 31, 1993	Vince L. Rotherham
Apr. 1, 1993–July 23, 2001	Jim Lemmon
July 2001 –	Michael Morava

Curators, Fort Robinson Museum

Mar. 1, 1956–Nov. 1959	Roger T. Grange
1960–1962	Floyd Urbach (seasonal)
1963–1964	Richard McGee (seasonal)
1965–Aug. 1985	Vance E. Nelson (seasonal until Aug. 1966)
Aug. 26, 1985–	Thomas R. Buecker

Superintendents, Trailside Museum

April 1991—	David A. Nixon

Notes

Abbreviations

AFBNM = Agate Fossil Beds National Monument   MIL = Monthly Information Letter

ARSW = Annual Report of the Secretary of War   NA = National Archives

FRM = Fort Robinson Museum   NSHS = Nebraska State Historical Society

GFWDT = General File, War Dog Training   PR = Post Returns

GPO = Government Printing Office   RDH = Remount Depot History

RG = Record Group   RG = Record Group

HVS = History of the Veterinary Service   UNL = University of Nebraska -Lincoln

IP = Inspection Report

Introduction

1. Ninetieth Congress, 2d. sess., Senate Committee on Labor and Public Welfare, *Medal of Honor, 1863–1968* (GPO: 1968), 7.

1. The Last of the Cavalry

1. Post Returns, Fort Robinson, July, December 1901 (National Archives Microfilm Publication M617, Returns from U.S. Military Posts), Records of the Office of the Adjutant General, Record Group 94, NA (copy in RG 501, Fort Robinson Records, NSHS, hereafter PR).

2. *Crawford Tribune*, Jan. 17, 1902.

3. Robert Lee, *Fort Meade and the Black Hills* (Lincoln: University of Nebraska Press, 1991), 156–57.

4. *Annual Report of the Secretary of War, 1912*, (GPO: 1913), 164, (hereafter ARSW).

5. *Crawford Tribune*, June 28, 1901.

6. Ibid.

7. Ibid., Apr. 19, 1901. Information on post hospital from Fort Building File, FRM.

8. *Crawford Tribune*, Sept. 20, 1901, Feb. 7, 14, 1902.

9. PR, Apr. 1902; *Crawford Tribune*, Apr. 25, 1902; Medical History, Fort Robinson, Apr. 1902, Records of U.S. Army Continental Commands, Record Group 393, NA, copy in RG 501, NSHS.

10. *Crawford Tribune*, Mar. 28, 1902; PR, May 1902.

11. Francis B. Heitman, *Historical Register and Dictionary of the United States Army* (1903; reprint, Urbana: University of Illinois Press, 1965), 175.

12. *Crawford Tribune*, June 6, 1902, July 28, 1905; Maj. E. L. N. Glass, *The History of the Tenth Cavalry* (Fort Collins, Colo: Old Army Press, 1972), 45–49.

13. *Crawford Tribune*, Mar. 13, 1903.

14. Ibid., Jan. 22, 1904.

15. Frank N. Schubert, *Buffalo Soldiers, Braves, and the Brass* (Shippensburg, Pa.: White Mane Publishing Co., 1993), 108, 150–51.

16. Thomas R. Buecker, "The Tenth Cavalry at Fort Robinson, 1902–1907," *Military Images* 7 (May–June 1991): 6; Regimental Returns, Tenth Cavalry, May 1903, RG 94, NA, copy at FRM.

17. PR, Sept., Oct. 1906.

18. Philip Eastman, "The Fort Riley Maneuvers," *Review of Reviews* 21 (Nov. 1903): 564–69; *Kansas City Journal*, Oct. 27, 1903; *Kansas City Star*, Oct. 23, 1903.

19. The Twenty-fifth Infantry from Fort Niobrara also had difficulties with the Texas troops. See Thomas R. Buecker, "Prelude to Brownsville: The Twenty-fifth Infantry at Fort Niobrara, Nebraska, 1902–1906," *Great Plains Quarterly* 16 (Spring 1996): 104–5.

20. For more on cavalry equipment and uniform changes see Randy Steffen, *The Horse Soldier 1776–1943: The United States Cavalryman, His Uniform, Arms, Accoutrements & Equipments*, 4 Vols. (Norman: University of Oklahoma Press, 1978–79). Vol. 3, "The Last of the Indian Wars, the Spanish American War, the Brink of the Great War, 1881–1916," is pertinent here.

21. Glass, *History of the Tenth Cavalry*, 90–92.

22. *Crawford Tribune*, May 1, 1903; Allen Splete, *Frederick Remington: Selected Letters* (Ogdensburg, N.Y.: Frederick Remington Art Museum, n.d.), 357.

23. Marvin E. Fletcher, *America's First Black General: Benjamin O. Davis, Sr., 1880–1970* (Lawrence: University Press of Kansas, 1989), 34–35; Frank N. Schubert, *On the Trail of the Buffalo Soldier: Biographies of African Americans in the U.S. Army, 1866–1917* (Wilmington, Del.: Scholarly Resources Inc., 1995), 114.

24. Glass, *History of the Tenth Cavalry*, 43.

25. Cpl. Charlie Simmons, "Thanksgiving Day in the Tenth Cavalry," *The Voice of the Negro* 2 (Jan. 1905): 663–64.

26. Frank N. Schubert, "The Fort Robinson Y.M.C.A., 1902–1907: A Social Organization in a Black Regiment," *Nebraska History* 55 (Summer 1974): 165–79.

27. *Crawford Tribune*, Sept. 18, 1903, Jan. 4, 1904. See also Frank N. Schubert, "Troopers, Taverns, and Taxes: Fort Robinson, Nebraska, and Its Municipal Parasite, 1886–1911," in Gary D. Ryan and Timothy K. Nenninger, eds., *Soldiers and Civilians: The U.S. Army and the American People* (Washington, D.C.: National Archives and Records Administration, n.d.), 91–103.

28. Rudyard Kipling, "Tommy," *Collected Verse of Rudyard Kipling* (Garden City, N.J.: Doubleday, Page & Co., 1918), 263.

29. *Crawford Tribune*, May 18, 1906. See also Wayne C. Lee, *Wild Towns of Nebraska* (Caldwell, Idaho: Caxton Printers, 1988), 104–8.

30. John Reid died of illness on Mar. 23, 1909, and is buried in the penitentiary cemetery.

31. Schubert, *Buffalo Soldiers*, 144–45.

32. Betty Loudon, ed., "Pioneer Pharmacist J. Walter Moyer's Notes on Crawford and Fort Robinson in the 1890s," *Nebraska History* 58 (Spring 1977): 99.

33. Schubert, *Buffalo Soldiers*, 144–45.

34. Ibid., 145.

35. *Crawford Tribune*, Apr. 12, 1907. All information on post buildings is from the Fort Building File, FRM.

36. *Crawford Tribune*, Mar. 30, June 29, 1906.

37. Ibid., July 20, August 17, 1906; ARSW, 1912, 162–63.

38. *Crawford Tribune*, Nov. 23, 1906, Feb. 1, Mar. 1, 1907.

39. Ibid., Apr. 19, 1901. Plans of the proposed 1906 brick expansion are in the Map File, FRM.

40. *Crawford Tribune*, June 15, 1906; interview with Red Cloud, Nov. 24, 1906, tablet 25, Eli S. Ricker papers, MS 8, NSHS.

41. For more on the wandering Utes, see Floyd A. O'Neil, "An Anguished Odyssey: The Flight of the Utes, 1906–1908," *Utah Historical Quarterly* 36 (Fall 1968): 315–27, and David D. Laudenschlager, "The Utes in South Dakota, 1906–1908," *South Dakota History* 9 (Summer 1979): 233–47. See also Lee, *Fort Meade*, 176–89. For an example of press sensationalism concerning the Utes in Wyoming, see *The Lincoln Daily Star*, Oct. 30, 1906.

42. Thomas R. Buecker, "An Excellent Soldier and an Efficient Officer," *NEBRASKAland*, 67 (June 1989): 16.

43. PR, Feb., May 1907.

44. *Crawford Tribune*, June 25, 1910, Sept. 11, 1908.

45. Ibid., Apr. 10, 1908.

46. ARSW, 1905, "Report of the Quartermaster General," 5.

47. Fort Building File, FRM.

48. Jerome A. Greene, "Fort Des Moines Historic District," Historic American Buildings Survey 1A–121 (Mar. 1987), 34.

49. *Crawford Tribune*, Jan. 12, 1906.

50. Ibid., July 10, Oct. 9, 1908.

51. Ibid., Dec. 16, 1910. Unless otherwise noted, all information on land issues is from the Military Reservation File, FRM.

52. Anthony J. Hytrek, "The History of Fort Robinson, Nebraska, from 1900 to the Present," (master's thesis, Chadron State College, 1971), 25–26; *Crawford Tribune*, Jan. 28, 1911.

53. *Crawford Tribune*, Aug. 11, 1911.

54. Ibid., Dec. 24, 1909; Schubert, "Troopers, Taverns, and Taxes," 100.

55. Schubert, "Troopers, Taverns, and Taxes," 97–98; *Crawford Tribune*, June 18, 1909.

56. *Crawford Tribune*, Mar. 31, 1911.

57. Ibid., Feb. 2, 1912.

58. Ibid., Oct. 28, Dec. 2, 1910.

59. Ibid., Dec. 2, 1910.

60. Heitman, *Historical Register*, 601, 886.

61. ARSW, 1914, "Report of the Adjutant General," 161.

62. W. F. Heck interview, July 4, 1963, FRM.

63. Ibid.

64. *Crawford Tribune*, Feb. 25, 1916, July 4, 11, 1913.

65. Ibid., Sept. 15, 1911.

66. Ibid., June 14, 1912.

67. Ibid., July 1, Nov. 25, 1910, July 28, 1911.

68. Andrea I. Paul, "Buffalo Bill and Wounded Knee: The Movie," *Nebraska History* 71 (Winter 1990), 183–90.

69. PR, Oct. 1913.

70. Richard J. Walsh, *The Making of Buffalo Bill* (Indianapolis: The Bobbs-Merrill Co., 1928), 346.

71. Paul E. Eisloeffel and Andrea I. Paul, "Hollywood on the Plains," *NEBRASKAland* 70 (May 1992): 42.

72. Gerald M. Adams, *The Post Near Cheyenne: A History of Fort D. A. Russell, 1867–1930* (Boulder, Colo.: Pruett Publishing Co., 1989), 157–58; Thomas R. Buecker, "In the Old Army: Harry K. Hollenbach at Fort Robinson, 1911–1913," *Nebraska History* 71 (Spring 1990): 16, 21.

73. Davidson B. McKibben, "Revolt of the Navaho, 1913," *New Mexico Historical Review* 29 (Oct. 1954): 259–89; *Crawford Tribune*, Nov. 21, 1913.

74. William A. Ganoe, *The History of the United States Army* (New York: D. Appleton-Century Co., 1942), 450; PR, May 1914–Jan. 1915; ARSW, 1914, "Report of the Chief of Staff," 136–37.

75. *Crawford Tribune*, Mar. 17, 1916; Ganoe, *History of the United States Army*, 453–56.

76. Buecker, "An Excellent Soldier," 17.

77. *Crawford Tribune*, Mar. 24, 1916, Apr. 27, 1917.

78. Ibid., Apr. 6, June 1, Aug. 3, 1917.

79. Thomas R. Buecker, "The Fort and the Railroad: Fort Robinson on the C&NW," *North Western Lines* 23 (Fall 1996): 31; William B. Quigley narrative on his service with the Fourth Nebraska Infantry at Fort Robinson, typescript, FRM.

80. Letter, Mrs. Ned Tecker, June 24, 1992, FRM; *Crawford Tribune*, Aug. 31, 1917.

81. William H. Carter, *The History of Fort Robinson, Nebraska* (Crawford, Nebr.: The Northwest Nebraska News, 1942), 15; *Crawford Tribune*, Oct. 19, 1917.

82. *Order of Battle of the United States Land Forces in the World War*, Vol. 3 (GPO:1949), paragraphs 313, 886; *Crawford Tribune*, May 17, 1918.

83. *Crawford Tribune*, June 14, 1918.

84. Ibid., June 14, 1918, Sept. 14, 1917; PR, Aug. 1918.

2. Robinson Quartermaster Depot, Remount

1. Capt. John T. Salee, "Developing the Horse at a Western Remount Depot," *The Quartermaster Review* 8 (Nov.–Dec. 1928): 23.

2. Ibid. A number of sources are available on the Quartermaster Remount, including articles in the *The Quartermaster Review*, the journal of the QM Corps. Also see Anna M. Waller, *Army Horses and Mules and National Defense* (Washington, D.C.: Office of the Quartermaster General, 1958).

3. Col. F. S. Armstrong, "The Remount Service," *The Quartermaster Review* 1 (July–Aug. 1921): 13–18.

4. "Remount Depot History," 1919, 21B, RG 501, NSHS, (hereafter RDH).

5. Letter, Col. Edwin Hardy, June 17, 1959, on the remount period of Fort Robinson, RG 501, NSHS.

6. RDH (1919), 22A.

7. Ibid.; RDH (1920), 25A–25B.

8. Department Inspection Report, Apr. 15, 1920, Records of the Office of the Inspector General, Record Group 159, NA.

9. Horse and mule numbers compiled from RDH, 1919 to 1931.

10. Hardy letter, June 17, 1959.

11. RDH (1924), 58B.

12. *Northwest Nebraska News* (Crawford), Nov. 8, 1934; *Sunday Journal and Star* (Lincoln), June 2, 1940.

13. "Introduction of an Army Horse," *The Cavalry Journal* 51 (July–Aug. 1942): 75–76; "History of the Veterinary Service at the Robinson Quartermaster Depot (Remount) Fort Robinson, Nebraska," Sept. 8, 1939, to Dec. 31, 1939," RG 501, NSHS, (hereafter HVS).

14. *Sunday Journal and Star*, June 2, 1940; Salee, "Developing the Horse," 25.

15. Ed Bieganski, "Condition and Issue Stable at Fort Robinson, Nebraska, 1938," *Dusting off the Saddles* (Gordon, Nebr.: Tri-State Old Time Cowboys Memorial, 1993), 11–15.

16. RDH (1926), 101A.

17. RDH (1928), 7.

18. Specific information on where animals were shipped is compiled from RDH, 1919 to 1931.

19. *Northwest Nebraska News*, Nov. 8, 1934.

20. RDH (1931), 22.

21. Ibid., 15.

22. *Northwest Nebraska News*, Nov. 8, 1934; *Sunday Journal and Star*, June 2, 1940.

23. Maj. R. M. Graham, "Our U.S. Army Remount Service,"*Nebraska Farmer* (May 4, 1940): 11.

24. RDH (1930), 10; Lt. Col. Edwin Hardy, "The Remount Service and the Army Breeding Plan," *The Quartermaster Review* 19 (Mar.–Apr. 1940): 12.

25. RDH (1927), 122A.

26. Capt. Ary C. Berry, ed., *A Souvenir History of Fort Robinson, Nebraska, 1930* (Crawford, Nebr.: Northwest Nebraska News, 1930), 10.

27. *Sunday Journal and Star*, June 2, 1940; Gerald Kennedy interview, 1976, FRM.

28. Ralph Knepper interview, 1976, FRM.

29. "Annual Report of Depot Veterinarian," RDH (1929), 1; RDH (1921), 35B; RDH (1925), 72B.

30. RDH (1926), 122A; *A Souvenir History of Fort Robinson, Nebraska, 1930*, 12.

31. RDH (1930), 12.

32. Nels Christensen interview, 1976, FRM.

33. RDH (1920), 30A; (1924), 52A.

34. "Memorandum for the Assistant Chief of Staff G-4," Aug. 19, 1927, Records of the Office of the Quartermaster General, Record Group 92, NA.

35. *Omaha World-Herald*, Mar. 12, 1975; *Crawford Tribune*, Apr. 20, 1978.

36. RDH (1920), 24B; Hardy letter, June 17, 1959; *Northwest Nebraska News*, Nov. 8, 1934.

37. RDH (1924), 54B–57B.

38. *Northwest Nebraska News*, July 20, 1939; Hardy letter, June 17, 1959.

39. RDH (1921), 33A; (1925), 76A; (1932), 2.

40. RDH (1920), 28B.

41. RDH (1929), 25.

42. Elmo Brangham interview, June 14, 1986, FRM.

43. Kenny Hutson interview, 1974, FRM.

44. *Northwest Nebraska News*, Sept. 3, 1936; Austin Muth veteran questionnaire, FRM.

45. RDH (1920), 31A; (1922), 42B; (1923), 48B.

46. George Mueller interview, July 7, 1989; Ed Bieganski interview, July 5, 1990, both FRM.

47. *Northwest Nebraska News*, Feb. 1, 1940, Aug. 10, 1937.

48. RDH (1932), 7–8.

49. *Sunday Journal and Star*, June 2, 1940.

50. RDH (1932), 4; Hardy, "The Remount Service," 70; letter, Leo Cooksley, Berwyn, Nebraska, May 23, 1990, FRM.

51. Capt. Charles J. Sullivan, *Army Posts and Towns* (Burlington, Vt.: Free Press Printing

Co., 1926), 180–81.

52. Waller, *Army Horses and Mules*, 49; Remount Officers file, FRM.

53. Christensen interview, FRM.

54. All information on building construction and removal compiled from the Fort Building File, FRM.

55. Department Inspection Report, Apr. 15, 1920, RG 159, NA.

56. RDH (1920), 27B–28B; (1921), 32A–32B; (1922), 37B.

57. RDH (1921), 32B–33A; (1923), 43B; (1924), 49B.

58. RDH (1926), 95B.

59. This story can be found in E. A. Brininstool, *Fighting Indian Warriors* (Harrisburg, Pa.: The Stackpole Co., 1953), 279. The neglected cemetery is also lamented in Joe E. Milner and Earle R. Forrest, *California Joe* (Caldwell, Idaho: Caxton Printers, 1935), 283.

60. Note on letter from Maj. J. McClintock to E. A. Brininstool, Nov. 6, 1928, James Cook papers, Agate Fossil Beds National Monument (hereafter AFBNM).

61. *Northwest Nebraska News*, July 25, 1935.

62. *Crawford Tribune*, Apr. 6, 1933.

63. Fort Building File, FRM.

64. Pat Davis interview, July 7, 1989, FRM; *Sunday Journal and Star*, June 2, 1940.

65. RDH (1932), 8; *Sunday Journal and Star*, June 2, 1940.

66. Herbert Hoover to War Department, Aug. 27, 1927, RG 501, NSHS.

67. William S. Koester, "Col. F. W. Koester, Noted Cavalryman, Thoroughbred Official," typescript, FRM.

68. Frequent mention is made in the *Crawford Tribune* and *Northwest Nebraska News* of official and nonofficial visitors to the post during the 1920s and the 1930s. Borglum visits are found in the *Northwest Nebraska News*, Aug. 28, Sept. 25, 1930.

69. Buecker, "Fort Robinson, Nebraska: The Country Club of the Army," paper for Center for Great Plains Studies 1998 symposium, "Health and Lifestyle, Sport and Recreation on the Great Plains," FRM.

70. *Omaha Sunday World-Herald*, Jan. 19, 1941. Several returning veterans have commented to the author about how glad they were to see the old "hitching post" still standing.

3. The 1930s

1. *Crawford Tribune*, Apr. 20, 1923.

2. "Memorandum for the Assistant Chief of Staff G-4," Aug. 19, 1927, RG 92, NA.

3. For a more complete history of the Fourth Field Artillery, see Chap. Paul B. Rupp, ed., *Fourth United States Field Artillery, History of Organization, 1907–1927* (San Antonio, Tex.: Ivan A. Britt, [1927?]).

4. RDH (1928), 1–2.

5. Ibid., 2.

6. "Inspection and Survey of Fort Robinson, Nebr.," June 21, 1930, June 22, 1929, RG 159, NA.

7. RDH (1931), 1–2.

8. *A Souvenir history of Fort Robinson, Nebraska, 1930*, 13.

9. *Northwest Nebraska News*, June 5, 1930, June 11, 1931; *Crawford Tribune*, May 24, 1929.

10. *Northwest Nebraska News*, Mar. 19, July 2, Apr. 16, 1931.

11. *A Souvenir History of Fort Robinson, Nebraska, 1930*, 13; *Northwest Nebraska News*, Mar. 6, 1930.

12. *Northwest Nebraska News*, Sept. 10, 1931.

13. "Inspection and Survey of Fort Robinson, Nebr.," June 22, 1929, RG 159, NA.

14. *Northwest Nebraska News*, July 3, 10, 1930, May 7, 1931; Fort Building File, FRM.

15. *Northwest Nebraska News*, Sept. 18, 1930, May 21, 1931; *Register of Graduates and Former Cadets of the United States Military Academy* (West Point Alumni Foundation, Inc., 1971), 448.

16. "Inspection and Survey of Fort Robinson, Nebr.," June 22, 1929, June 21, 1930, July 8, 1931, RG 159, NA.

17. *Crawford Tribune*, May 24, 1929.

18. *Northwest Nebraska News*, Jan. 29, 1931, Dec. 18, 1930.

19. Ibid., May 8, 15, Aug. 14, 1930.

20. *Crawford Tribune*, Nov. 22, 1929.

21. Ibid., Nov. 15, 1929, June 5, 1931.

22. *Northwest Nebraska News*, Aug. 20, 1931; *Crawford Tribune*, Aug. 21,1931.

23. RDH (1932), 2; *Northwest Nebraska News*, Sept. 17, 24, 1931; Carter, *The History of Fort Robinson*, 14.

24. RDH (1931), 3–4.

25. *Northwest Nebraska News*, Aug. 25, 1932.

26. *Official Army Register, January 1, 1934* (GPO: 1934), 292.

27. *Crawford Tribune*, Jan. 26, 1933; *Northwest Nebraska News*, Jan. 9, 1930, Oct. 20, 1932.

28. *Northwest Nebraska News*, Nov. 30, Dec. 14, 1933; Fort Building File, FRM; *Crawford Tribune*, July 20, 1934.

29. Fort Building File, FRM.

30. Maurice Matloff, ed., *American Military History* (GPO:1969), 413–14. For more on the CCC, see Leslie Alexander Lacy, *The Soil Soldiers: The Civilian Conservation Corps in the Great Depression* (Radnor, Pa.: Chilton Book Co., 1976).

31. Gordon C. Golden CCC questionnaire, July 29, 1988, FRM.

32. *Northwest Nebraska News*, May 18, 1933; PR, May 1933.

33. Fort Building File, FRM.

34. *Northwest Nebraska News*, Aug. 17, 1933.

35. *Crawford Tribune*, Aug. 11, 1933.

36. Work report, June 28, 1935, Harold Cook papers, AFBNM; *Northwest Nebraska News*, Apr. 26, 1934; CCC questionnaires and interview transcripts at FRM.

37. *Crawford Tribune*, July 27, 1934; *Northwest Nebraska News*, Jan. 24, 1935.

38. Unidentified newspaper articles, S-201 File, CCC, Records of the Civilian Conservation Corps, Record Group 35, NA; *Crawford Tribune*, Feb. 15, 1934.

39. PR, May, Apr., July 1934; *The Butte Trail*, May 24, 1935, RG 501, NSHS.

40. *The Butte Trail*, May 24, 1935.

41. PR, Oct. 1935; *Northwest Nebraska News*, Oct. 24, 1935.

42. Bill Mallon and Ian Buchanan, *Quest for Gold* (New York: Leisure Press, 1984), 90. Guy, Jr., like his father, had a distinguished career in the U.S. Cavalry. He graduated from West Point in 1898 to eventually become chief of cavalry. He retired as a major general in 1939, but was recalled for active duty during World War II. Henry died in 1967.

43. David Wallechinsky, *The Complete Book of the Olympics* (New York: Penguin Books, 1984), 224, 235; Margaret Phipps Leonard, "Exhibition at Fort Robinson," typescript, RG 501, NSHS.

44. *The Rasp 1922* (Fort Riley, Kan.: The Cavalry School, 1922), 159–60; *Northwest Nebraska News*, Dec. 27, 1934.

45. *Northwest Nebraska News*, Dec. 27, 1934.

46. Ibid., May 30, June 6, 1935.

47. *Crawford Tribune*, June 21, 28, 1935; *The Butte Trail*, June 29, 1935.

48. *Northwest Nebraska News*, Aug. 22, 1935; "1936 United States Olympic Equestrian Team," scrapbook compiled by 2nd Lt. R. T. Abernethy, copy at FRM.

49. Wallechinsky, *The Complete Book*, 215, 225, 230.

50. *Crawford Tribune*, June 10, 1937, June 18, 1938; *Northwest Nebraska News*, Sept. 8, 1938, June 22, 1939.

51. PR, June 1939; *Northwest Nebraska News*, June 22, 1939.

52. *Northwest Nebraska News*, Sept. 7, 1939.

53. *Crawford Tribune*, Oct. 6, 27, 1939; "Intimate Glimpses Behind the Olympic Team Jumping," typescript, RG 1517.AM, NSHS.

54. Fort Building File; letter, Lt. Col. Sumner Williams to A. P. Howe, Aug. 21, 1934; joint letter to: President, Crawford Chamber of Commerce; Mayor, City of Crawford; Post Commander, Arch Cullers Post 138, American Legion; Editor, *Crawford Tribune*; Editor,

Northwest Nebraska News, June 28, 1934, all FRM.

55. *Crawford Tribune*, May 13, 1932.

56. *Northwest Nebraska News*, June 28, 1934.

57. Roy V. Mahlman, "The Last Roundup of the Great Sioux Nation," WPA Federal Writers Project, Sept. 15, 1939, FRM.

58. *Crawford Tribune*, Aug. 3, 1934.

59. Ibid.; *Northwest Nebraska News*, Aug. 30, Sept. 6, 1934.

60. *Northwest Nebraska News*, Aug. 30, 1934.

61. Ibid., Sept. 6, 1934; "Souvenir Program, Dedication of Twin Monuments in Honor of Lieut. Levi Robinson and Crazy Horse," Sept. 5, 1934, RG 501, NSHS.

62. Letter, Henry Standing Bear to George Gorton, Oct. 22, 1934, FRM.

63. Mahlman, "The Last Roundup," 7.

64. Letter, Maj. Edwin N. Hardy to QM Gen. Louis Bash, Mar. 19, 1935, RG 92, NA.

65. Letter, Bash to Hardy, Mar. 28, 1935, ibid.

4. War Comes to Fort Robinson

1. Robert McCaffree veteran questionnaire, FRM; *Northwest Nebraska News*, Aug. 15, 1940.

2. Waller, *Horses and Mules*, 10.

3. Inspector General's Report, Oct. 21, 1939, comments of Maj. James Adamson and Maj. Gen. P. P. Bishop, RG 92, NA.

4. Waller, *Horses and Mules*, 10; Col. Edwin Hardy, "Remount Procurement Operations," *The Quartermaster Review* 20 (Jan.– Feb. 1941): 26–27.

5. HVS, Sept. 8, 1939, to June 30, 1942.

6. *Crawford Clipper*, Sager obituary, n. d.; Elburne Luehrs interview, Dec. 28, 1987; George Richmond, "Work and Play at Ft. Robinson, Nebraska, Remount Station During World War II," typescript, all FRM.

7. All information on new buildings erected 1941–42 compiled from Fort Building File, FRM.

8. *Northwest Nebraska News*, Aug. 15, Mar. 28, 1940, July 7, 1938.

9. Ibid., June 6, 1940; Robert McCaffree, "A Military Retrospect," typescript, FRM.

10. *Northwest Nebraska News*, Jan. 12, Nov. 16, 1939; *Sunday Journal and Star*, June 2, 1940.

11. *Northwest Nebraska News*, Apr. 21, 1941; inspection report by Col. Edwin Hardy, May 8, 1941, RG 92, NA.

12. Information on new troop facilities compiled from Fort Building File, FRM; *Northwest Nebraska News*, July 10, 1941.

13. Inspection Report, Oct. 3, 1941, endorsement by Col. E. M. Daniels, Nov. 10, 1941; "Completion Report, November 10, 1941, Construction of Fencing and Illumination of Critical Areas," RG 501, NSHS.

14. Hardy Inspection Report, May 8, 1941; "Memorandum to All Officers, July 17, 1941;" "Schedule Officers' School Fort Robinson, Nebraska," both FRM.

15. McCaffree, "A Military Retrospect," 7.

16. "Depot Instructions Number 53, September 30, 1941;" "Depot Instructions Number 66, October 13, 1941;" "Daily Information Letter, October 7, 1941," all FRM.

17. McCaffree veteran questionnaire, FRM.

18. Letter, Robert McCaffree, May 4, 1992, FRM.

19. Harry Schneider interview, June 6, 1990, FRM.

20. Ibid.

21. Letter, Robert McCaffree, Mar. 4, 1989, FRM.

22. John K. Kerr and Edward S. Wallace, *The Story of the United States Cavalry, 1775–1942* (New York: Bonanza Books, 1984), 248–52.

23. *Northwest Nebraska News*, Apr. 16, 1942.

24. *Omaha World-Herald*, Apr. 3, 5, 1942.

25. Ibid., Apr. 7, 1942.

26. *Crawford Tribune*, Apr. 10, 1942; Thomas R. Buecker, "The Dismounting of the Fourth Cavalry at Fort Robinson, 1942," *Rural Electric Nebraskan* 43 (Feb. 1989): 12–14.

27. Glen Daugherty, phone conversation, Nov. 9, 1988; letter, Col. Harry A. Clark, Nov. 28, 1988, FRM.

28. John Dvergsten interview, Aug. 19, 1988, FRM.

29. Nels Christensen interview, FRM.

30. HVS, semiannual reports, Jan. 1, 1941, to June 30, 1943; Floyd Sager interview, July 2, 1979, FRM.

31. HVS, reports for 1943; Fort Building File, FRM.

32. "Monthly Information Letter," Feb.–Oct. 1944, RG 501, NSHS (hereafter MIL).

33. Waller, *Horses and Mules*, 19; MIL, Jan.–June 1944.

34. MIL, May 1944, Jan., Apr., July, Aug. 1945.

35. *Hoofbeats and Barks* (post newspaper, issues available only from February 19 to July 10, 1943), June 4, 1943, RG 501, NSHS.

36. Herman Wulf interview, June 9, 1988, FRM.

37. Waller, *Horses and Mules*, 24.

38. *Sunday World-Herald* (Omaha), Aug. 12, 1945; Wulf interview; Paul Burdett file, both FRM.

39. *Hoofbeats and Barks*, Mar. 12, 1943.

40. Luehrs interview; Lyman Gueck File, both FRM.

41. Waller, *Horses and Mules*, 27; "Visit to Fort Robinson, Nebraska," Mar. 1–9, 1945, Geographic File, RG 92, NA.

42. *Hoofbeats and Barks*, Apr. 2, 23, 1943.

43. Ibid., June 18, 1943; L. Harmon Wilmoth, "Wyoming Doctor," typescript, 62, FRM.

44. *Hoofbeats and Barks*, May 14, 1943.

45. Ibid., July 10, 1943.

46. Samuel Mitchell, "Narrative," typescript, FRM.

47. Luehrs interview, FRM.

48. "A Brief History of the 88th Glider Infantry Regiment," FRM.

49. *Crawford Tribune*, Aug. 13, 1943.

50. Lt. Col. William Blythe, *Thirteenth Air Borne Division*; "History of the 326th Glider Infantry Regt.," both FRM.

51. Letter, Homer Blank, Oct. 20, 1987; letter, Robert Fischer, Nov. 20, 1987, both FRM.

52. *Crawford Tribune*, Aug. 20, 1943; Wulf interview, FRM.

53. List of Post Officers 1944 ; Mueller interview; Luehrs interview, all FRM.

54. *Hoofbeats and Barks*, June 11, 1943.

55. Information on new construction compiled from Fort Building File, FRM.

56. John Findley veteran questionnaire, FRM.

57. Fort Building File; Wulf interview, both FRM.

58. For more on WAC life at Fort Robinson, see Esther Edmonson and Gladys Hoefner interviews, July 7, 1989, FRM.

59. Margerete Runge interview, Dec. 28, 1987, FRM. Margerete Franklin married Sgt. Walter Runge on Oct. 10, 1945, just before they left Fort Robinson.

60. Confidential Report on Disloyal Statements, Sept. 21, 1944, and "Monthly ISS Report, 31 December 1944," Geographic File, RG 92, NA.

61. *Hoofbeats and Barks*, June 18, 1943.

62. Ibid., Mar. 8, 1943.

63. Sadie Barker scrapbook, copy at FRM.

64. *Crawford Tribune*, Aug. 7, Dec. 25, 1942, July 2, 1945.

65. *Hoofbeats and Barks*, June 4, 1943; *Crawford Tribune*, July 27, 1945.

66. McCaffree, "A Military Retrospect," 20–21; Bob Grier, "Whitney Lake," *NEBRASKAland* 72 (Dec. 1994): 10.

67. Luehrs interview; James C. Stratton interview, 1974; "Remount Soldier's Guide, Detachment Quartermaster Corps, Robinson QM Depot," typescript, all at FRM.

68. Ralph Knepper interview; Stratton interview, both FRM; *Hoofbeats and Barks*, Apr. 2, 1943.

69. *Crawford Tribune*, July 13, 1945.

70. *Robinson Roundup*, July 18, 1946.

71. *Crawford Tribune*, Dec. 25, 1942; Leland Hughes interview, May 25, 1976; McCaffree veteran questionnaire, both FRM. Luther was later killed in action in Italy. Herman Rohrig, who also played halfback on the team, was the remount company clerk. He once told the author, "My big job was keeping Butch Luther out of trouble." Herman F. Rohrig veteran questionnaire, FRM.

72. *Crawford Tribune*, Dec. 25, 1942; Knepper interview, FRM.

73. Richmond, "Work and Play at Fort Robinson," 5.

74. Wulf interview; Homer Blank letter, Oct. 20, 1987, both FRM. Sally Rand's visit was an event recalled by almost every post veteran who was there at the time.

75. James B. Young interview; Sager interview, both FRM; HVS, July 1, 1943.

76. "Memorandum for Lieutenant Colonel Elwin A. Spencer, Headquarters Army Service Forces, 22 May 1944," U.S. Army Quartermaster Museum, Fort Lee, Virginia, copy at FRM.

5. War Dogs

1. Anna M. Waller, *Dogs and National Defense* (Washington, D.C.: Office of the Quartermaster General, 1958), 2–3.

2. *TM 10-396, Technical Manual, War Dogs* (GPO: 1943), 7.

3. Fairfax Downey, *Dogs for Defense* (New York: Dogs for Defense, Inc. 1955), 15–24.

4. Erna Risch and Chester L. Kieffer, *The Quartermaster Corps: Organization, Supply and Services* Vol. 2 (GPO: 1955), 325–27. For a complete overview of U.S. Army dog use, see Michael G. Lemish, *War Dogs: Canines in Combat* (Washington, D.C.: Brassey's Inc., 1996).

5. Letter, adjutant general to commanding general, Services of Supply, July 16, 1942, General File 454.3 of War Dog Training, RG 92, NA (hereafter GFWDT).

6. Risch and Kieffer, *The QM Corps*, 326–27.

7. Waller, *Dogs and National Defense*, 8.

8. Bob Burger interview, July 16, 1988; Donald Stuber interview, Oct. 9, 1987, both FRM.

9. Clayton G. Going, *Dogs at War* (New York: The Macmillan Co., 1945), 17–18.

10. Letter, Col. E. M. Daniels to commanding officer, Fort Robinson, Aug. 3, 1942, GFWDT.

11. Ibid., July 24, 1942.

12. All information on K-9 facilities is from the Fort Building File and from Semiannual Veterinary Section reports, 1942–43, both FRM.

13. Lt. Col. Frank L. Carr to Daniels, Oct. 27, 1942, GFWDT.

14. Daniels to commanding officer, Front Royal, Aug. 4, 1942, GFWDT.

15. Col. Charles Hoss to Daniels, Sept. 10, 1942, GFWDT.

16. Semiannual Veterinary Section Report, July 1, 1942, to Dec. 31, 1942, 15–16, FRM.

17. Surgeon general to commanding officer, Fort Robinson WDRTC, Mar. 11, 1943, GFWDT.

18. Letter, Ira Kunkel, Mar. 12, 1995, FRM; Wiley S. Isom, *Diary of a War Dog Platoon* (Shelbyville, Tenn.: Bible & Missionary Foundation, 1997), 226–27.

19. "War Dog Reception & Training Center, Fort Robinson, Nebraska," typescript, n.d. (trainee orientation booklet), FRM.

20. Semiannual Veterinary Section Report, July 1, 1942, to Dec. 31, 1942, 11–12.

21. *Technical Manual, War Dogs*, 44.

22. Lt. M. B. Godsol, "Pal Joins the Army," *The Quartermaster Review* 22 (Mar.–Apr. 1943): 54; W. A. Young, "A Visit to Fort Robinson," *The North American Veterinarian* (May 1944): 294, both FRM. By the fall of 1943 the two-week classroom period was combined with the basic dog training period.

23. Going, *Dogs at War*, 21–24.

24. *Technical Manual, War Dogs*, 113, 121; Downey, *Dogs for Defense*, 57.

25. Inspection reports, Feb. 9–10, 25, 1945, Geographic File, RG 92, NA; letter, John Matovich, June 20, 1982, FRM.

26. Young, "A Visit to Fort Robinson," 294; Semiannual Veterinary Section Report, Jan. 1, 1943, to June 31, 1943, 5, FRM.

27. Information compiled from veteran questionnaires at FRM.

28. Letter, Leonard Fullerton, Mar. 6, 1993; Richard Dietrick interview, n.d., both FRM.

29. Dennis L. Noble, *The Beach Patrol and Corsair Fleet* (Washington, D.C.: Coast Guard Historian's Office, 1992), 14–15; Randall Buckley statement, n.d.; Alex Robertson veteran questionnaire, both FRM.

30. *Hoofbeats and Barks*, Apr. 9, 1943; Sgt. J. Weston Woodbury, "Personal Daily Log of Tour of Duty," entry for July 1, 1943, copy at FRM.

31. *Hoofbeats and Barks*, Mar. 12, 1943.

32. Anonymous, "The Canine Corps," RG 501, NSHS.

33. *Hoofbeats and Barks*, June 18, 1943.

34. Richmond, "Work and Play at Fort Robinson," 5; *Crawford Tribune*, Feb. 12, 19, 1943.

35. *Hoofbeats and Barks*, Feb. 26, Mar. 5, 1943.

36. Ibid., Apr. 9, 1943; Richard J. Zika, "Dog Days in the CBI," *CBIVA Sound-off* (Winter 1991): 40–42.

37. "Use of War Dogs in Prisoner of War Camps," Dec. 23, 1944; Brig. Gen. Ralph Talbot to Daniels, Dec. 9, 1944, both GFWDT.

38. *Omaha World-Herald*, Mar. 15, 1943.

39. Young, "A Visit to Fort Robinson," 294.

40. *Omaha World-Herald*, July 4, 1943.

41. Going, *Dogs at War*, 10.

42. *Omaha World-Herald*, Jan. 29, 1945.

43. Clarence J. Pfaffenberger, "No Casualties," *The Shepherd Dog Review* (July 1944): 15–17; Waller, *Dogs and National Defense*, 27; Robert Johnson interview, June 11, 1992; Art Tyler interview, June 11, 1992, all FRM.

44. "SOP For Training of Scout Dog Platoons," and training schedules, FRM.

45. Risch and Kieffer, *The QM Corps*, 333.

46. "K-9 Mine Detection," *QM Training Service Journal* (Sept. 1944): 7; Risch and Kieffer, *The QM Corps*, 331.

47. "Instructions Issued During Recent Inspection, 11 Dec. 1944," GFWDT; Inspection reports, Mar. 1–9, Apr. 25–26, 1945, Geographic File, RG 92, NA.

48. "General Instructions for Field Exercises," July 3, 1944, Geographic File, RG 92, NA.

49. "Verbally to assembled staff and Att. Troops at Division CP," July 11, 1944, Geographic File, RG 92, NA.

50. "Instructions Issued During Recent Inspection, 11 Dec. 1944," GFWDT.

51. Risch and Kieffer, *The QM Corps*, 333–34; *Sunday Journal and Star*, June 17, 1945.

52. "Maintenance of Dog Kennels," June 6, 1945; June 21, 1945, endorsement to June 6, 1945 letter, both GFWDT.

53. *Sunday Journal and Star*, June 17, 1945.

54. Risch and Kieffer, *The QM Corps*, 334; W. C. Thompson interview, July 8, 1978; Roger F. Holding interview, n.d., both FRM.

55. Table of Organization and Equipment No. 7–167, "Infantry Scout Dog Platoons," War Department, Dec. 14, 1944, with corrections Feb. 1, 22, 1945, FRM.

56. Training Circular No. 35, "Infantry Scout Dog Platoons," War Department, Aug. 20, 1945, FRM.

57. *Crawford Tribune*, Aug. 10, 24, 1945; *Omaha World-Herald*, Aug. 19, 1945.

58. Lester Gertsch veteran questionnaire, FRM.

6. Prisoners of War

1. The best sources on prisoners of war in this country are Arnold Krammer, *Nazi Prisoners of War in America* (New York: Stein & Day, 1979) and Judith Gansberg, *Stalag U.S.A.* (New York: Thomas Y. Crowell Co., 1977).

2. Krammer, *Nazi Prisoners*, 271–72.

3. Ibid., 81.

4. "Memorandum for the Chief of Engineers," Nov. 26, 1942, RG 393, NA.

5. Memoranda on "Layout of War Internment Camp, Fort Robinson," Dec. 4, Dec. 12, 1942, RG 393, NA.

6. "Entry for the Diary," Dec. 21, 1942, RG 393, NA.

7. Personal conversation with John Southard, Springfield, Mo., Jan. 11, 1994; *Crawford Tribune*, Dec. 18, 1942.

8. *Crawford Tribune*, Jan. 5, 1943; "Entry for the Diary," May 14, 1943, RG 393, NA.

9. All information on camp buildings and facilities is compiled from Camp Buildings File, FRM; "Memorandum to General Clemens," Apr. 28, 1943, RG 393, NA.

10. Enemy PW Information Bureau, Subject File 1942–46, "Other Inspection Reports, Robinson, Fort - Nebraska" (hereafter IR) Jan. 30, 1944, Records of the Office of Provost Marshal General, Record Group 389, NA.

11. Ibid., Dec. 19, 1943.

12. Ibid., Feb. 5, 1945.

13. Ibid.

14. Alfred Thompson, "A Characterization of the Educational and Recreational Diversions of PW Camp, Fort Robinson, Nebraska," typescript, FRM.

15. IR, July 31, 1944.

16. Ibid.

17. Ibid., Feb. 8, 1945.

18. Lt. Col. Lester Vocke memorandum, Apr. 28, June 21, 1943, RG 393, NA.

19. IR, Dec. 19, 1943.

20. Royal E. Draime, "Historical Sketch," manuscript, FRM.

21. Constitution and By-laws of the Windy Flats Enlisted Men's Club, copy at FRM.

22. *Hoofbeats and Barks*, July 3, 1943.

23. Draime, "Historical Sketch;" Mitchell "Narrative," both FRM; IR, Jan. 21, 1944.

24. *Order of Battle of the German Army* (GPO: 1943), 202; Wolfgang Dorschel interview, Aug. 22, 1987, FRM.

25. "Fort Robinson Prisoner of War Camp Revisited, Part 2," *Northwest Nebraska Post*, Oct. 1987.

26. Letter, Dietrich Kohl, Aug. 24, 1985, FRM.

27. "Aus Dem Leben Eines Prisoners" (Episodes from a Prisoner's Life) *Neuer Horizont* (camp newspaper), Sept. 21, 1945, trans. by Dr. Hans Waecker, former PW, Cliff Island, Maine, May 16, 1988, FRM.

28. List by Dietrich Kohl, copy at FRM.

29. Letter, Dietrich Kohl, Nov. 25, 1993, FRM.

30. Mitchell, "Narrative," FRM; Fritz Esenwein collection, museum # 11467, NSHS; "Administrative Memorandum No. 51," headquarters, prisoner of war camp, Fort Robinson, Nebraska, Sept. 23, 1944, FRM.

31. Mitchell, "Narrative," FRM.

32. "Episodes from a Prisoner's Life," *Neuer Horizont*, Sept. 21, 1945.

33. Hans Wallendorf papers, RG 501, NSHS.

34. "Prisoner of War Camp Fort Robinson Guard Regulations," Oct. 1943," RG 389, NA.

35. Gen. Archer L. Lerch, "The Army Reports on Prisoners of War," *The American Mercury* 55 (May 1945): 537–38; IR, Jan. 21, 1944.

36. IR, Jan. 30, July 19, 1944.

37. Ibid., Jan. 30, Feb. 21, June 21, 1944.

38. Ibid., Feb. 22, June 21, July 19, 1944.

39. Mitchell, "Narrative;" Thompson letter, Dec. 15, 1945, both FRM.

40. Transfer requests of Erich Waltenberger, Heinz Unglaube, and Franz Erpeldinger, Enemy PW Information Bureau, Subject File, RG 389, NA.

41. IR, Dec. 19, 1943, Feb. 24, 1944; Letter, Dietrich Kohl, Jan. 1, 1944, FRM.

42. Band transfer request dated Feb. 21, 1944, Enemy PW Information Bureau, Subject File, RG 389, NA; IR, June 21, 1944.

43. Mitchell, "Narrative;" Kurt Kohler interview, June 13, 1978, both FRM.

44. "Field Service Camp Survey, February 15, 1945, Report on Camp Spokesman," RG 389, NA.

45. Benjamin Lemlich interview, Aug. 20, 1988; Herman Wulf interview; Beverly Humbert Chiasson, "My Life at Fort Robinson," typescript, all FRM.

46. Mitchell, "Narrative;" Wolfgang Loesche interview, Aug. 27, 1987, both FRM.

47. Letter, Austrian prisoners to the War Department, Washington, D.C., n. d., translated copy ; Chiasson, "My Life at Fort Robinson;" Mitchell, "Narrative," all FRM.

48. IR, June 21, 1944.

49. Ibid.

50. Ibid., Mar. 30, 1945.

51. "Instructions For Persons Using PW labor," 1944, RG 501, NSHS.

52. IR, Dec. 19, 1943; Draime, "Historical Sketch," FRM.

53. IR, Jan. 30, 1944.

54. Ibid., Mar. 30, 1945, June 21, 1944.

55. HVS, July 1 – Dec. 31, 1944, Jan. 1 – Sept. 3, 1945.

56. Report of Roscoe Craig to post engineer, Mar. 30, 1945, FRM.

57. IR, June 21, 1944.

58. Ibid., Jan. 24, 1945.

59. Ibid., Feb. 5, 1945.

60. Ibid., Jan. 21, Feb. 21, 1944.

61. Ibid., July 19, 1944, Jan. 24, 1945.

62. Ibid., July 31, 1944.

63. Ibid., Jan. 24, 1945.

64. Ibid.; Gerald Kennedy interview, FRM.

65. Wolfgang Dorschel interview, Aug. 22, 1987; Mitchell, "Narrative," both FRM.

66. Personal commentary on Varista performers by Dr. Hans Waecker, 1989, FRM.

67. IR, Jan. 24, Feb. 5, 1945; Draime, "Historical Sketch," FRM.

68. IR, Feb. 5, 1945, July 31, 1944.

69. Ibid., July 31, 1944.

70. Ibid., Jan. 30, Feb. 5, July 19, 1945.

71. Letter, Dietrich Kohl, Aug. 24, 1985, FRM.

72. Carl Still interview, July 11, 1978, FRM.

73. Letter, Kurt Kohler to family, Apr. 15, 1944, RG 501, NSHS.

74. IR, July 31, 1945.

75. Camp Population File, FRM.

76. "Special Equipment Authorization" and "Report on War Dog Installation," RG 393, NA.

77. Krammer, *Nazi Prisoners*, 149. For a more detailed study of Nazism at the Fort Robinson camp, see Thomas R. Buecker, "Nazi Influence at the Fort Robinson Prisoner of War Camp During World War II," *Nebraska History*, 73 (Spring 1992): 32–41.

78. IR, Feb. 5, 27, 1945; Buecker, "Nazi Influence," 35, 37.

79. Wolfgang Dorschel interview, Aug. 22, 1987, FRM.

80. Gansberg, *Stalag U.S.A.*, 59; Buecker, "Nazi Influence," 38.

81. Letters, Alfred Thompson, Jan. 30, 1946, June 30, 1945; Thompson, "A Characterization," FRM. A wealth of information on special projects is found in the Special Projects Letters file at FRM.

82. Wolfgang Dorschel diary, RG 1517. AM, NSHS; Dorschel interview; Thompson letter, June 30, 1945, both FRM.

83. Thompson letters, June 30, July 27, 1945, FRM.

84. IR, Feb. 27, 1945, Jan. 30, 1945.

85. Lee, *Fort Meade*, 228–33; Draime, "Historical Sketch," FRM.

86. Copies of both proclamations found with Alfred A. Thompson papers, FRM.

87. Lemlich interview, FRM; Buecker, "Nazi Influence," 39.

88. Buecker, "Nazi Influence," 39; Thompson letter, June 30, 1945, FRM.

89. *Crawford Tribune*, May 18, 25, 1945.

90. List of donations from Alfred Thompson papers.

91. Letter, Mrs. R. E. Oglesby, York, Nebr., Oct. 18, 1987, FRM.

92. *York Daily Times*, May 21, 1945; *York Republican*, May 24, 1945.

7. Abandonment, Transfer to the USDA

1. James Mansheim interview, July 26, 1978; Burl Minton interview, 1976; Donald Stuber interview, Oct. 9, 1987, all FRM.

2. MIL, Apr.–Sept. 1945.

3. HVS, Jan. 1 – Sept. 3, 1945, 7–8; *Robinson Roundup*, Nov. 2, 1945, 5–6.

4. MIL, July–Dec. 1944, Oct. 1945–July 1946.

5. Numbers of enlisted men with the remount detachment were reported in MIL.

6. MIL, June, Aug. 1946, Jan. 1947, Sept. 1946; *Crawford Tribune*, Jan. 3, 1947.

7. MIL, Aug. 1947; *Crawford Tribune*, July 5, 1946.

8. *Crawford Tribune*, Sept. 28, 1945; Letter, Alfred Thompson to Royal Draime, Nov. 28, 1945, FRM.

9. Thompson letter, Dec. 7, 1945, FRM; GO 2, Robinson Quartermaster Depot, Jan. 31, 1946, GFWDT.

10. Krammer, *Nazi Prisoners*, 221–24; *Crawford Tribune*, Aug. 30, 1946. The warehouse remained standing on site until it was demolished in the mid-1960s. At this writing, a number of former camp buildings that were moved into town are still standing and in use.

11. Letter, QM general to Col. Brisbane Brown, Oct. 26, 1945, GFWDT.

12. *Sunday Journal and Star,* June 17, 1945.

13. Letter, Lt. James Ferguson to Harlan Heitz, Nov. 28, 1945, FRM.

14. *Robinson Roundup*, Nov. 2, 1945; Dog numbers file, FRM.

15. MIL, Aug. 1946, June 1947; *Robinson Roundup*, Feb. 8, 1946; *Crawford Tribune*, Aug. 15, 1947.

16. *Omaha Morning World-Herald*, Nov. 13, 1947; *Crawford Tribune*, Feb. 20, 1948.

17. Letter, R. I. Ivins to Byron Cherry, May 23, 1947, RG 501, NSHS.

18. *Omaha World-Herald*, Jan. 11, 1948.

19. *Crawford Tribune*, Apr. 19, 1946; Waller, *Army Horses and Mules*, 31.

20. News release, Horse and Mule Association of America, May 14, 1948, RG 501, NSHS

21. *Crawford Tribune*, Apr. 19, 1946.

22. *Chadron Record*, Apr. 23, 1946.

23. *Crawford Tribune*, Feb. 20, 1948; Marvel Baker, "One Goosenest Wasp," typescript, University of Nebraska-Lincoln Archives and Special Collections (hereafter UNL Archives), 343.

24. *Chadron Record*, Apr. 23, 1946; *Crawford Tribune*, Apr. 4, 1947.

25. *Crawford Tribune*, Jan. 3, 1947.

26. Copy of HR 3484 is found in RG 501, NSHS.

27. *Crawford Tribune*, May 30, 1947; letter, Col. Edwin Hardy, June 17, 1959, RG 501, NSHS.

28. *Omaha World-Herald*, June 30, 1947; *Crawford Tribune*, Aug. 1, 1947.

29. Poem, "Old Fort Robinson," found in *Robinson Roundup*, Apr. 17, 1947.

30. *Crawford Tribune*, Oct. 4, 1946.

31. Herman Wulf interview, June 9, 1988, FRM.

32. *Crawford Tribune*, July 9, 1948.

33. Buecker, "The Fort and the Railroad," 32.

34. Information compiled from Post Cemetery file and Moses Milner file, FRM. Born in 1834, Milner left his Kentucky home and went west at a young age. For years he hunted and trapped with fur traders and mountain men, and searched for gold in California and Idaho. In the 1860s he relocated to the southern Plains and began to scout and guide for the army. Tall, dark-bearded, with a taste for liquor and a jovial personality, he became a favorite with army officers. In 1868 he scouted for Custer in the Washita campaign, and later for the 1875 Jenney exploration to the Black Hills. After prospecting in the Hills, Milner went to Camp Robinson in the fall of 1876 as a scout for Ranald Mackenzie's winter campaign. For some months he had been accused by Tom Newcomb, a quartermaster employee at the post, of murdering John Richard and his nephew at the Niobrara Crossing in 1875. On the afternoon of October 29, a confrontation between the two at the post trader's store nearly ended in a gunfight. Although both left the bar in apparent friendship, Newcomb shot Milner from ambush a short time later behind the quartermaster corral. California Joe died instantly.

35. PW Deaths and Cemetery file, FRM.

36. *Crawford Tribune*, Sept. 26, Oct. 3, 1947.

37. Ibid., Oct. 3, 1947; "Fort Robinson Horse and Colt Exhibition," FRM.

38. MIL, Dec. 1947.

39. *Crawford Tribune*, Apr. 2, June 1, 25, 1948.

40. Confirmation copy of telegram dated Apr. 9, 1948; Joint Army and Navy Bulletin No. 18, June 7, 1948; telegram, QM general to Robinson QM Depot, May 28, 1948, RG 501, NSHS.

41. Unidentified newspaper article, FRM; *Omaha World-Herald*, Jan. 11, 1948, Mar. 16, 1947.

42. For statements on continuation of remount operations by USDA, see *Crawford*

Tribune, Apr. 19, 1946, May 30, Dec. 12, 1947, Feb. 20, July 9, 1948, and *Omaha World-Herald*, May 13, 1946.

43. *The Fort Robinson Beef Cattle Research Station*, bulletin, University of Nebraska College of Agriculture, Agricultural Experiment Station, n. d., FRM; *Alliance Daily Times-Herald*, Mar. 8, 1952.

44. *Omaha World-Herald*, Dec. 3, 1948. For the USDA reorganization involving the remount program, see letter, E. J. Overly to Clinton Anderson, July 21, 1948, RG 501, NSHS.

45. *Omaha World-Herald*, Feb. 26, 1949.

46. *Omaha Sunday World-Herald*, Jan. 11, 1948; Elvin F. Frolik and Ralston J. Graham, *The University of Nebraska-Lincoln College of Agriculture: The First Century* (Lincoln: The Board of Regents of the University of Nebraska, 1987), (hereafter *The First Century*).

47. Letter, Lee O. Hill, June 23, 1998; Eugene Lessman interview, 1978, both FRM.

48. MIL, May–June 1949.

49. Letter, Lee O. Hill to Ed Bieganski, Dec. 5, 1992, FRM; Baker, "One Goosenest Wasp," 300.

50. R. M. Koch, "Fort Robinson," *Nebraska Experiment Station Quarterly*, 7 (Spring 1960): 3–6; *Crawford Tribune*, May 12, 1950.

51. Frolik, *The First Century*, 334; Koch, "Fort Robinson."

52. Baker, "One Goosenest Wasp," 305; George Round interview with Robert Koch, Sept. 15, 1976, UNL Archives, 7.

53. "The Fort Robinson Beef Cattle Research Station in Nebraska," remarks of James E. Ingalls, superintendent, *Congressional Record*, June 21, 1961, 10991.

54. Robert Koch, personal conversation, Jan. 19, 1994; Koch interview, 7–8.

55. *Plattsmouth Journal*, Dec. 23, 1954; Frolik, *The First Century*, 335; letter, Harold Cook to William Manton, Jan. 17, 1962, Harold Cook papers, AFBNM.

56. *Crawford Tribune*, Aug. 7, 1953, Aug. 10, 1956.

57. SCS Training file, FRM.

58. Ingalls, *Congressional Record*, 10991.

59. "List of Buildings and Improvements" and "Cross-Index Reference of Buildings and Improvements at Robinson QM Depot," both 1948, and "Surplus Buildings Located at Beef Cattle Research Station, Fort Robinson," all RG 501, NSHS.

60. *Omaha World-Herald*, Nov. 18, 1951; Marvel Baker, "Present Use of Fort Robinson," Apr. 1953, Elvin F. Frolik research file, FRM.

61. *Omaha Sunday World-Herald*, May 31, 1953; *Alliance Daily Times-Herald*, Mar. 8, 1952; letter, Marvel Baker to Gov. Robert Crosby, Apr. 24, 1953, Frolik research file, FRM.

62. Letter, Harold Cook to Monroe Bixler, Feb. 2, 1953, Harold Cook papers; *Scottsbluff Star-Herald*, Apr. 3, 1953; *Alliance Daily Times- Herald*, Jan. 17, 1952.

63. *Alliance Daily Times-Herald*, Mar. 10, 1952.

64. Ibid., Mar. 10, Apr. 29, 1952.

65. Letter, Harold Cook to Monroe Bixler, Dec. 12, 1952, Harold Cook papers.

66. *Crawford Clipper,* Jan. 18, 1990.

67. *Alliance Daily Times-Herald,* July 28, 1950.

68. Ibid., May 2, 1952.

69. Ibid., Jan. 24, 1952.

70. *Crawford Tribune,* Aug. 4, 1950; *Alliance Daily Times-Herald,* Mar. 14, Apr. 19, July 15, 1952.

71. *Crawford Tribune,* May 22, 1953; Frolik, *The First Century,* 336; Baker, "One Goosenest Wasp," 343–34.

72. *Alliance Daily Times-Herald,* Mar. 10, 1952.

73. Letter, Marvel Baker to Bruce Snyder, Dec. 5, 1958, Frolik research file, FRM.

74. Frolik, *The First Century,* 335; Baker, "Present Use of Fort Robinson," 4; *Scottsbluff Star-Herald,* Apr. 3, 1953.

75. *Omaha World-Herald,* Nov. 13, 1947; *Crawford Tribune,* Dec. 19, 1952; *Omaha Sunday World-Herald Magazine,* May 31, 1953.

76. Harold Cook, "Some Possibilities For The Practical Use of the Fort Robinson Area;" letter, Cook to Terry Carpenter, Jan. 30, 1953, both Harold Cook papers.

77. "Excerpts from Ft. Robinson Survey Committee Report, May 11, 1953," Frolik research file, FRM; *Scottsbluff Star-Herald,* Nov. 16, 1953.

78. Letter, Monroe Bixler to Harold Cook, Jan. 29, 1953, Harold Cook papers; *Alliance Daily Times-Herald,* Jan. 14, 1953.

79. *Alliance Daily Times-Herald,* June 14, 1956.

80. *Crawford Tribune,* Nov. 20, 1953, Jan. 15, 1954; *Alliance Daily Times-Herald,* June 13, 1956.

81. *Plattsmouth Journal,* Dec. 23, 1954.

82. Frolik, *The First Century,* 337; *Scottsbluff Star-Herald,* Nov. 17, 1954.

83. Frolik, *The First Century,* 336.

84. *Crawford Tribune,* Feb. 11, 1955.

85. Letter, Harold Cook to Lt. Col. Edwin Hardy, May 27, 1955, Harold Cook papers.

86. "Survey Report of James Olson, Apr. 16, 1953," Frolik research file, FRM.

87. The University of Nebraska Trailside Museum opened July 3, 1961. Since the early 1950s, university paleontology crews had used the fort for their field headquarters.

88. *Crawford Tribune,* Apr. 27, May 18, 1956; *Alliance Daily Times-Herald,* May 18, 1956; *Chadron Record,* May 31, 1956.

89. *Crawford Tribune,* June 8, 1956; *Alliance Daily Times-Herald,* June 4, 5, 1956.

90. *Alliance Daily Times-Herald,* June 8, 9, 12, 18, 1956. Legal notice of the building sale appeared in the *Alliance Daily Times-Herald,* Apr. 18, 1956.

91. Ibid., Dec. 9, 1960; Koch interview, 11.

92. Letter, Lavon J. Sumption to Chancellor Clifford Hardin et al., July 30, 1965, Frolik research file, FRM; Baker, "One Goosenest Wasp," 344; *Alliance Daily Times-Herald*, Feb. 18, 1963.

8. The Evolution of a State Park

1. *Alliance Daily Times-Herald*, Nov. 16, 1959; Frolik, *The First Century*, 337.

2. *Lincoln Journal and Star*, Nov. 14, 1959; letter, W. J. Lambert to Bruce Snyder, Dec. 5, 1958, Frolik research file, FRM.

3. Letter, T. C. Byerly to M. O. Steen, July 1, 1959; letter, W. J. Lambert to Byerly, May 27, 1959, both Frolik research file, FRM.

4. "Report of Legislative Council Committee on Outdoor Recreation, November 1960," 10, Frolik research file, FRM.

5. *Alliance Daily Times-Herald*, Dec. 9, 1959; *Crawford Tribune*, Dec. 11, 1959.

6. "Report of Legislative Council Committee," 10; letter, Frank Welsh, asst. to secretary, USDA, to U. S. Senator Wayne Morse, Apr. 4, 1969, S. C. Eittreim research file, RG 1517.AM, NSHS.

7. Frolik, *The First Century*, 342–44.

8. *Alliance Daily Times-Herald*, Aug. 12, 1965.

9. Frolik, *The First Century*, 337–38; letter, Elvin W. Schleicher to Frolik, Feb. 8, 1963; letter, Lavon J. Sumption to Chancellor Clifford Hardin et al., July 30, 1965, both Frolik research file, FRM. Rangeland research subsequently benefited from the Gudmundsen Sandhills Laboratory established north of Whitman.

10. Letter, Lee Galbreath to S. C. Eittreim, Jan. 31, 1968, Eittreim research file, NSHS; *Chadron Record*, Feb. 4, 1963.

11. Frolik, *The First Century*, 338–39; letter, Senator George Gerdes to James Thornton, asst. to secretary, USDA, June 14, 1966; letter, Thornton to Frolik, June 6, 1966, both Eittreim research file, NSHS.

12. Letter, S. C. Eittreim, July 14, 1997; FRM; *Crawford Tribune*, Mar. 7, 1965, Sept. 5, 1968; *Omaha World-Herald*, Apr. 2, 1968.

13. "Fort Robinson Multiple Use Complex," n.d., Frolik research file; Eittreim letter, July 14, 1997, both FRM.

14. Letter, Sumption to Hardin, et al., Aug. 3, 1965, Frolik research file, FRM.

Epilogue

1. *Alliance Daily Times-Herald*, Feb. 2, 1968.

2. *Omaha World-Herald*, n.d. (1967).

3. *Crawford Tribune*, Jan. 3, 1947.

Bibliography

Manuscripts and Government Records
Fort Robinson Museum, Crawford, Nebraska
(Some material was copied from sources listed elsewhere.)

Abernethy, Lt. R. T. "1936 United States Olympic Equestrian Team." Scrapbook.

Barker, Sadie. Scrapbook.

Buecker, Thomas R. "Fort Robinson, Nebraska: The Country Club of the Army." Typescript

Blythe, Lt. Col. William. *Thirteenth Air Borne Division*. N.p., n.d.

"A Brief History of the 88th Glider Infantry Regiment." N.p., n.d.

Camp Buildings File (PW).

Camp Population File (PW).

Chaisson, Beverly. "My Life at Fort Robinson." Typescript.

Constitution and By-Laws of the Windy Flats Enlisted Men's Club. n.d.

Dog Numbers File

Draime, Royal. "Historical Sketch." Manuscript.

Fort Building File-Information on each building or structure erected, 1874–1948.

Frolik, Elvin. Research File.

Harmon, L. Wilmoth. "Wyoming Doctor." Typescript.

"History of the 326th Glider Infantry Regiment." N.p., n.d.

Koester, Fred W. "A Historical Perspective of the U. S. Army Remount Service." Typescript.

Koester, William S. " Col. F. W. Koester, Noted Cavalryman, Thoroughbred Official." Typescript.

Mahlman, Roy V. "The Last Roundup of the Great Sioux Nation." WPA Federal Writers Project, September 15, 1939.

Map File-Plats, reservation maps, and building plans, Fort Robinson and PW camp.

McCaffree, Robert. "A Military Retrospect." Typescript.

Military Reservation File - Information about military reservation and Wood Reserve lands, 1874–1948.

Milner, Moses. Research File.

Mitchell, Samuel. "Narrative." Typescript.

Oral Interview Tapes and Transcripts.

Post Cemetery File.

PW Deaths and Cemetery File.

Quigley, William B. "Narrative." Typescript.

Remount Officers File.

"Remount Soldiers Guide, Detachment Quartermaster Corps, Robinson QM Depot." Typescript, n.d.

Richmond, George. "Work and Play at Fort Robinson, Nebraska, Remount Station During World War II." Typescript.

SCS (Soil Conservation Service) Training File.

Special Projects Letters File.

Thompson, Alfred E. Correspondence, 1944–46; "A Characterization of the Educational and Recreational Diversions of PW Camp, Fort Robinson, NE." Typescript.

Veteran and CCC Questionnaires.

"War Dog Reception and Training Center, Fort Robinson, Nebraska." Typescript, n.d.

Woodbury, J. Weston. "Personal Daily Log of Tour of Duty." Manuscript.

Agate Fossil Beds National Monument, Agate, Nebraska
Cook, Harold. Papers.

Cook, James. Papers

National Archives and Records Administration
Record Group 35. Records of the Civilian Conservation Corps.

Record Group 92. Records of the Office of the Quartermaster General. General Correspondence, "Geographic File."

Record Group 94. Records of the Office of the Adjutant General. Post Returns, 1900–1939; Returns from Regular Army Cavalry Regiments.

Record Group 153. Records of the Office of the Judge Advocate General.

Record Group 159. Records of the Office of the Inspector General.

Record Group 389. Records of the Office of the Provost Marshal General, 1941–46.

Record Group 393. Records of the U. S. Army Continental Commands, 1821–1920.

Nebraska State Historical Society, Lincoln, Nebraska
MS 8, Ricker, Eli S. Papers.

RG 501 and RG 1517. AM, Fort Robinson, Nebraska Records and Research Files.

Dorshel, Wolfgang. Diary.

Eittreim, S. C. Research File.

Eisenwein, Fritz. Collection.

University of Nebraska-Lincoln Archives and Special Collections
Baker, Marvel. "One Goosenest Wasp." Typescript.

Koch, Robert. Interview.

Unpublished Materials
Greene, Jerome A. "Fort Des Moines Historic District." Historic American Buildings Survey 1A-121, March 1987.

Hytrek, Anthony J. "The History of Fort Robinson, Nebraska, from 1900 to the Present." Master's thesis, Chadron State College, 1971.

Government Publications
Annual Reports of the Secretary of War, 1905, 1912, 1914. GPO: 1906–15.

Baker, Marvel, Leslie Johnson, and Russell L. Davis. *Beef Cattle Breeding Research at Fort Robinson*. Miscellaneous Publication 1. The University of Nebraska College of Agriculture, Agricultural Experiment Station, April 1952.

Congressional Record, 1961.

FM 25-6, Basic Field Manual, Dog Training. GPO: 1941

The Fort Robinson Beef Cattle Research Station. The University of Nebraska College of Agriculture, Agricultural Experiment Station, n.d.

Medal of Honor, 1863–1968. GPO: 1968.

Official Army Register, January 1, 1934. GPO: 1934.

Order of Battle of the German Army. GPO: 1943.

Order of Battle of the United States Land Forces in the World War, Vol. 3. GPO: 1949.

Outline Descriptions of Military Posts and of National Cemeteries. GPO: 1904.

Table of Organization and Equipment No. 7–167, "Infantry Scout Dog Platoons." GPO: 1945.

TM 10-390, Technical Manual, Operation of the Remount Breeding Service. GPO: 1941.

TM 10-395, Technical Manual, Remount. GPO: 1941.

TM 10-396, Technical Manual, War Dogs. GPO: 1943.

TM 19-500, Technical Manual, Enemy Prisoners of War. GPO: 1944.

Training Circular No. 35, "Infantry Scout Dog Platoons." GPO: 1945.

Newspapers and Newsletters
Alliance Daily Times-Herald

The Butte Trail (CCC camp)

The Chronilian (Fort Robinson)

Chadron Record

Crawford Clipper

Crawford Courier

Crawford Crescent

Crawford Tribune

Hoofbeats and Barks (Fort Robinson)

Kansas City Journal

Kansas City Star

Lincoln Daily Star

Neuer Horizont (PW camp)

Northwest Nebraska News (Crawford)

Northwest Nebraska Post (Crawford)

Omaha World-Herald

Omaha Progress

Plattsmouth Journal

Robinson Roundup (Fort Robinson)

Scottsbluff Star-Herald

Sunday Journal-Star (Lincoln)

Sunday World-Herald (Omaha)

Valentine Democrat

York Daily Times

York Republican

Books
Adams, Gerald M. *The Post Near Cheyenne: A History of Fort D.A. Russell, 1867–1930.* Boulder, Colo.: Pruett Publishing Co., 1989.

Berry, Capt. Ary C., ed. *A Souvenir History of Fort Robinson, Nebraska, 1930.* Crawford, Nebr.: Northwest Nebraska News, 1930.

Brinninstool, E. A. *Fighting Indian Warriors.* Harrisburg, Pa.: The Stackpole Co., 1953.

Carroll, John M. *The Black Military Experience in the American West.* New York: Liveright Publishing Co., 1971.

Carter, William H. *The History of Fort Robinson, Nebraska.* Crawford, Nebr.: Northwest Nebraska News, 1942.

Cavalry School. *The Rasp, 1922.* Fort Riley, Kan.: The Cavalry School, 1922.

Downey, Fairfax. *Dogs for Defense.* New York: Dogs for Defense, Inc., 1955.

Fletcher, Marvin E. *America's First Black General: Benjamin O. Davis, Sr., 1880–1970.* Lawrence: University Press of Kansas, 1989.

_____. *The Black Soldier and Officer in the United States Army.* Columbia, Mo.: University of Missouri Press, 1974.

Frolik, Elvin F., and Ralston J. Graham. *The University of Nebraska-Lincoln College of Agriculture: The First Century.* Lincoln: The Board of Regents of the University of Nebraska, 1987.

Ganoe, William A. *The History of the United States Army.* New York: D. Appleton-Century Co., 1942.

Gansberg, Judith M. *Stalag U.S.A.: The Remarkable Story of German POWs in America.* New York: Thomas Y. Crowell Co., 1977.

Glass, Maj. E. L. N. *The History of the Tenth Cavalry.* Fort Collins, Colo.: Old Army Press, 1972.

Going, Clayton G. *Dogs at War.* New York: The Macmillan Co., 1945.

Heitman, Francis B. *Historical Register and Dictionary of the United States Army,* 1903. Reprint. Urbana: University of Illinois Press, 1965.

Isom, Wiley S. *Diary of a War Dog Platoon.* Shelbyville, Tenn.: Bible & Missionary Foundation, 1997.

Kerr, John K. and Edward S. Wallace. *The Story of the United States Cavalry, 1775–1942.* New York: Bonanza Books, 1984.

Kipling, Rudyard. *Collected Verse of Rudyard Kipling.* Garden City, N.J.: Doubleday, Page & Co., 1918.

Krammer, Arnold. *Nazi Prisoners of War in America.* New York: Stein & Day, 1979.

Lacy, Leslie Alexander. *The Soil Soldiers: The Civilian Conservation Corps in the Great Depression.* Radnor, Pa.: Chilton Book Co., 1976.

Lee, Robert. *Fort Meade and the Black Hills.* Lincoln: University of Nebraska Press, 1991.

Lee, Wayne C. *Wild Towns of Nebraska.* Caldwell, Idaho: Caxton Printers, 1988.

Lemish, Michael G. *War Dogs: Canines in Combat.* Washington, D.C.: Brassey's Inc., 1996.

Lewis, Lt. Col. George G., and Capt. John Mewha. *History of Prisoner of War Utilization by the United States Army, 1776–1945.* GPO: 1955.

Mallon, Bill, and Ian Buchanan. *Quest for Gold.* New York: Leisure Press, 1984.

Matloff, Maurice, ed. *American Military History.* GPO: 1969.

Milner, Joe E., and Earle R. Forrest. *California Joe.* Caldwell, Idaho: Caxton Printers, 1935.

Noble, Dennis L. *The Beach Patrol and Corsair Fleet.* Washington, D.C.: Coast Guard Historian's Office, 1992.

Risch, Erna, and Chester L. Kieffer. *The Quartermaster Corps: Organization, Supply, and Services,* Vol. 2. GPO: 1955.

Rupp, Chap. Paul B., ed., *Fourth United States Field Artillery: History of Organization, 1907–1927.* San Antonio, Tex.: Ivan A. Britt, [1927?].

Schubert, Frank N. *Buffalo Soldiers, Braves, and the Brass.* Shippensburg, Pa.: White Mane Publishing Co., 1993.

_____. *On the Trail of the Buffalo Soldier: Biographies of African Americans in the U.S. Army, 1866–1917.* Wilmington, Del.: Scholarly Resources, Inc., 1995.

Splete, Allen. *Frederick Remington: Selected Letters.* Ogdensburg, N.Y.: Frederick Remington Art Museum, n.d.

Steffen, Randy. *The Horse Soldier, 1776–1943: The United States Cavalryman, His Uniform, Arms, Accoutrements, and Equipments*, 4 vols. Vol. 3, "The Last of the Indian Wars, the Spanish American War, the Brink of the Great War, 1881–1916." Norman: University of Oklahoma Press, 1978.

Sullivan, Capt. Charles J. *Army Posts and Towns.* Burlington, Vt.: Free Press Printing Co., 1926.

Wallechinsky, David. *The Complete Book of the Olympics.* New York: Penguin Books, 1984.

Waller, Anna M. *Army Horses and Mules and National Defense.* Washington, D.C.: Office of the Quartermaster General, 1958.

_____. *Dogs and National Defense.* Washington, D.C.: Office of the Quartermaster General, 1958.

Walsh, Richard. *The Making of Buffalo Bill.* Indianapolis: The Bobbs–Merrill Co., 1928.

West Point Alumni Foundation. *Register of Graduates and Former Cadets of the United States Military Academy.* West Point, N.Y.: West Point Alumni Foundation Inc., 1971.

Articles
Armstrong, Col. F. S. "The Remount Service." *The Quartermaster Review* 1 (July–Aug. 1921): 13–18.

Bieganski, Ed. "Condition and Issue Stable at Fort Robinson, Nebraska, 1938." *Dusting Off the Saddles.* Gordon, Nebr.: Tri-state Old Time Cowboys Memorial, 1993: 11–15.

Buecker, Thomas R. "The Abandonment of Fort Robinson." *NEBRASKAland* 76 (Apr. 1998): 22–27.

_____. "An Excellent Soldier and an Efficient Officer." *NEBRASKALand* 67 (June 1989): 12–17.

_____. "The Dismounting of the Fourth Cavalry at Fort Robinson, 1942." *Rural Electric Nebraskan* 43 (Feb. 1989): 12–14.

_____. "The Fort and the Railroad: Fort Robinson, Nebraska, on the C & NW." *North Western Lines* 23 (Fall 1996): 23–52.

_____. "The Fort Robinson War Dog Reception and Training Center, 1942–1946." *Military History of the West* 27 (Spring 1997): 1–23.

_____. "In the Old Army: Harry K. Hollenbach at Fort Robinson, 1911–1913." *Nebraska History* 71 (Spring 1990): 16–21.

_____. "Marking History at Fort Robinson." *NEBRASKAland* 73 (Mar. 1995): 42–47.

_____. "Mules, Horses, and Dogs: Fort Robinson in World War II." C.A.M.P. *Periodical* 16 (Apr. 1989): 34–49.

_____. "Nazi Influence at the Fort Robinson Prisoner of War Camp During World War II." *Nebraska History* 73 (Spring 1992): 32–41.

_____. "Prelude to Brownsville: The Twenty-fifth Infantry at Fort Niobrara, Nebraska, 1902–1906." *Great Plains Quarterly* 16 (Spring 1996): 95–106.

_____. "The Tenth Cavalry at Fort Robinson, 1902–1907." *Military Images* 7 (May–June 1991): 6–10.

_____. "When the Olympics Came to Fort Robinson."*NEBRASKAland* 68 (Oct. 1990): 16–21.

Clement, Thomas J. "Athletics in the American Army." *The Colored American Magazine* 8 (Jan. 1905): 21–29.

Curtis, K. D. "Frontier Fort for Tourists." *Ford Times* 49 (June 1957): 32–35.

Deitemeyer, Carl. "Better Steaks at Stake." *Nebraska Farmer* (Aug. 1, 1953): 1, 7, 35.

Eastman, Philip. "The Fort Riley Maneuvers." *Review of Reviews* 21 (Nov. 1903): 564–69.

Eisloeffel, Paul E., and Andrea Paul. "Hollywood on the Plains." *NEBRASKAland* 70 (May 1992): 42–47.

Farnham, Rob Roy. "Fort Robinson, From Army Post to Experiment Station." *The Cornhusker Countryman* 23 (Feb. 1951): 4, 13.

Godsol, Lt. M. B. "Pal Joins the Army." *The Quartermaster Review* 22 (Mar.–Apr. 1943): 54, 134–37.

Graham, Maj. R. M. "Our U.S. Army Remount Service." *Nebraska Farmer* (May 4, 1940): 3, 11, 14.

Grange, Roger T. "Fort Robinson: Outpost on the Plains." *Nebraska History* 39 (Sept. 1959): 191–241.

Grier, Bob. "Whitney Lake." *NEBRASKAland* 72 (Dec. 1994): 8–13.

Hall, Edith. "Historic Fort Robinson." *Nebraska Farmer* (Mar. 17, 1956): 10, 92.

_____. "The Preservation of Fort Robinson." *The Nebraska Cattleman* 12 (June 1956): 74, 76, 83, 84–85.

Hardy, Lt. Col. Edwin N. "The Remount Service and the Army Breeding Plan." *The Quartermaster Review* 19 (Mar.–Apr. 1940): 7–12, 69–71.

_____. "Remount Procurement Operations." *The Quartermaster Review* 20 (Jan.– Feb. 1941): 25–29, 61, 64–65.

"Introduction of an Army Horse." *The Cavalry Journal* 51 (July–Aug. 1942): 75–76.

"K-9 Mine Detection." *The Quartermaster Training Service Journal* 5 (Sept. 1944).

Koch, R. M. "Fort Robinson." *Nebraska Experiment Station Quarterly* 7 (Spring 1960): 3–6.

Laudenschlager, David D. "The Utes in South Dakota, 1906–1908." *South Dakota History* 9 (Summer 1979): 233–47.

Lerch, Gen. Archer L. "The Army Reports on Prisoners of War." *The American Mercury* 55 (May 1945): 536–47.

Loudon, Betty, ed. "Pioneer Pharmacist J. Walter Moyer's Notes on Crawford and Fort Robinson in the 1890s." *Nebraska History* 58 (Spring 1977): 88–117.

Lowe, Albert S. "Camp Life in the Tenth U.S. Cavalry." *The Colored American Magazine* 7 (Mar. 1904): 203–8.

McKibbin, Davidson B. "Revolt of the Navaho, 1913." *New Mexico Historical Review* 29 (Oct. 1954): 259–89.

O'Neil, Floyd. "An Anguished Odyssey: The Flight of the Utes, 1906–1908." *Utah Historical Quarterly* 36 (Fall 1968): 315–27.

Paul, Andrea I. "Buffalo Bill and Wounded Knee: The Movie." *Nebraska History* 71 (Winter 1990): 183–90.

Peterson, Marx. "Beef Research at Fort Robinson." *The Cornhusker Countryman* 25 (Oct. 1952): 11.

Pffaffenberger, Clarence J. "No Casualties." *The Shepherd Dog Review* (July 1944): 15–17.

Salee, Capt. John T. "Developing the Horse at a Western Remount Depot." *The Quartermaster Review* 8 (Nov.–Dec. 1928): 23–25.

Schubert, Frank N. "The Fort Robinson Y.M.C.A., 1902–1907: A Social Organization in a Black Regiment." *Nebraska History* 55 (Summer 1974): 165–79.

———. "Troopers, Taverns, and Taxes: Fort Robinson, Nebraska, and its Municipal Parasite, 1886–1911." In *Soldiers and Civilians: The U.S. Army and the American People*. Edited by Gary D. Ryan and Timothy K. Nenninger, 91–103. Washington, D.C.: National Archives and Records Administration, n.d.

Simmons, Cpl. Charlie. "Thanksgiving Day in the Tenth Cavalry." *The Voice of the Negro* 2 (Jan. 1905): 663–64.

Stewart, Miller J. "Fort Robinson, Nebraska, Army Remount Depot, 1919–1945." *Nebraska History* 70 (Winter 1989): 274–82.

Wade, Barc. "Western Nebraska Wonderland." [Cornhusker] *Motor Club News* 13 (May 1955).

Wheelock, Joseph. "Our Own Editors and Publishers." *The Colored American Magazine* 8 (Jan. 1905): 29–30.

Wight, Willard E., ed. "A Young Medical Officer's Letters from Fort Robinson and Fort Leavenworth, 1906–1907." *Nebraska History* 37 (June 1956): 135–48.

Young, W. A. "A Visit to Fort Robinson." *The North American Veterinarian* (May 1944): 292–94, 296.

Zika, Richard. "Dog Days in the CBI." *CBIVA Sound-Off* (Winter 1991): 40–42.

Index